GU00786415

Library Service

04. SE 95

added
11/0

14/8/13

Please remember that this item will attract overdue charges if not returned by the latest date stamped above. You may renew it by personal call, telephone or by post quoting the bar code number and your personal number. I hope you enjoy all of your library services.

Peter Herring, Head of Arts and Libraries

unless a renewal has been obtained by personal call or post, quoting the above number and the date due for return.

MAYFAIR
A SOCIAL HISTORY

By the same author

HAREWOOD
The Life and Times of an English Country House

MAYFAIR
A SOCIAL HISTORY

CAROL KENNEDY

Hutchinson
London Melbourne Auckland Johannesburg

First published in Great Britain in 1986 by Century Hutchinson Ltd
Brookmount House, 62–65 Chandos Place, London WC2N 4NW

Century Hutchinson Publishing Group (Australia) Pty Ltd
16–22 Church Street, Hawthorn, Melbourne, Victoria 3122

Century Hutchinson (NZ) Ltd
32–34 View Road, PO Box 40–086, Glenfield, Auckland, 10

Century Hutchinson Group (SA) Pty Ltd
PO Box 337, Bergvlei 2012, South Africa

Phototypeset in Linotron Palatino
by Input Typesetting Ltd, London

Printed and bound in Great Britain by
Butler & Tanner Ltd, Frome and London

ISBN 0 09 155590 6

*To my mother, Grace Kennedy, who
saw the last of Mayfair's golden age*

CONTENTS

BIBLIOGRAPHY

The Survey of London, Vols XXXIX and XL: The Grosvenor Estate in Mayfair (1977, 1980)

Berkeley Square to Bond Street. B. H. Johnson (1952)

London Life in the Eighteenth Century. M. Dorothy George (1925)

The Growth of Stuart London. N. G. Brett-James (1935)

London Improved and Westminster Improved. John Gwynn (1766)

Georgian London. Sir John Summerson (1962)

Old and New London. Edward Walford (1876)

Victorian Duke: The Life of Hugh Lupus Grosvenor, First Duke of Westminster. Gervas Huxley (1967)

Lost London. Hermione Hobhouse (1971)

Lady Elizabeth and the Grosvenors. Gervas Huxley (1965)

The Great Landlords of London. Frank Banfield (1888)

Evelyn's Diaries.

Pepys' Diaries. ed Robert Latham

The Greville Diaries.

Boswell's London Journal 1762–63. ed. Frederick Pottle (1950)

Hanoverian London. George Rudé (1971)

The Great Fire of London. Walter G. Bell (1920)

London: 2000 Years of a City and Its People. Felix Barker (1974)

Grace and Favour. Loelia, Duchess of Westminster (1961)

Chips: The Diaries of Sir Henry Channon. ed. Robert Rhodes James (1967)

Mayfair. Reginald Colby (1966)

History of the Squares of London. E. B. Chancellor (1907)

Horace Walpole's Correspondence. Yale Edition (1965) ed. W. S. Lewis

Letters and Journals of Lady Mary Coke (1896)

Mary Davies and the Manor of Ebury. C. T. Gatty (1921)

Coburg Hotel Prospectus (1898)

A History of Grosvenor Square. A. I. Dasent (1935)

Piccadilly in Three Centuries. A. I. Dasent (1914)

The Buildings of England. London: The Cities of London and Westminster. Nikolaus Pevsner (1957)

A Tour Through the Whole Island of Great Britain. Daniel Defoe (1724)

Florence Nightingale. Cecil Woodham-Smith (1950)

The Siren Years. Charles Ritchie (1974)

Peace in Piccadilly: The Story of Albany. Sheila Birkenhead (1958)

The West End of Yesterday and Today. E. B. Chancellor (1926)

London Past and Present. H. B. Wheatley (1891)

A Short History of Bond Street. H. B. Wheatley (1911)

London: The Unique City. Steen Eiler Rasmussen (1934, 1937, 1960)

A History of London. Robert Gray (1978)

London: Biography of a City. Christopher Hibbert (1969)

Georgiana, Duchess of Devonshire. Brian Masters (1981)

Mayfair: The Years of Grandeur. Mary Cathcart Borer (1975)

Romance and Realities of Mayfair and Piccadilly. P. R. Broemel (1927)

Landlords to London. Simon Jenkins (1975)

Mid-Georgian London. Hugh Phillips (1964)

The Autobiography of Margot Asquith. (1920)

Lord of London. Michael Harrison (1966)

The Face of London. Harold P. Clunn (1961)

A Letter from Grosvenor Square. John G. Winant (1947)

London War Notes. Mollie Panter-Downes (1972)

The Smith of Smiths. Hesketh Pearson (1934)

Sydney Smith. Alan Bell (1980)

The London of Thackeray. E. B. Chancellor (1923)

The Sweet and Twenties. Beverley Nichols (1958)

Castlerosse. Leonard Mosley (1956)

The Long Weekend. Robert Graves and Alan Hodge (1940)

London West. Francis Marshall (1944)

Melbourne. David Cecil (1965)

The Companion Guide to London. David Piper (1970)

Goodbye London. Christopher Booker and Candida Lycett Green (1973)

Ward Lock Guides to London (1925 and 1937)

Muirhead's London and Its Environs (1927)

Baedeker's London and Its Environs (1905)

The Way We Live Now. Anthony Trollope

The Literary Ghosts of London. E. B. Chancellor (1933)

A Village in Piccadilly. Robert Henrey (1942)

Sinister Street. Compton Mackenzie (1913)

Hugh Walpole. Rupert Hart-Davies (1952)

Vanity Fair. William Thackeray (1848)

Barnaby Rudge. Charles Dickens

Unquiet Souls. Angela Lambert (1984)

Mountbatten. Philip Ziegler (Collins 1985)

The People's War. Angus Calder (1969)

The Capital Companion. Peter Gibson (1985)

The London Encyclopedia. ed. Ben Weinreb and Christopher Hibbert (1983)

The Dance Band Era. Albert McCarthy (1971)

Discretions and Indiscretions. Lady Duff-Gordon (1932)

Edwardian Daughter. Sonia Keppel (1958)

Duveen. S. N. Behrman (1952)

The Works of Oscar Wilde.

The Life and Letters of Walter H. Page. (1923)

We Danced All Night. Barbara Cartland (1970)

Diaries and Letters 1930–1945. Harold Nicolson

The Randlords. Geoffrey Wheatcroft (1985)

The Blitz. Constantine FitzGibbon (1957)

Jack the Ripper: The Final Solution. Stephen Knight (1976)

Champagne and Chandeliers. Charles Graves (1958)

Matthew Arnold. Park Honan (1982)

The London Ritz. Hugh Montgomery-Massingberd and David Watkin (1980)

The London Journal of General Raymond E. Lee 1940–41. ed. James Leutze (1971)

Kelly's Handbook to the Titled, Landed and Official Classes, (1954, 1959)

The Devonshire House Circle. H. Stokes (1917)

Great Hostesses. Brian Masters (1982)

Debrett's Peerage, Baronetage, Knightage and Companionage, 1925

Who's Who and Who Was Who.

A History of Regent Street. Hermione Hobhouse (1975)

Dictionary of National Biography

Survey of London Vols XXXI and XXXII: The Parish of St. James, Westminster. Part Two; North of Piccadilly.

The Private Palaces of London. E. B. Chancellor (1908)

Mayfair and Belgravia. G. Linch (1892)

The Life of Edward Earl of Clarendon, by himself. (1827)

Elinor Glyn. Anthony Glyn (1955)

The Streets of London. Thomas Burke (1940)

Swans Reflecting Elephants. Edward James (1982)

Mrs Dizzy. Mollie Hardwick (1955)

Few Eggs and No Oranges. Vere Hodgson (1976)

The Golden Age of British Hotels. Derek Taylor and David Bush (1974)

Syrie Maugham. R. B. Fisher (1978)

The Ghosts of Piccadilly. G. S. Street (1914)

The Selected Letters of Thomas Babington Macaulay. ed. Thomas Pinney (1982)

Self Portrait with Friends: The Selected Diaries of Cecil Beaton 1926–1974. ed. Richard Buckle (1980)

Agnew's 1817–1967. Geoffrey Agnew (1967)

Beau Brummell. Hugo Cole (1977)

Brown's Hotel. David Tennant (1968)

Kelly's Post Office Directories.

Files of the Times, Harper's Bazaar, The Queen.

LIST OF ILLUSTRATIONS

ACKNOWLEDGEMENTS

I am grateful to many people for their help in my researches for this book. Among them I would particularly like to thank the Duke of Westminster, the Hon. Lady Lindsay (formerly Loelia, Duchess of Westminster), Margaret, Duchess of Argyll, Lady Freda Valentine, Francis Sitwell, Brigadier Gordon Viner (founder of the Mayfair Residents' Association), Cyril Ray, Major W. Ellery Anderson, secretary of the In and Out Club, Peter Aldersley, secretary of the Savile Club, Tommy Joy of Hatchards, Patrick Chalkley of the May Fair Hotel, Agnew's of Bond Street and Marjorie Lee of the Dorchester.

I owe much to the enthusiasm and creative support of Max de Trensé, and to the diligent research of Elizabeth Hennessy in the final stages. My mother tirelessly read and checked the manuscript and Jim Cochrane, formerly of Hutchinson, and Giles Gordon, my agent, buoyed me up with their own enthusiasm and confidence in the book throughout many long months. The London Library, as ever, was indispensable. So was the Survey of London, that splendidly detailed and scholarly work on which I have relied for much solid information. To its various authors I owe a great debt; any errors or omissions are certainly not theirs.

Carol Kennedy

London. Spring 1986.

INTRODUCTION

Some dreams, for no good reason, stick like burrs in the memory, especially when they leave a sense of something undiscovered and you wake with the key, as it were, half-turned in the lock. I still recall in vivid detail one that occurred at least ten years ago, a time-warp experience in which, walking in Hyde Park, I come upon a huge pair of ivy-encrusted iron gates. Pushing them open with difficulty, I emerge on a sunlit stretch of grass facing Park Lane – but a Park Lane of some indeterminate period before this. There is no Hilton, no Playboy Club, no cliff-like office blocks to break the undulating vista of Regency bow fronts glittering in the sun, their balconies bright with flowers. Yet the traffic has a modern air – double-decker buses, taxis, cars – and as I jump on a bus travelling north I become obsessed with the desire to find out what year I have strayed into. Newspaper billboards offer tantalizing clues, flashing past, but the head-lines are never legible. At the point where the bus sweeps round Marble Arch I wake up with a curiously poignant sense of loss – for what? More, surely, than a vanished urban landscape which, in any case, has not looked like that for the best part of a century.

When I came to plan this book, the fragment of dream rose out of my subconscious as if released by a depth-charge, and I realized that its significance to me lay somewhere in a childhood spent in west London to which the shining face of Park Lane represented the frontier to a land of mysterious glamour. I rarely ventured into it from the other side of the Bayswater Road, but it was associated with treats – an exquisitely flavoured strawberry ice cream, once, at

Gunter's, then in its last days of glory in Curzon Street, or a grown-up feast of smoked salmon sandwiches in the Premier, a darkly fascinating dive bar-restaurant in Dover Street. From naively romantic British films like *Spring in Park Lane* and *Maytime in Mayfair*, which were still doing the rounds, I had an image of that glittering square mile east of the Park as populated exclusively by beautiful people in evening dress attending grand balls at the Dorchester or Grosvenor House – an image not entirely anachronistic, because my parents would occasionally take their own prewar finery out of mothballs and go off to such an evening.

I don't remember particularly wanting to live in Mayfair, being perfectly happy in our sunny 1930s sixth-floor flat in Queensway from the roof of which, I later learned, suicides used to leap with alarming frequency in the bleak years after the war. But those Park Lane apartments were another world, all bleached oak panelling, fake Adam fireplaces, wall-to-wall carpet and Parker-Knoll sofas, through which Anna Neagle and Michael Wilding glided in impeccable clothes, maids and menservants in discreet attendance as if the People's War and the Attlee austerity had never happened. That physical world still exists – you can see it almost any week in the glossy house-agents' ads in *Country Life* or *The Tatler*; only now the dream tends to cost a quarter of a million pounds – renting in Mayfair, as elsewhere in residential London, having become the dwindling preserve of a few long-established tenants, many elderly and on fixed incomes which year by year fall back as the rents inexorably advance.

The image of Mayfair as a dream-world populated by glamorous couples foxtrotting to Ambrose or Sydney Lipton was a potent one, even in the early 1950s. Before the war, radio had spread it to every household in the land, broadcasting dance music from the grand West End hotels; from Pinner to Penzance, Dollis Hill to Darlington, they tuned in to the vicarious party that went band-hopping every night, its guests no doubt ending the evening at that fabled Hyde Park Corner coffee stall immortalized in novels of and about the period from Michael Arlen to Anthony Powell.

Mayfair has a somewhat different image now. It is still

shorthand for a moneyed way of life, but these days the money comes from expense accounts and Middle East oil wells, and the desirable properties in the glossy ads are more likely to be offices than private homes, except for those quarter-million-pound apartments and the odd Georgian house that is sold to a Central African diplomat. The privileged night-life centres around the gaming tables of the Clermont or Crockford's rather than the dance floors of grand hotels. Except for the great charity balls and the discreet richness of the Connaught grill room – where the voices are still redolent of 'old money' from the shires – class has become much less of a factor dividing Mayfair from Marylebone or Pimlico. Mayfair has become part of the cosmopolitan, adman's world, its Georgian drawing rooms given over to publicity parties and its hidden mews to fashionable restaurants or PR consultants' offices.

Here and there, though, tantalizing glimpses remain of another, unchanging world: the cavernous red-brick mansion flats of Down Street with their two-storey libraries and mysterious inhabitants, among them Arab sheikhs and a White Russian princess; the subtly florid doorways of Half Moon Street, still a place that wears an air of raffish bachelor chambers to which debutantes might be lured after an evening at Ciro's or the Kit-Cat Club; stretches of the eighteenth-century streets between Berkeley Square and the Park where, if you half-close your eyes on a twilit evening to shut out the parking meters and yellow lines, you might fancy a lamplighter going about his business or a carriage setting down Sydney Smith or Disraeli for a dinner party flashing with political and bookish wit.

Mayfair is a palimpsest on which every age in the last 250 years has scrawled its signature, some more elegantly than others. In the 1880s the first Duke of Westminster rebuilt Mount Street and Davies Street in crimson brick and terracotta. Heavy-handed 1930s neo-classicism is everywhere, from the motor showrooms of Berkeley Street which replaced the tree-shaded gardens of Devonshire House to the discreetly rich apartment blocks of Grosvenor Square and the cliff of flats that stands in place of Isaac Ware's magnificent eighteenth-century Chesterfield House in South Audley Street.

The 1960s destroyed lower Park Lane's remaining Regency houses and the last great society mansion, Londonderry House, to make a concrete canyon of hotels – a fitting monument to the transient society of the late twentieth century. Stretches of Georgian terraces are infilled like dental bridgework with ponderous facsimiles. But it is the ornately confident presence of Edwardian London that leaves the most lasting impression; nearly every Mayfair street felt the impact of the new rich from South Africa and the American Midwest who rebuilt, redecorated, fitted sprung maple ballroom floors and threw two houses into one with exuberant disregard for cost or architectural probity.

There is little left now of the Mayfair of the first great building boom of 1720 to 1760 – a few individual houses like 44 Berkeley Square – and even less of the vibrant social mix that once marked this community. There are still, surprisingly, working-class flats in north Mayfair, built by the Grosvenor family but administered now by the Peabody Trust. But when Mayfair was first populated it resembled a cutaway layer-cake of society with millionaires, marquesses and ministers of the Crown living literally back to back with the grooms, house servants and artisans who serviced the gentry from mews and alleys behind the great houses. And leavening the whole mix of classes was a cultural yeast of politicians, writers, poets, architects; the Albany chambers off Piccadilly being, as Macaulay contentedly observed, the nearest thing to college life in London.

It was the discovery of this lost village of all the talents, in its graceful brick streets and squares, which took me through the frontiers of my brittle dream Mayfair to the reality of the past and made me want to write this book.

PROLOGUE

'BRIGHTNESS FALLS
FROM THE AIR'

MAYFAIR in the late summer of 1939 showed little outward sign that its brilliant life as the playground and town estate of the British upper classes was about to be extinguished. Six years of war and a profound social revolution would change everything except the physical fabric of the area (most of it suffered comparatively little bomb damage) and its identification in the popular mind with money – though the money would no longer in future spring from the wealth of individuals but from international commerce and business. August 1939, before the sirens sounded, saw the last of that old, intimate society, celebrated by participants as different as Sydney Smith, Thackeray and Michael Arlen, which had lived, shopped, dined and disported itself in the odd-shaped quadrilateral bounded by Park Lane, Piccadilly, Regent Street and Oxford Street.

It was still, in those last weeks of peace, a district thickly populated by titles, most of whose holders knew each other. Grosvenor Square was lined with private houses whose residents included Katherine, Duchess of Westminster, Lord de Saumarez, the Marquess of Bath, the Honourable Clive Pearson, Lord Charles Montagu, the Honourable Claude and Lady Dorothy Hope Hope-Morley, Viscountess

Tredegar, Lord Illingworth and Sir Frank Sanderson. The influx of foreign fortunes that had come in Edwardian times was still represented by Pierpont Morgan Junior and Joel Jack Barnato at 12 and 34 Grosvenor Square respectively. The Earl of Rosebery, whose horse Blue Peter won the Derby that summer of 1939, maintained his town house at 38 Berkeley Square, where his aristocratic neighbours included Lord Mildmay of Flete, Viscountess Castlerosse and the Honourable Rupert Mitford. Viscount Cranborne, heir to Lord Salisbury, lived in Charles Street, as did Evelyn, Marchioness of Downshire and the Honourable Mrs John Bowes-Lyon, along with two noted men of letters, the playwright Frederick Lonsdale, who had apartments at Number 6, and Major Ian Hay Beith (Ian Hay) at Number 47. The Duke of Portland had recently moved from Grosvenor Square to a more modest terraced house in Hill Street, where his neighbours included Viscount Esher and the Broadway impresario Gilbert Miller. Even on Park Lane itself, where Dorchester House and Grosvenor House had a decade earlier made way for glossy international hotels, the Marquess of Londonderry still lived at Londonderry House, the Earl of Scarbrough at Number 21, Sir Philip Sassoon at Number 45 and Major the Honourable John Ward at Dudley House. The American film star Douglas Fairbanks Junior lived in style at Number 99 and two famous names from the world of commerce, Harry Gordon Selfridge, heir to the department-store fortune, and Sir Henri Deterding of Royal Dutch/Shell had flats in Park Lane.

The social mix of Mayfair in the late 1930s was very different from the vibrant village community that grew up with the district in the late eighteenth century; from a blend encompassing peers, writers, politicians, pastrymakers, builders, poets and grooms it had narrowed to a few categories of money and caste, but the houses were still homes and not yet offices. And it was indisputably the hub of West End society, with a thriving infrastructure of service industries, from court dressmakers to poulterers, which existed to serve its needs. In August 1939 all that was about to be swept away.

'The crisis', as everyone called it, hung heavy in the air that August like the blanket of unseasonable grey cloud which covered London, with the bloated silver shapes of barrage balloons floating lazily beneath it. The King had reviewed a massive rally of volunteer defence services in Hyde Park; the glossy women's magazines carried advertisements for military tailors and 'Emergency Bread' in sealed tins ('guaranteed to remain crisp and fresh for at least 10 years'), and urged fashionable young ladies to order 'your beau's regimental badge in diamond and enamel' from Asprey's. Dressed by Mainbocher and Molyneux, hatted by Schiaparelli and shod by Delman, the women of Mayfair continued to maintain the facade of the social calendar; to lunch at the Ritz and to take tea at Gunter's.

It was still an age of sartorial formality for both sexes; a note of mildly shocked surprise was evident when *Harper's* reported that the young film actress Penelope Dudley Ward had been observed walking down Dover Street with a red kerchief tied over her head instead of a hat. But the leaders of fashion (popular that autumn was a white silk blouse printed with silhouettes of Neville Chamberlain's homburg hat) were now reading in *Harper's* and *The Queen* how they could prepare for far tougher tests of initiative.

> What you can do . . . apply to the ARP offices as an ambulance or fire service driver. . . . If you have your own car, you can volunteer as an owner-driver either in the AFS (Auxiliary Fire Service) or for the evacuation of patients from hospitals to convalescent homes. . . . There is much good work to be done in getting children out of London and the big cities.

Still the surface continued to coruscate. Jack Jackson and his orchestra played nightly for dancing at the Dorchester; Sydney Lipton and his band at the Grosvenor House; Harry Roy at the Mayfair and Roy Fox at the Monseigneur restaurant at Marble Arch. It was the last of white-tie-and-tails Mayfair; the habit of formal evening wear disappeared with the coming of war and was never regained. Mayfair social happenings continued to make news. Lord and Lady Louis Mountbatten opened their eighth-floor penthouse on Park Lane and Upper Brook Street for a charity reception, and *The Queen* devoted two pages to a rapturous description

of its lavish decorations by Rex Whistler, its terrace running
round two floors, thickly bordered with sweet stocks, its
sweeping staircase, Van Dyck portraits and Lord Louis'
bedroom designed like the cabin of a ship, high over Hyde
Park. The Douglas Fairbankses gave a farewell party for the
actress Constance Bennett at their Park Lane house and the
young Jack Kennedy, son of the American Ambassador, was
mentioned among the eligible bachelors in the throng of
duchesses, peers of the realm and Hollywood stars.

The ordered progression of debutante balls and charity
dances wound its stately way to the end of the Season,
which was later than usual that year because the return of
the King and Queen from Canada on 22 June had given a
delayed impetus to the social round. A frisson of alarm ran
round Mayfair drawing rooms when it was rumoured that
Mrs James Corrigan, the vastly wealthy American hostess,
was thinking of going to Australia instead of taking her
customary London house for the Season – perhaps because,
as everyone still thought, the Duke of Kent would be taking
up his appointment that autumn as Governor General in
Canberra. Mrs Corrigan did stay in London, however,
renting Dudley House on Park Lane for two months at a
cost of £5000, where she threw one of the summer's most
splendid private balls. Its guest list was headed by the
Marquess and Marchioness of Londonderry, the Duke and
Duchess of Buccleuch and the Duke and Duchess of
Marlborough; he, indulging in a favourite trick, turned up
disguised in beard and glasses. On Ascot Gold Cup Day
Mrs Corrigan, who had taken a house for the week at nearby
Englemere, gave a huge cocktail party with six other society
hostesses: guests danced the Big Apple and the Lambeth
Walk on the terrace and the Duke of Marlborough, this time
sporting a Basque beret, conducted the band and executed
a flashy Charleston with Laura Corrigan.

The leaders of society were the royal duchesses, Kent and
Gloucester. Marina, Duchess of Kent, was the star attraction
that season at the Theatrical Garden Party, wearing a ruby
and diamond feather brooch four inches long in her lapel.
Derby Day television parties were a successful novelty. On
10 August, as the Season neared its end, all London's lights
except for the railway termini were shut off for a practice

blackout, an eerie foretaste of what was to come. The King and Queen left for Balmoral and society scattered in their wake, some to the grouse moors of Scotland and Yorkshire, others to continental playgrounds – preferably those nearest to home. The Channel resorts of Deauville and Le Touquet were particularly crowded: it was felt they would be handy to get out of in a hurry should the crisis break. In Le Touquet, the smarter of the two, which was now served by a daily Imperial Airways service from Croydon, the Hermitage Hotel advertised itself as 'the chosen residence of the Smart Set', while the Westminster claimed to be 'where British and French society meet'. Even the taxis in Le Touquet were old Rolls-Royces and Hispano-Suizas.

Mayfair was left slumbering under overcast skies. London, a society columnist noted, seemed 'duller, drearier and dustier' than in previous Augusts. The Georgian squares and terraces echoed to desultory footsteps; taxi drivers nodded in their stationary cabs, and Bond Street awnings shaded shop-window displays of interest now only to passing tourists – the new transatlantic air service had been inaugurated in June with Pan American's *Yankee Clipper* flying boat, eighteen hours and forty-two minutes from London to New York.

There was some unusual activity. Anti-aircraft guns were being lugged into position in Hyde Park, strips of brown paper being pasted over windows and glass doors against bomb blast, and cliffs of sandbags being filled and stacked by sweating men stripped to the waist in the humid air. Elsewhere in London art treasures were being carried out of the British Museum and loaded into vans for transport to hidden destinations carved out of the Welsh hills, and on 25 August trainloads of children, wearing luggage labels and carrying gas-masks, left Waterloo for evacuation to country billets. Still, unbelievably, magazine advertisements touted the attractions of the Sudetenland, a cruise in RMS *Andes* and even 'Germany, Land of Hospitality'.

The spellbound atmosphere was short-lived. On 3 September, the day Chamberlain's downcast voice resounded through a million fretworked radio sets declaring war, a mere six guests checked in at the Dorchester Hotel, but by 6 September Mayfair was bursting at the seams as its residents rushed back into town. Still the bands played on as service uniforms replaced tails and dinner jackets. The wistful melody 'Wishing Will Make It So' was a hit that September; never was there more ironic timing for a popular song. Six weary and anxious years later, no amount of wishing could restore what had been, in Mayfair or anywhere else.

MAKERS OF MAYFAIR

1

'WE WHO LIVE IN THE SUBURBS'

*I*N 1660, when King and Court returned to London after the six dour years of Cromwell's republic, and society resumed its accustomed order, the fashionable places to live were Lincoln's Inn Fields, St Martin's Lane and Inigo Jones's splendid, gravelled piazza in Covent Garden, with its handsome houses and arcaded sides, completed about thirty years before.

A few great houses remained in the Strand with their gardens stretching down to the Thames, still in the hands of the nobility who had appropriated them from the princes of the Church. Round the Court, now increasingly centred on St James's Palace – built the previous century on the site of a leper hospital – and away from Whitehall where Charles I had met his end, new colonies of fashion were springing up. As early as 1656 there were a few brave residents paying rates in Pall Mall, while a handful had been established since 1627 in Piccadilly, when the name itself was still new, derived from the 'pickadils', collars or hems, made by its first resident, a tailor called Robert Baker. Wits of the time found this appropriate, as Piccadilly, formerly known as the Way to Reading, was regarded as the outer limit of civilized London.

The West End owed its beginnings to Charles II's gratitude

for the support of his friends in exile. At Michaelmas 1660 Henry Jermyn, Earl of St Albans, who had been a close companion of the exiled King, was granted a sixty-year Crown lease on forty-five acres at St James's Fields to build houses 'fit for the dwellings of noblemen and gentlemen of quality'. Jermyn himself scarcely qualified for that description, being a notorious gambler and lecher who, according to the poet Andrew Marvell, looked like a butcher and had 'a drayman's shoulders'. He would soon become the first resident in the grandly planned St James's Square, development of which began in 1662, and achieve a niche in London history as the founder of the West End.

But the man who first set up home on the southern fringe of what became Mayfair was the Earl of Clarendon, the powerful and ambitious Lord Chancellor and head of the post-Restoration government. Clarendon, who had earlier owned Dorset House in Fleet Street, did not consider himself housed grandly enough in the Strand, where he leased Worcester House with its sloping riverside garden for £500 a year from Edward Somerset, second Marquess of Worcester. In August 1664 he managed to obtain a grant by Letters Patent from Charles II, 'in consideration of his eminent and faithful services', of twenty-nine and a half acres on the north side of Piccadilly, roughly at the point where St James's Street enters it today. On about eight and a half acres of this site he planned to build a palatial mansion, selling off the remaining acres (the day after his own grant went through on the Patent Rolls) to three fellow aristocrats with a shrewd eye for speculation – Lord Berkeley of Stratton, soldier, diplomat, and recently ennobled scion of a West Country family; Sir William Pulteney, a member of one of London's oldest merchant families, with extensive properties in Bath; and Sir John Denham, minor poet and Sir Christopher Wren's predecessor as Surveyor-General of the King's Works. In time these three sites were to become, respectively, those of Devonshire House, Bath House and Burlington House and Albany.

Work on Clarendon's mansion proceeded briskly, and by mid-October 1664 the diarist John Evelyn, after dining with the Lord Chancellor at Worcester House, was taken by coach to advise on the garden layout at Piccadilly. London society gossiped about Clarendon's source of money for the project; there was so much rumour about him accepting French bribes over the return of Dunkirk to French sovereignty that it was popularly nicknamed 'Dunkirk House'. Marvell, who subscribed to the belief that Clarendon had bought with his ill-gotten gains stone originally designated for rebuilding St Paul's well before the Great Fire, commented sardonically in a poem for 'Clarendon's House Warming': 'Behold, in the depth of our Plague and our Wars, He built himself a Palace that outbraves the Stars.'

On the advice of his fellow diarist Evelyn, Samuel Pepys visited the site early in 1666 and described it as 'the finest pile I ever did see in my life, and will be a glorious house'. A month later he was able to admire the view from the roof, a landscape still mainly pastures and farms to north and west, with the crenellated Tudor outline of St James's Palace in the dip directly to the south, and beyond it the roofs and spires of Westminster. Pepys thought it 'the noblest prospect that I ever saw in my life, Greenwich being nothing to it'. Evelyn, in a letter to Clarendon's son Viscount Cornbury on 20 January 1666, extolled it as 'the best contrived, the most usefull, gracefull, and magnificent house in England. Here is state and use, solidity and beauty, most symmetrically combined together: Nothing abroad pleases me more, nothing at home approaches it. . . . I pronounce it the first Palace in England.' Later, he qualified his initial enthusiasm by noting that it had 'many defects as to ye architecture, yet plac'd most gracefully'. Designed by Sir Roger Pratt, who was knighted by Charles II for his services in the post-Fire rebuilding of London, Clarendon House with its projecting wings and noble courtyard facing Piccadilly became the model for a generation of English country houses.

The move westward by Restoration society, then, had already begun in earnest from the old City – still, in these last months before the Great Fire, the walled City Shakespeare knew, with its crammed and gabled streets, their wood and plaster houses almost touching at the upper storeys, its boisterous, balconied taverns and a hundred spired churches, crowned by Old St Paul's on its hill. Although a number of the capital's wealthiest merchants and bankers still lived in style on the slopes of St Laurence

Pountney Hill and the aristocracy retained a foothold in Aldersgate Street, which boasted several great houses, London had become so overcrowded, dirty and plague-ridden that the social divide between the City (and the 'Cits', as its inhabitants were witheringly known in Court circles) and the Court at Westminster was growing wider by the year.

Old London's industrial activities, among them brewing, dyeing, lime-burning and soap-boiling, contributed to its social undesirability. Churches, palaces, clothes and gardens, as John Evelyn complained, were grimed with 'horrid smoke' from the riverside furnaces, with the effects reaching as far as Whitehall. One needed to go a considerable distance west before the prevailing south-west wind ensured freedom from 'that Hellish and dismal Cloud of Seacoal' about which Evelyn urged King Charles II to act by moving all the noisome traders five or six miles out beyond Greenwich. The King was sympathetic, but a combination of bureaucratic lethargy and vested interests managed to delay any action. After September 1666 the matter of pollution became academic amid the smoking ruins of the City.

The Fire changed everything. When the ashes cooled, 13,200 houses had been destroyed in more than 400 streets and courts of the medieval City, and only 9000 could be rebuilt after the new safety laws controlling street widths came into force. Moreover, despite the boasts of contemporary historians that the City was rebuilt in four years (the Monument still records falsely that it was achieved in three), it was to remain disfigured with ruins for the best part of two decades, and those who could afford to move west did so in increasing numbers. Ironically, it was largely pressure from traders fearing such a shift of custom and wanting to retain their old business quarters that blocked the plans by Evelyn, Wren and others to build a new model city. Had Wren's majestic Renaissance boulevards and piazzas been realized, they might well have tempted back the wealthy residents.

Some did remain loyal to their former neighbourhoods, rebuilding more magnificently than before. Sir Robert Clayton, a self-made man of great wealth who became Lord

Mayor in 1679, built a splendid house in Old Jewry where he entertained on a lavish scale, and other imposing residences went up near the Royal Exchange. They were described in Hatton's *New View of London*, forty-two years after the Fire, as 'magnificent with courts, offices and all the other necessary apartments inclosed to themselves, and noble gates and frontispieces towards the streets, richly furnished within'. In general, however, there was such reluctance to return to the scene of the greatest catastrophe in London's history that the City Corporation was obliged to impose heavy penalties on any alderman and his family moving outside the City limits. Eight years after the Fire, there were as many as 3000 empty sites and uninhabited houses; Wren himself commented on the number of rebuilt dwellings that remained empty.

Even fashionable Lincoln's Inn was affected by the exodus; the Fire had swept as far west at the corner of Fetter Lane before it was finally halted, enveloping the Temple on two sides and gutting the lawyers' quarter of King's Bench Walk. Today Number 55 Fleet Street marks the limits of the Fire's advance; its overhanging Jacobean frontage and that of Staple Inn, Holborn, are the last relics of pre-Fire London (though several times restored), miraculously surviving the Blitz of 1940–41. The palatial mansions that had lined the Strand from the Temple to Westminster also lost their charms when it was feared the Fire was unstoppable: some were blown up by gunpowder to provide fire-breaks, and in due course Essex, Arundel and York houses were pulled down and their gardens built over.

Some of the aristocratic refugees settled to the north, in the heavy clay fields of Clerkenwell, which had been a favoured suburban area for some years; St John's Square boasted the Earl of Carlisle, the Earl of Essex, Lord Townshend and the Bishop of Durham as residents, while the Duke of Newcastle lived on Clerkenwell Green. But fashion for the most part chose to follow the Earl of St Albans to St James's Square and its adjoining streets: among the 'noblemen and gentlemen of quality' who moved in were the Earl of Arlington, Viscount Halifax, Lord Bellasis, the Honourable Thomas Jermyn, Sir Thomas Clarges, the French Ambassador, Lord Cavendish (later the first Duke of

Devonshire), Colonel John Churchill (later the first Duke of
Marlborough), Sir Isaac Newton, Lord Sunderland, the Earl
of Feversham and Sir John Duncombe, Chancellor of the
Exchequer. Some of these would soon take part in the development of southern Mayfair around and behind Clarendon
House; even obscure cronies of Charles II who benefited
from land or other rewards in the area left their names
permanently on the street map of a later age, like Colonel
James Hamilton, whose office as Ranger of Hyde Park
brought him the piece of ground now known as Hamilton
Place.

Clarendon himself had moved from the Strand to Berkshire (later Bridgewater) House in St James's as the walls of
his Piccadilly mansion went up, but so terrifying was the
Fire's advance that he doubted whether even those western
outskirts were safe as the nine-day holocaust raged. 'We
who live in the suburbs,' he wrote to Lord Winchilsea,
'preparing for the same fate, fled from our lodgings and
have hardly yet recovered our goods or our wits.'

Meanwhile the buyers of Clarendon's surplus land were
developing their sites with equal speed. East of Clarendon
House Sir John Denham, described unkindly by Evelyn as
'a better Poet than Architect' (though his merits as a versifier
hardly matched those in whose company he was buried in
St Paul's – Chaucer, Cowley and Dryden) was supervising
the construction of a plain, red-brick house with a spacious
garden, but it was never finished in time for him and his
second wife Margaret to occupy it. Following Margaret's
sudden death in January 1666 – it was rumoured she had
been poisoned by a cup of chocolate – Denham sold the
partly-built property to Richard Boyle, first Earl of
Burlington and second Earl of Cork, Lord Treasurer of
Ireland and friend of Clarendon.

Completion took some time – building materials were in
short supply during the reconstruction of the burned-out
City, and the arrival of the Dutch Fleet in the Thames forced
concentration upon larger matters. Lord Burlington's son,
Lord Clifford, and the family's agent Richard Graham
commented in a report on the work that they were doing
'all wee can to quicken ye workmen, whoe in these unsetled
[sic] times are generally very backward to work'. It was 1668

before Burlington was able to hold a house-warming, which was graced by the presence of the Archbishop of Canterbury and the bishops of Lincoln and Winchester. A few years later, on the adjoining plot to the east, Sir Thomas Clarges MP, the brother-in-law of General Monk, put up another house set back behind a courtyard from Piccadilly; eventually it became Melbourne House and then Albany, the secluded apartment building, while Burlington House was completely remodelled by Burlington's grandson, the architect third Earl.

To the west of Clarendon House, Lord Berkeley's mansion, which had been completed at a cost of £30,000 by the time the Fire broke out, was described by Evelyn, whom Berkeley employed to advise on his financial affairs, as 'well built and has many noble roomes, but they are all not very convenient . . . they are all roomes of state, without clossets . . .' Like Burlington House, it was built of brick, but more ornately trimmed, with stone pilasters and a Corinthian pediment adorned with a white marble figure of Britannia. Like its fellows, it sat back behind a noble courtyard in the fashion that only vanished finally from Piccadilly in 1925, when its successor Devonshire House was pulled down. It had a terrace at the back, planted on Evelyn's advice with holly hedges, and a garden the diarist thought incomparable. He was less complimentary about the design of the house; its porticoes, he remarked, were done in imitation of a house described by Palladio, 'but it happens to be the worst in his booke, tho' my good friend Mr Hugh May effected it'. May, now a largely forgotten Carolean architect, was also brought in by Burlington to finish his house. He was one of the King's Commissioners appointed along with Pratt and Wren to advise on the rebuilding of burned-out London, and later carried out extensive alterations at Windsor Castle; otherwise, his career was short and relatively undistinguished.

John Berkeley, first Baron Berkeley of Stratton, was a man considered by his contemporaries to have succeeded more than he deserved by his abilities. An aggressive, short-tempered character – Pepys described him as 'the most hot, fiery man in discourse, without any cause, that ever I saw' – he was Charles I's Ambassador to Sweden at the early age

of thirty, served as an MP in the Short Parliament of 1640
and commanded the Royalist forces in Devon and Cornwall
during the Civil War. He chose Stratton for his title from
the name of a Cornish village near the scene of several
Royalist victories, and it survives today on the map of
Mayfair, though not as prominently as Berkeley, in the short
street that came to flank the grounds of his Piccadilly
mansion. After the Restoration, for which he helped in the
negotiations with Cromwell and Ireton, he married the
daughter of Sir Andrew Riccard, chairman of the East India
Company, and by 1663 had made a fortune of £50,000 out
of a clutch of eminent sinecures. As well as building Berkeley
House he bought the fine country estate of Twickenham
Park, whose house had once belonged to Francis Bacon, and
was an early investor in land in America.

Clarendon's fortunes, by contrast, were about to collapse
dramatically, both financially and politically. His self-
confessed 'rash enterprise' in building Clarendon House –
in his autobiography he blamed it on 'weakness and vanity'
– ran him into a mountain of debt. His architect, Pratt, had
expected to finish the work for £18,000, but the final bill was
nearer £50,000, according to Evelyn. Frost and water damage
in the harsh winter of 1665–6 accounted for part of the
additional expense, but a large amount was also due to the
decision by Clarendon's heir, Viscount Cornbury, to have
the height of the first-floor rooms raised by another foot –
an aesthetic gain, but a costly one.

For all his 'entanglement of debt', however, Clarendon
was reluctant to sell the house, even after moves to impeach
him for treason over his conduct of the Dutch war forced
him into sudden exile in December 1667. On the ninth of
that month Evelyn visited him and found him sitting discon-
solately in a wheelchair, suffering from gout and gazing out
over the gardens: 'The next morning I heard that he was
gone.' The house was rented for a while to the Duke of
Ormonde and after Clarendon's death in 1674 it was sold for
half of what it had cost to build. The buyer was Christopher
Monck, second Duke of Albemarle, who renamed it Albemarle House, but he ran through his own fortune so rapidly
that by 1683 he was forced to sell. This time it was no
aristocratic denizen of St James's who made the successful

bid of £35,000, but a consortium of property speculators described waspishly by Evelyn as 'certain inferior people, rich bankers and mechanics'.

Their first intention, it was rumoured around town, was to demolish the house and build on its site a 'stately square, equal to that at St James's', as Evelyn recorded. The grand piazza would be known as Albemarle Square and be surrounded by a whole 'new towne'. The project was never realized, but the house was indeed pulled down and four streets laid out on the cleared site and on some additional land around Hay Hill Farm which had belonged to Clarendon on a ninety-nine-year lease. These were Dover Street, Albemarle Street, Stafford Street and what is now Old Bond Street. The man who gave his name to Mayfair's principal shopping street, the Peckham baronet Sir Thomas Bond, was not the head of the consortium, as is often popularly assumed, but played a relatively minor role in the development. Though Evelyn claimed he demolished Clarendon House to 'build a street of tenements to his undoing' (Bond Street was not a successful development at the start), Bond's activities seem to have been limited to acquiring some freeholds from the three principals in the consortium. These men, primarily responsible for the first development of Mayfair north from Piccadilly, do not, to this day, have their names on the Mayfair map.

Evelyn's 'bankers and mechanics' were in fact a goldsmith and financier (two occupations often entwined in the early days of banking) named John Hinde; a Southwark timber merchant and property speculator called Cadogan Thomas; and a professional bricklayer and builder called Richard Frith. The last two had been in business together in Soho, developing Soho Square and some of the surrounding streets, including Frith Street. Hinde was in his forties when he acquired Clarendon House, a prosperous professional man with a residence attached to his place of business in Cornhill and another large house on Highgate Hill which boasted a considerable collection of pictures, plate and fine furniture and where he entertained lavishly, even playing host, it was said, to Charles II and Nell Gwyn.

Early in the development of Albemarle Ground, as the site of Clarendon House became known, Hinde and his

associates disposed of several building leases; as well as Sir
Thomas Bond, two other purchasers were destined to be
remembered in Mayfair street names – Baron Dover, a
kinsman of the St Albans family, and Margaret Stafford,
daughter of a Northamptonshire landowner and a shrewd
businesswoman. The carved stone sign for Stafford Street,
dated 1686, is the earliest in Mayfair and can still be seen,
attached to the wall of the Duke of Albemarle public house
on the corner of Stafford and Dover streets.

Bond himself is a shadowy figure. He came of a Catholic
family, well connected in the City; his great-grandfather, Sir
George Bond, was Master of the Haberdashers Company
and Lord Mayor of London in 1587–8, while his grandfather,
Sir William Bond, had been a City alderman. Thomas Bond
Senior was an untitled physician practising in Hoxton, but
his son, who served as Controller of the Household to
Queen Henrietta Maria and became a great Court favourite,
was created an hereditary baronet by Charles I in 1658. Later
he seems to have acted as unofficial banker to the monarch,
his papers recording loans amounting to £40,000 during the
year 1667–8. He had a town house in Pall Mall and a country
estate at Peckham, where he built himself a fine house with
a garden full of fruit trees imported from France. An avenue
of majestic elms opened on to the distant prospect of St
Paul's, the Tower of London and the clustered masts of
shipping towards Greenwich.

Bond's fortunes faded, however, when he became associated with the Clarendon House consortium. Hinde and his
partners recouped their capital investment through selling
materials and land on the site, but by 1685 Hinde personally
was in deep debt and had been forced to mortgage unsold
parts of the site. The following year he died in the Fleet
debtors' prison. Frith and Thomas also fell into difficulties
and died in debt. Bond himself died suddenly in the early
summer of 1685, before any of the house built on his part
of the site had found occupiers. Most of the buildings had
not even been finished, the work delayed by an abnormally
hard winter in 1683–4 when the Thames was frozen over
throughout most of January and February.

Hinde's bankruptcy effectively put a stop to development
for years as lawyers wrangled over ownership of the leases.

As late as 1720, when much of the district had been built up, John Strype in his edition of Stow's famous *Survey* was still able to remark that a considerable area was 'not to this Day finished, and God knows when it will'. Strype likened the scene to the ruins of Troy, with many houses still at foundation stage, others roofless and desolate. Only the finished houses near Portugal Street, as that stretch of Piccadilly had been named in 1663 in honour of Charles II's Portuguese-born Queen, Catherine of Braganza, attracted tenants without difficulty. London's newest suburb resembled a building site, with smoking brick kilns and half-built streets petering out into the fields. But an advance guard of aristocratic society was already on the march, snapping up bargains from the builders and joiners who had bought the first leases cheaply from Hinde's hapless consortium. Unpromising though the unfinished streets looked to the passer-by on Portugal Street heading to or from St James's, they would soon be the best investment and part of the best address in London.

2

'INHABITED BY PERSONS OF QUALITY'

WEST of Berkeley House in the 1670s and 1680s all was still rural along Piccadilly, or Hide Park Road as this stretch was known. A stone bridge arched over the Tybourne stream where it emerged to dive into what is now Green Park; after that the road petered out towards the dusty crossroads of Hyde Park Corner and Tyburn Lane, edged with stonemasons' yards and taverns serving the drovers who brought their herds up from the west to market. The celebrated Hercules Pillars mentioned in Fielding's *Tom Jones* stood roughly where the Athenaeum Hotel does today – a low, comfortable hostelry frequented by farmers and the grooms of the gentry.

North of the three great Piccadilly mansions lay open country dotted with farms, the nearest being Hay Hill Farm, where the Tybourne turned south west after its long descent from the heights of Hampstead. A man could still shoot woodcock over the site of Regent Street. Oxford or Tyburn Road was a deeply rutted track, muddy in wet weather, along which the execution processions rumbled every six weeks to the dreaded 'Triple Tree'. Within the next half-century, however, the development boom started by the cronies of Charles II would change London's western rim out of all recognition; by 1684 John Evelyn was already complaining of the 'mad intemperance' of building going on. The city, he grumbled, was 'by far too disproportionate already to the nation; I having in my time seene it almost as large again as it was within my memory.'

North-east of Hyde Park Corner a meadow called Brookfield became notorious in the late 1680s as the site of the May Fair, held from every May 1st for fourteen or fifteen days. This old-established cattle market and carnival had been held since the time of Edward II in St James's Fields, but by the Restoration it was deemed to be undesirably close to the Court and, after a spell in abeyance, the new King, James II, granted letters patent permitting it to be held in Brookfield 'for ever'. It covered about thirteen acres, with its epicentre lying roughly where today's Curzon Street runs into Shepherd Market. Live cattle were bought and sold on the first three days, then booths and stalls were set up, spreading as far west as Tyburn (now Park) Lane, offering sideshows, gambling, boxing matches and every variety of prostitution, or 'vice and impurities not to be mentioned', as one censorious contemporary noted. Puppet shows, often with a political message, were popular; after the Jacobite rebellion of 1745 there was a booth devoted to mock executions, with puppets representing the Scottish chieftains being ritually beheaded.

Bloodlust was more directly satisfied by the sport of duck hunting, which took place, always with large and enthusiastic crowds of onlookers, at a pond by the public house called the Dog and Duck, which stood at the foot of present-day Hertford Street. Here the market butchers gambled on whose dog would be the first to catch a duck which was thrown on the pond after having its wings tied down. The desperate bird could only escape by diving, but the spaniels that excelled at this game soon dragged it out, exhausted and dying, to the cheers and yells of the excited spectators.

In 1708 Westminster magistrates who hoped to suppress the Fair called it a place where 'many loose, idle and disorderly persons do rendez-vous and draw and allure young persons and servants to meet to game and commit lewd and disorderly practices'. Some citizens who were persuaded to join the revels hated every minute, as a surviving account vividly shows.

By the help of a great many slashes and hey-ups, and
after as many jolts and jumbles, we were dragg'd to the
Fair, where the harsh sound of untunable trumpets, the
catterwauling scrapes of thrashing fiddlers, the
grumblings of beaten calves-skin, and the discording
toots of broken organs set my teeth on edge, like the
filing of a hand-saw. . . . We order'd the coach to drive
through the body of the Fair, that we might have the
better view of the tinsey heroes and the gazing
multitude, expecting to have seen several corporations
of strolling vagabonds, but there prov'd but one
company, amongst whom Merry Andrew was very
busy in coaxing the attentive crowd into a good opinion
of his fraternities and his own performances. . . .
Beyond these were a parcel of scandalous boosing-kens,
where soldiers and their trulls were skipping and
dancing about to most lamentable music, perform'd
upon a crack'd crowd by a blind fiddler. In another hut,
a parcel of Scotch pedlars and their moggies, dancing a
highlander's jig to a hornpipe. Over against 'em the
Cheshire Booth, where a gentleman's man was playing
more tricks with his heels in a Cheshire Round than
ever were shown by the Mad Coffee Man at Sadler's
Music House. . . . We now began to look about us, and
take a view of the spectators; but could not, amongst the
many thousands, find one man that appear'd above the
degree of a gentleman's valet, nor one whore that could
have the impudence to ask above sixpence wet and
sixpence dry, for an hour of her cursed company. In all
the multitudes than ever I beheld, I never, in my life,
saw such a number of lazy lousie-lock'd rascals, and so
hateful a throng of beggarly, sluttish strumpets. . . .

Others, however, enjoyed themselves innocently enough.
'I wish you had been at May Fair,' wrote Brian Fairfax to a
friend in 1701.

All the nobility in town were there, and I am sure even
you, at your years, must have had your youthful wishes
to have beheld the beauty, shape and activity of Lady
Mary when she danced. Pray ask my Lord Fairfax about

her, who, though not the only lord by twenty, was every
night an admirer of her while the Fair lasted.

Fairfax was particularly taken with the rope-dancing, a
famous feature of the May Fair, and with a beautifully
detailed model of the City of Amsterdam, ten yards in diam-
eter, in which 'every street, every individual house, was
carved in wood in exact proportion one to another.'

But the following year the Fair erupted in tragic violence
when a constable attempting to arrest some young women
as prostitutes was killed by a rapier thrust. Thomas Cook,
a butcher, was found guilty after being pursued to Ireland,
and was hanged at Tyburn. Meanwhile the dead constable,
John Cooper, was given a public funeral at St James's, Piccadilly, in the hope that popular feeling would be aroused
against the Fair.

Queen Anne, who as Princess Anne of Denmark had lived
in Mayfair, renting Berkeley House for £600 a year from 1692
to 1696, disapproved strongly of the May Fair and soon after
ascending the throne issued a Royal Proclamation
suppressing it. But not even her writ could abolish James
II's grant in perpetuity, and the early Georgian years saw a
return of the sideshows, pedlars, jugglers and Tiddy-Dol,
the gingerbread seller whose name, connected with a
doggerel song he used to chant, is commemorated in a
Shepherd Market restaurant popular with American tourists. What killed the Fair in the end was not so much pious
denunciations of its wickedness as the rising tide of bricks
and mortar covering the district which by 1749 had taken
its name from the notorious event (a by-election that year
recorded several voters' addresses as being in 'May Fair').

Edward Shepherd, the architect and builder who designed
many distinguished houses in Georgian Mayfair including a
low, elegant white mansion for himself which, much altered,
eventually became Crewe House and still miraculously
survives, gleaming amid green lawns off Curzon Street, was
the first developer of Brookfield, on land he leased from Sir
Nathaniel Curzon. As building progressed after 1715, the
new residents objected to the yearly disruption and undesirable characters which the Fair brought to the neighbourhood. The Earl of Coventry, who bought a house nearby on

Piccadilly, was particularly vocal about the nuisance, and by the latter half of the eighteenth century the showmen and stall-holders were folding their tents and stealing away. Also victims of the new respectability were the boisterous old taverns along Piccadilly; the Half Moon (on the corner of present-day Half Moon Street), the White Horse, still remembered in a street name, the Greyhound Inn and, of course, the Pillars of Hercules. Shepherd Market, however, was destined with neighbouring Curzon Street to enjoy a permanently raffish, nudge-and-wink reputation as a discreet red-light district, as if the ghostly lords of misrule still lingered on in their long-vanished meadow.

Undesirable though the May Fair undoubtedly was to its immediate area, some of the grandest families in the land wanted a town house on Piccadilly. One of these, Berkeley House, became the centre of a colourful legal battle in the 1690s which held London society fascinated for the best part of two years. The first Lord Berkeley of Stratton had died in 1678 and left four sons, three of whom succumbed to untimely deaths after inheriting the title in succession. Berkeley's widow, the shrewdly businesslike daughter of the East India Company's chairman, sold off strips of the glorious gardens planned by Evelyn for the building of Stratton and Berkeley Streets, a move which increased her income from ground rents by £1000 a year. When the second Baron Berkeley died in 1692 the family rented the house for four years to Princess Anne and Prince George of Denmark, after which the third Lord Berkeley decided to sell it. Unfortunately, his attempts to play off two wealthy and aristocratic buyers against each other backfired and landed all three parties in the courts. To add piquancy to the battle, the two contestants for the house were celebrated political opponents – the Marquis of Normanby, leader of the Tories under William III, and the Whig grandee William Cavendish, first Duke of Devonshire.

Both were controversial, larger-than-life characters. Normanby, a former suitor for Princess Anne's hand (to the strong displeasure of the King) was a man of whom Dr Johnson remarked, 'his principles concerning property were such as the gaming table supplies', while Devonshire was also a gambler, a lover of racing and duelling, but a man of wide culture who wrote verse and had the inclinations of a Medici in his patronage of art and architecture. Johnson made his own partialities plain: Devonshire, he opined, was a man of such 'dogged veracity that if he had promised an acorn and not one had grown in his woods that year, he would have sent to Denmark for one.'

Normanby was convinced that he had clinched a deal with Lord Berkeley, pending only the final formalities, but even as the case went to court in July 1696 Berkeley transferred ownership of the house to the Duke of Devonshire for £11,000. It was not until December 1697 that judgement was delivered by the Lord Chancellor and the Lord Chief Justice, and it dismissed Normanby's claim. In the meantime the Duke of Devonshire had busied himself with the building of Chatsworth, his Renaissance palace in the Derbyshire Peak District. On his visits to London he lived in Arlington House, a pleasant, countrified house south-east of Hyde Park Corner which he rented from the Duchess of Grafton. When Normanby lost the Berkeley property he bought Arlington House, rebuilding it as Buckingham House after he was created Duke of Buckingham and Normanby by Queen Anne. (Its transformation by George IV into Buckingham Palace added millions in value to the Grosvenor family's properties in the area later known as Belgravia.)

The new owner of Berkeley House renamed it Devonshire House and it passed down his heirs until October 1733, when it was gutted by a fire that broke out on an upper floor where renovation was going on. A pot of workmen's glue boiled over on a brazier and ignited some wood shavings. The family was at breakfast with the Prince of Wales, who was a house guest, and he immediately offered a reward of thirty guineas to anyone who helped to save the Duke's books, furniture and pictures. One work of art which escaped, a *trompe l'oeil* Dutch painting of a violin hanging on a door, is now at Chatsworth. But the famous cedar staircase with its sweetly aromatic scent was totally destroyed. The house was rebuilt to a plain brick design by William Kent and endured behind its high wall facing Piccadilly until its demolition in 1925.

One curious by-product of the court case over the sale of

Berkeley House was the stipulation that no heirs of Lord Berkeley should build on its gardens abutting Berkeley Square in such a way as to 'annoy' the house. In effect, this prevented the completion of Berkeley Square until 1925, and it certainly gave Robert Adam problems when he came to design a grand new house in 1762 for the Earl of Bute. Instead of being able to site it on the south side of Berkeley Square, as Lord Bute wanted, Adam had to place it at right angles to the garden of Devonshire House.

Lansdowne House, as Bute House became known after its sale (before completion) to the Earl of Shelburne, later Marquess of Lansdowne, was originally an elegant mansion with two well-proportioned wings, but it was brutally cut back in 1935 to accommodate the extension of Curzon Street. Between its garden and that of Devonshire House, with its statues and elm trees, ran Lansdowne Passage, a shadowy and rather sinister path cut below ground level and terminated at either end by steps leading up to Berkeley and Curzon streets. After a highwayman made his escape on horseback down the passage, looping back into Piccadilly to evade the pursuing constables, an upright iron bar was installed at its entrance. Lansdowne Passage, now a mundane kitchen exit to the May Fair Hotel, can still generate a shiver or two from its dank stonework, where murder and violence were once common occurrences.

By the beginning of the eighteenth century, May Fair (it continued to be spelled as two words until well into Thackeray's time) had undeniably become the most fashionable address in London. The unfinished Bond estate was taking shape and in Hatton's *New View of London* (1708) Dover Street was described as 'a street of very good Buildings, mostly inhabited by Gentry'. Albemarle Street was 'a Street of excellent new Building, inhabited by Persons of Quality between the Fields and Portugal Street', while Bond Street was ' a fine new street, mostly inhabited by Nobility and Gentry'.

Sir Henry Bond, Sir Thomas's heir, found his career as Vice-Treasurer and Receiver-General in Ireland ending ignominiously with the fall of James II in 1688, as did Baron Dover, but before the deluge both of them managed to sell several freehold plots complete with newly built houses in

Dover, Albemarle and Bond streets. One of the first residents was Dame Catherine Wyndham, who paid Lord Dover £2500 for a house on the fashionable west side of Dover Street. Plots in Albemarle and Bond streets sold for a few hundred pounds, some of the first buyers being humble craftsmen – two joiners, a carpenter, a bricklayer and the former sergeant-printer to William III. The last recorded sale by Sir Henry Bond was that of his own house and garden in Dover Street, to a scrivener called Huntley Bigg who paid £1150 for the property in 1706. Two generations later the Bond baronetcy became extinct.

Lord Dover, who had gone into exile following the overthrow of James II by Dutch William, returned in due course and lived until his death in a large house with a garden at the corner of Dover Street and Hay Hill. (His first London home, Number 8 St James's Square, was demolished as recently as 1938). He had no heirs and after his widow's death in 1726 the house was sold at auction with all its contents. A fine property, according to the auctioneer's description, with seven rooms, three coach-houses and stables for ten horses 'and all manner of Conveniencies for a great Family', it was knocked down for £4000 to an agent called Christopher Cook.

The sale and resale of plots and houses in Bond Street and Albemarle Street went on continuously in the early eighteenth century. The Duke of Albemarle public house was sold in 1706 to its tenant, William Edge, for £240. By now the aristocracy was moving in: Henrietta, Countess of Dalkeith, and the Earl of Orkney paid £200 each for plots on the east side of Dover Street with ruined buildings on them – the site was to become that of Brown's Hotel. Among the first residents in Albemarle Street were Lady Elizabeth Egerton, daughter of the third Earl of Bridgewater, Robert Mansfield and the Earl of Dalkeith, heir to the Duke of Buccleuch. The freehold of their houses was owned by Benjamin Jackson, master mason to the Queen, who paid £174 each for the building plots in 1707. Among them was the site of 50 Albemarle Street, which was first inhabited successively by Mansfield and the Earl of Dalkeith, and in 1812 passed into the ownership of the publisher John Murray, whose firm flourishes there to this day.

From the start Bond Street's residents had a more raffish air than those in the neighbouring developments: one of the earliest was Charles Beauclerc, son of Charles II by Nell Gwyn, first Duke of St Albans. Lavinia Fenton, the original Polly Peachum in John Gay's *The Beggar's Opera*, who pioneered show-business marriages into the aristocracy by becoming the Duchess of Bolton, moved there in 1730. The street soon became a fashionable place for young blades to promenade; by 1717 popular newspapers were referring to 'Bond Street loungers'.

Meanwhile a very different character – that of the Whig establishment, solidly loyal to the new House of Hanover – was being stamped on the first of the great Mayfair squares rising north-east of Bond Street on land owned by the Earl of Scarborough (and still regarded as so far out in the sticks that it sold for only 2s. 6d. a foot). Originally intended to be named Oxford Square, Hanover Square was to be, in Sir John Summerson's words, 'the foundation stone of Mayfair', and in 1717 its first residents were moving in to its distinctive four-storey houses built of dark grey, red and yellow stock brick. They were a group of Whig generals who had served in Marlborough's campaigns, the best-known being Lord Cadogan, a large, burly Irishman recently raised to the peerage who had been Marlborough's quartermaster-general and most trusted subordinate. But the pioneer of the Hanover Square development seems to have been the elderly General Stewart, commander-in-chief in Ireland under Queen Anne and a landowner of substance in both Ireland and England. In 1712 he had given the site for the building of St George's Church, and he was certainly among the first to take up residence in the square in 1717, when he was seventy-three years old.

From the beginning Hanover Square was fashionable – in the 1720s thirteen of its twenty-five inhabitants had titles, and St George's remained well into this century *the* place for society weddings. Its residents, said a commentator in 1734, were 'persons of distinction'; among the earliest was Lord Cowper, the former Lord High Chancellor who had opposed the ill-fated South Sea investment scheme and was known as 'silver-tongued Cowper'. Besides Marlborough's generals, the ratepayers in 1725 included the dukes of

Roxburghe, Montrose and Bolton; lords Hillsborough, Falk-land, Carpenter, Dunmore, Pontefract, Londonderry and Lichfield; Lady Dashwood, Sir Adolphus Oughton, and Count Staremberg. It was small wonder that John Strype, the London topographer, predicted Tyburn gallows would soon be moved elsewhere to save this new neighbourhood 'inconvenience or annoyance' from the journeys of the condemned along the Oxford Road.

Its Hanoverian respectability did not, however, preclude some racy activities among the square's aristocratic resi-dents, notably Lord Hillsborough, whose son became the Marquess of Downshire. His family house at the corner of Hanover Square and Brook Street, later the scene of famous diplomatic and literary dinners hosted by Talleyrand, the French Ambassador, was frequented about the year 1730 by a private society at whose gatherings, according to one eye-witness account:

Each gentleman came masked, and brought with him one Lady – either his mistress, or any other man's wife, or perhaps a woman of the town – who was also masked. They were on oath not to divulge names, and continued masked the whole time. There were tables set out for supper, artificial arbours, couches &c., to which parties retired when they pleased, and called for what refreshment they chose. . . .

Another notorious resident of Hanover Square in the 1770s was Lord Le Despenser, a member of the Hell Fire Club. The site of his house was rebuilt in 1827 as the Oriental Club, an institution irreverently known to hackney coachmen as 'the Horizontal Club'.

Hanover Square had a continental flavour to its architec-ture – some thought it Germanic, though the engraver Thomas Malton considered that the view of St George's from the upper end of the square possessed 'more the air of an Italian scene than any other in London'. This vista was much admired by topographical writers: in 1734 James Ralph, author of *A Critical Review of the Public Buildings in and about London*, waxed almost lyrical about it.

I must own that the view down George Street, from the upper end of the Square, is one of the most entertaining in this whole city; the sides of the square, the area in the middle, the break of the buildings that form the entrance to the vista, the vista itself, but above all the beautiful projection of the portico of St George's Church, are all circumstances that unite in beauty and make the scene perfect.

The poet Wordsworth thought the view from Harewood Place, the same vantage point as Ralph's, one of the finest in old London. (Today only Number 24 survives in the square among the offices and dress manufacturers' show-rooms to suggest what the original houses looked like, though something of the charm of that view down St George's Street remains.)

Mayfair was now, in the second decade of the eighteenth century, about to become a ferment of architectural genius, with a young patron of taste and public spirit setting the tone at the Piccadilly end. About the time that Marlbor-ough's generals were settling into their Hanover Square homes, Richard Boyle, third Earl of Cork and Burlington, was embarking on the transformation of his family mansion, Burlington House, from the plain, classic brick structure chosen by his great-grandfather in Restoration times to the Palladian magnificence, all exuberant arcades and colon-nades, which he had so admired as an architectural student in Italy. The house was accordingly encased in a new coat of stone, and curved colonnades connected it with an imposing arched gateway on to Piccadilly. Horace Walpole, seeing it for the first time by daylight after attending a ball at Burlington House, gazed at sunrise out of his bedroom window and exclaimed: 'It seemed one of those edifices in fairy tales that are raised by genii in a night time.' Other contemporaries were less impressed. The sharp-tongued Lord John Hervey, who lived on Burlington's estate at 31 Old Burlington Street, commented that the house was 'possessed of one great hall of state, Without a room to sleep or eat'. (Hervey also remarked sardonically that Burlington's Palladian villa, Chiswick House, was 'too small to live in and too large to hang on a watch-chain'.)

In 1717 Burlington was only twenty-three, but he had already been a member of the Privy Council for four years and was well advanced on his influential career as a patron of architecture, painting, literature and music; through gathering a circle about him of such architects as Colen Campbell and William Kent, he stamped the Palladian image on English buildings for more than a century. While Campbell, under his supervision, was transforming Burlington House into an Italian palazzo straight out of Vicenza or Verona, Burlington himself was laying out a new residential quarter on the land directly behind it; Old and New Burlington streets, Clifford Street and Savile Row. He badly needed revenue to defray his mounting pile of debt, for which he had already had to mortgage land in Ireland, but the London estates were entailed, and it was necessary to obtain a private Act of Parliament before he could sell leases there. Curiously, in view of Burlington's architectural flair, the new quarter was never conceived as an entity, but there were some extremely fine individual houses within its boundaries, designed by the foremost architects of the day: Colen Campbell, William Kent (who lived for a while in Savile Row, surrounded by a fine collection of Italian paintings), Henry Flitcroft and Nicholas Hawksmoor, the great church builder. The area attracted eminent inhabitants, among them General Wade, pacifier of the Highland clans, Field Marshal Lord Ligonier, and Queen Anne's favourite Court physician, the author and wit Sir John Arbuthnot, friend of Pope and Swift.

General Wade, a lifelong bachelor, had the distinction of having his house designed by the Earl of Burlington himself at 29 Old Burlington Street. It was very splendid, but uncomfortable: the Earl of Chesterfield suggested that he should live in the house opposite and just look at it. Wade lived there for twenty-three years, however, and the house survived, as part of the Burlington Hotel, until 1935. Arbuthnot lived at 11 Cork Street and his friend Pope considered taking a house in the area but decided against it, although his doctor, Simon Burton, lived nearby at 19 Savile Row. The quarter was popular not only with retired military commanders and their widows, but before the rise of Harley and Wimpole streets it was also the favoured area for the top reaches of the medical profession.

By 1720 Mayfair was gradually being filled in, but there remained a large vacant area of fields to the north-west, about a hundred acres sloping gently from Tyburn to the edge of the Berkeley lands. Its owner, Sir Richard Grosvenor, wanted it to be the best-planned unit in London, laid out on an elegant grid pattern with, as its centrepiece, a square larger than any then seen in the capital, to which the grandest names in society would be attracted as residents. By 1721 he had granted the first of many building leases which in half a century would cover the remaining corners of rural Mayfair with bricks and mortar. Once Hanover Square was completed, he could envisage a splendid thoroughfare linking it with Grosvenor Square and offering a vista from the Park which would culminate in the spire of St George's. Unfortunately another landlord, building on the bulge off Maddox Street, spoiled this grand design for later generations, but it captivated contemporary writers. Daniel Defoe, making a tour of the Grosvenor estate for *Applebee's Weekly Journal* in September 1725, recorded passing 'an amazing Scene of new Foundations, not of Houses only, but as I might say of new Cities, New Towns, New Squares and fine Buildings, the like of which no City, no Town, nay, no Place in the World can shew; nor is it possible to judge where or when they will make an end or stop of Building'. Four years later a popular versifier wrote: 'Pease, cabbages, and turnips once grew where Now stands New Bond Street, and a newer Square; Such piles of buildings now rise up and down, London itself seems going out of Town.'

The east side of Berkeley Square began to rise in 1737; all were demolished two centuries later to make way for office blocks and car showrooms. A few houses on the west side still look as they did in the early 1740s, the gem being Number 44, in Sir Nikolaus Pevsner's view possibly the finest terrace house in London. Built by William Kent for Lady Isabella Finch, its interior, with a magnificent Venetian staircase and vaulted drawing room, was described by Horace Walpole as 'a beautiful piece of scenery'. Today enjoyed by the well-heeled gamblers of the Clermont Club, it remains a treasure house of interior design which, as Sir

Sacheverell Sitwell has remarked, would be famous in any other city but London.

Berkeley Square and the streets which sprang west from it – Hill Street, Charles Street, John Street (now Chesterfield Hill) and Farm Street – were immediately fashionable places to live. The first ratepayer in the square was Sir Charles Frederick, Surveyor-General of the Ordnance, who lived in the present Number 35. Clive of India died of an overdose of laudanum at Number 45 in 1774 and this and its neighbour Number 46 were inhabited continuously by the same families (Clives and the Earls of Powis, and Blighs and Mildmays respectively) from the mid eighteenth century to the mid twentieth century. Number 47 Berkeley Square was the home of William Pitt in December 1783 when he became Britain's youngest prime minister at the age of twenty-four. It was rebuilt in the 1890s by Edward Steinkopff, the managing director of the Apollinaris mineral water firm, who sold his share in the company for more than £1 million. Number 40, residence of the fourth Duke of Newcastle in 1815, had earlier been the home of the unfortunate Admiral Byng, executed in 1757 (*'pour encourager les autres'*, as Voltaire said) after he had failed to relieve Minorca from French attack. Colley Cibber, the playwright, lived at No. 20, on the corner of Bruton Street, and died there in 1757 as Poet Laureate, aged eighty-four.

But like so much of Mayfair in the early days of its intimate, village-like character, Berkeley Square was also the home of tradesmen – a wax chandler, a woollen draper, an undertaker, a distiller and a hosier were all among the earliest residents. There was Gwynn's Coffee House, a fishmonger's shop and, from 1760 right up to 1931, the celebrated ice-cream and pastry-maker Gunter, founded by an Italian immigrant called Dominicus Negri at Number 7 on the east side of the square. In 1762 the square's most aristocratic resident, the Earl of Bute, bought two small plots of land from the fifth Lord Berkeley for £115 and commissioned Robert Adam to design Bute House at the southern end. Before the house was finished, Lord Bute sold it to William Petty, second Earl of Shelburne and first Marquess of Lansdowne, who changed its name first to Shelburne House and then to Lansdowne House, under which

name it became a famous centre of political entertaining in
the nineteenth century. Much truncated, and shorn of its
delightful garden which used to abut that of Devonshire
House and give the south side of Berkeley Square a countrified air up to the mid–1920s, it survives now as the
Lansdowne Club, with only a handful of rooms retaining a
Georgian character and much of the rest still redolent of its
mid-thirties conversion. One of its original marble fireplaces
now graces the reading room of the London Library in St
James's Square; the original drawing room was acquired by
the Museum of Arts in Philadelphia and the dining room
went to the Metropolitan Museum in New York.

The last Lord Berkeley of Stratton died in 1773 and his
estates reverted to the main branch of the family, the Earls
of Berkeley, whose ancestral seat was Berkeley Castle on the
Severn. The family's London home, 16 Berkeley Square,
was demolished in 1937 along with several other historic
dwellings, including Walpole's at Number 11, to provide the
site for Berkeley Square House, a massive block of offices
on the east side. Five years later the line died out with
Randal Thomas Mowbray, the eighth Earl. The last Berkeley
of Stratton was not to be granted the wish expressed in his
will that his family stock 'may continue to Flourish and put
forth new Branches as long as any kind of Civil Government
shall subsist in this Country'. The Grosvenor family was to
be more fortunate, as indeed it had been from the very
beginning, when a twist of fateful match-making ensured
that Grosvenors rather then Berkeleys would lord it over
Mayfair.

3

SIR THOMAS GROSVENOR'S GOLDEN ACRES

*I*N 1672 the first Baron Berkeley had every reason to feel pleased with the prospects for his family. He had signed an agreement for the marriage five years hence of his eldest son Charles, then aged ten, to Mary Davies, the seven-year-old heiress to 500 acres on the western edge of London, adjoining the Berkeley estates. Mary was the daughter of Alexander Davies, whose occupation of scrivener, technically concerned with the drafting of deeds, also involved the management of investments for clients. In his case it had also lately included acting as confidential clerk to his famously rich great-uncle, Hugh Audley or Awdeley, as it was sometimes spelled. Audley was a clerk to the Court of Wards and Liveries in the City, but his immense wealth had come from a secondary career as a money-lender, for which he was so renowned that after his death in 1662 a pamphlet was sold by street-vendors proclaiming 'The way to be rich, according to the practice of the great Audley. . . . Who begun with *two hundred Pound* in the year 1605 and dyed with *four hundred thousand Pound* this instant November'.

Samuel Pepys noted in his diary for 23 November 1662 that 'old rich Audley' had, by his will, 'made a great many

poor families rich', including Pepys's old schoolfellow at
St Paul's, the bookseller Thomas Davies. But Audley was
constantly changing his will in his last years and it was
Thomas's younger brother Alexander who eventually came
off best. His inheritance, still swampy meadowland, had
once formed the ancient manor of Eia or Eye (from which
the name Ebury derives) and its boundaries had stretched
from the Roman road following the line of present-day
Oxford Street and Bayswater Road to the Thames in the
south, the Westbourne stream in the west and the Tybourne
in the east. After the Norman Conquest the land was given
to Geoffrey de Mandeville for his services to William; it then
passed to the monks of Westminster Abbey for 500 years,
returning to Crown ownership at the dissolution of the
monasteries. Under Henry VIII the manor was divided and
part of it enclosed to make Hyde Park, where the sporting
monarch liked to ride and keep herds of deer.

The estate's next owner, in 1618, was Sir Lionel Cranfield,
the ambitious, self-made merchant who became Lord High
Treasurer of England under James I but was impeached for
corruption. The decline in his fortunes forced him to sell the
leasehold cheaply to Audley in 1626 for £9400. Audley, a
miserly and unloved character, lived for so long that several
generations of his family saw their hopes of wealth blighted
before he finally died in his eighties. His great-nephew Alexander Davies had joined his service only a short time before
the old man's death.

With his unexpected inheritance, Davies planned to go
in for speculative building on the estate, starting with a
development on Millbank, where he built a handsome town
house for himself. But three years later, aged only twenty-
nine, Davies became a victim of the Great Plague. His
daughter Mary was six months old; his widow, also named
Mary, was twenty-two. He left a mountain of debts, having
borrowed heavily to finance his building projects. Mary
Davies soon married again, a shrewd businessman named
John Tregonwell, and the couple devised a plan to retrieve
a slice of capital through trading off young Mary's future
inheritance.

It was Tregonwell who drew up the agreement with Lord
Berkeley, in which Berkeley agreed to pay £5000 down on

signature of the contract and to transfer a further settlement of land worth £3500. The latter proved the undoing of the Berkeley family ambitions, because for some reason – perhaps the expense of building Berkeley House – he was unable to complete the terms of the deal, and it was called off. The Tregonwells, by this time having spent the first £5000, were forced to look elsewhere for a husband of suitable substance. There was no shortage of offers and their choice fell on the twenty-one-year-old baronet Sir Thomas Grosvenor, scion of an old Cheshire family claiming descent from Hugh Lupus, a nephew of William of Normandy.

The Grosvenors owned land in three counties along with valuable lead mines in Wales. Thomas, the third Baronet, was a short, good-looking young man with dark eyes, curly hair and a lively, educated mind. His father had died when he was six and his grandfather three years later. In the company of a guardian trustee, he had made the Grand Tour of Europe when he was fourteen, with a passport signed personally by Charles II 'for Sir Thomas Grosvenor of Eaton Boat, Baronet, to travel beyond the seas for his education and experience'. He had studied with the great Danish mathematician Nicolaus Mercator and he collected books on astronomy, mathematics, military affairs and navigation. He was busy with a plan to rebuild his family's ancestral home, the ramshackle manor house known as Eaton Boat, and it was while visiting his architect in London that he received the Tregonwells' offer, on which he had to make up his mind within six weeks. The treaty, elaborately drafted by the Tregonwells' lawyers, required him first to repay Lord Berkeley's £5000, plus £1500 interest. Grosvenor accepted the terms and after the marriage the Grosvenor lawyer, William Thomas, drew up a receipt which read:

I, Sir Thomas Grosvenor of Eaton in the County of Chester Baronet do acknowledge that I have had and received from the Right Honble John Ld Berkeley a certain Deed bearing date the twelfth day of December 1672 whereby William Thomas gent with the consent of John Tregonwell Esqre assigned a certain term of one hundred years of and in the Reversion or Remainder one third part of certain lands tenements and hereditaments

late of Alexander Davies Esqre deceased unto the said
Ld Berkeley. Witness my hand the 31th day of Octr
1677. T. Grosvenor.

The wedding took place on 10 October 1677 at St Clement
Danes in the Strand, where the bride's grandfather was
rector. She was twelve years and eight months old, the
bridegroom twenty-one. Mary Davies's dowry was not quite
so extensive as when the manor of Eye was owned by the
Crown. At some stage the southern portion of what is now
Mayfair had been sold – ironically, to the Berkeleys, who,
if their own Davies marriage bargain had gone through,
would have ended up as landlords of an area greater than
the Grosvenors acquired – and odd parcels of land had been
detached elsewhere, like the present site of the Dorchester
Hotel, which to this day lies just outside the edge of the
Grosvenor estate. Some had also been sold, by special Act
of Parliament in 1675, to reimburse John Tregonwell for
debts incurred by Alexander Davies which he had settled
out of his own pocket. These lands included the site of what
was to become Buckingham Palace, seven acres of Mayfair
to the north of Brick Street, and twenty-two acres of Knights-
bridge – later repurchased by the Grosvenor family. In 1677
the total annual income from Mary Davies's London estates
was £2170, less than half the return from the Grosvenor
lands in Cheshire.

Because of her extreme youth, Mary Grosvenor remained
in the guardianship of her aunt for two years after her
marriage, during which time her husband busied himself
with the building of his new seat, Eaton Hall, to the north
of the old manor on the banks of the Dee, and had his
portrait painted by Lely. About the time he finally brought
his bride home to the new house with its square courtyard
and wings of local brick and stone, Sir Thomas was returned
as Tory MP for Chester, and during the rest of his short life
he spent much of his time in politics, serving in six parlia-
ments and on many committees.

Mary Grosvenor took a close and informed interest in
her London estates – letters to her mother reveal a shrewd
knowledge of rents and leases – and found the life of the
Cheshire gentry tedious. 'Though Chester is so near I scarce

ever see it, so can tell little what is done there, never enquiring after it,' she wrote plaintively to a visitor to the county. 'The players are gone to Shrewsbury from thence. I saw none of their plays, but am told they acted well enough. There have been three Balls. . . . The Ladies play at Cards every week att one another's houses, and raffle att the Indian house is all I can tell you. . . .'

In the mid–1680s, when anti-Popery fever was still high, she converted to Roman Catholicism, a traumatic event for the politically active Grosvenor family and one which was to have a profound effect on the future of the London estates, as did her deteriorating mental condition. A few months after Sir Thomas died of 'a feavour' in July 1700 Mary Grosvenor announced her intention to travel abroad with her Catholic chaplain. To the horror of the family she was persuaded into marrying the chaplain's brother Edward Fenwick while visiting Paris; four years of legal battles ensued, in which Fenwick unsuccessfully tried to get his hands on Mary's fortune, even petitioning the Court of Chancery, until the marriage was finally annulled in 1705. In the same year Dame Mary, as she was known, was committed into the care of a guardian as insane: from then until her death in 1730 revenues from her estates were paid into the Court of Chancery for investment on her behalf, and no changes in the use or disposal of the land could be made without the court's permission, which considerably restricted her son Richard's plans to attract developers to his grand new residential quarter round Grosvenor Square. Dame Mary's mother, Mrs Tregonwell, continued to hold one-third of the estate in dower until she died in 1717, when her portion passed to her daughter, to be administered in Chancery.

Sir Richard Grosvenor, eldest son of the Grosvenor-Davies union, married twice; the first time at eighteen and both times to the daughters of other country baronets. Neither wife gave him children, but he acquired settlements through his marriages of a handsome £20,000. He was a country squire by temperament, closely tied to his Cheshire roots and, like his father, representing Chester in the House of Commons, but by 1710 he had set in train plans for the boldest piece of town planning yet seen north of St James's, a plan that would determine the pattern of Mayfair and its social axis. The centrepiece was to be the grandest square in London, six acres in area, with two new streets, Audley Street and Grosvenor Street, giving access from the Oxford Road and Bond Street. Grosvenor brought in Colen Campbell, who styled himself Architect to the Prince of Wales, to advise on the layout of the square on a piece of land known by the charmingly bucolic name of Pursey Close.

The time was propitious for a building boom: England had settled into a stable and prosperous spell following the Hanoverian succession, the Peace of Utrecht and the crushing of the Jacobite rising of 1715. Plenty of capital was available for mortgages and the steady westward migration from the older, crowded parts of London (where the Plague was still within living memory) to the fresh air and spaciousness of the rising ground between Piccadilly and Oxford Road, combined to induce a feverish spate of speculative building. In 1725 Daniel Defoe described the construction work going on in west London as a 'kind of Prodigy'. Within a dozen years the builders had advanced from Hanover Square through the Grosvenor lands and north of Oxford Road to begin work on Cavendish Square. 'How much farther it may spread, who knows?' pondered Defoe in his *Tour Thro' London About the Year 1725*.

> New squares and new streets rising up every day to such a prodigy of buildings, that nothing in the world does, or ever did, equal it, except old Rome in Trajan's time, when the walls were fifty miles in compass and the number of inhabitants six million eight hundred thousand souls.

The first lease on the Grosvenor estate was granted in July 1721 to a master builder called Thomas Barlow, who had executed some of the handsome new houses in Hanover Square. It was for two parcels of land in what later became Davies Street, and ran for a term of sixty years. Sir Richard Grosvenor was concerned that the term might not be long enough to tempt builders into the area, but his hands were tied until his mother's death, after which he was able to extend the lease to the now familiar ninety-nine years. Several of this length were granted during Dame Mary's lifetime by special permission of her guardian, Robert Myddelton, and the system became the linchpin of the Grosvenors' success down the generations in keeping the estate intact and under family control. Even at sixty-year leases, however, builders proved eager to move in, recouping their investment by selling the shells of houses to wealthy residents who then had the interiors tailored to their taste. The Grosvenors were helpful ground landlords, advancing money for sewer construction, granting mortgages and occasionally turning a blind eye to arrears of ground rent, which by Christmas 1731 had mounted up to £3600. By the time of Mary Grosvenor's death in 1730 money spent on the estate had exceeded income received by more than £4500, and in 1732, the year of his own death, Sir Richard negotiated a loan of £10,000 at 4 per cent interest from one of his tenants, the collateral being ground rents on houses in Brook Street, Grosvenor Street, and Grosvenor Square.

Robert Grosvenor, who succeeded to the baronetcy in 1733 – his brother Thomas had held it for only a year before dying in Italy – continued the family policy of providing mortgages and at his death in 1755 was owed £7700 by builders. He was the most directly involved in Mayfair of all the family, living in a house in Upper Grosvenor Street and running the day-to-day business of the estate while Sir Richard squired it in Cheshire, and acting as head lessee for most of the south side of Grosvenor Square. He helped John Simmons, builder of the east side, by buying up ground rents from him at enhanced values, thus providing finance for the construction of four important houses between 1731 and 1733.

The man most responsible for shaping the street map of Mayfair as we know it was the builder Thomas Barlow, who, with the Grosvenors' estate manager Richard Andrew, laid out a grid pattern of streets sloping gently down from the north-west corner, now Marble Arch, to the top of Berkeley Square. Barlow received £50 for his initial work and a stipend of £50 a year plus 'reasonable expenses' of about £10. It took nearly half a century to cover the area with Georgian brown brick houses, the north-west corner being shunned by developers for years because of its proximity to the Tyburn gaallows, where public executions continued until 1783.

By the summer of 1725, however, building was well advanced in and around the grand centrepiece, Grosvenor Square. An item of news in the *Daily Journal* for 12 July that year recorded:

> The several new streets designed in Grosvenor Building lying between New Bond Street and Hyde Park were lately particularly named: upon which occasion Sir Richard Grosvenor, Bt, gave a very splendid entertainment to his tenants and others concerned in these buildings. . . . There is now building a Square called Grosvenor Square, which for its largeness and beauty will far exceed any yet made in and about London.

In June Sir Richard Grosvenor had undertaken to lay out at his own expense a garden in the centre of the square – the money to be recovered later from the builders who had taken leases around it. The cost was £350, with a further £262.10s. for the splendid gilded statue of King George I, dressed as a Roman emperor, which dominated the centre of the garden. The King's statue had an historical irony about it, for its site in the Civil War had been a Cromwellian strong point known as Oliver's Mount, the origin of Mount Street's name.

The area was an immediate attraction for the 'People of Fascination', as the novelist Tom Fielding called them in 1752:

> Within the memory of many now living the circle of the people of Fascination included the whole parish of Covent Garden and a great part of St Giles in the Fields; but here the enemy broke in and the circle was presently contracted to Leicester Fields and Golden Square. Hence the People of Fashion again retreated before the foe to Hanover Square; whence they were once more driven to Grosvenor Square and even beyond it, and that with so much precipitation, that had they not been stopped by the walls of Hyde Park, it is

more than probable they would by this time have arrived at Kensington.

Sir Richard Grosvenor must have been gratified at how quickly the titled and the wealthy moved in. Of the first fifty-one ratepayers in Grosvenor Square, sixteen were peers, thirty-five had a title of some sort and nineteen were MPs. Their average age was around forty. George II himself was rumoured to be thinking of buying a house in the square for the Prince of Wales. In the square and its principal adjoining streets, Brook and Upper Brook streets, Grosvenor and Upper Grosvenor streets, 117 of the total 277 houses boasted residents of title, either in their own right or by marriage. Nearly one-fifth had a seat in Parliament at one time or another.

One of the earliest inhabitants of the neighbourhood was George Frederick Handel, who took a small house at the Bond Street end of Brook Street (now Number 25, a much-restored brick building housing a dealer in Oriental art) in 1723 and lived there for thirty years. The *Messiah* was composed there. Number 60 Grosvenor Street was sold to Anne Oldfield, a celebrated actress of the time, for £2200 in 1725, a huge sum of money then for a town house. In Grosvenor Square the first duchess had moved in by 1728 – the Duchess of Kendal, one of George I's mistresses, so tall and thin she was known as 'the Maypole'. She had been one of the fortunate few to make money out of the South Sea Bubble, and after she and another royal mistress, the enormously fat Countess of Darlington ('the Elephant and Castle') had to leave St James's Palace on the King's death in 1727, the Duchess immediately elected to live in Mayfair. She stayed for a while in a house on the east side of Old Bond Street which had belonged to Nell Gwnn's son, the Duke of St Albans, and then took a lease from Thomas Barlow of 43 Grosvenor Square, one of the first houses to be completed on the south side.

Grosvenor Square was not built to an architectural design like Inigo Jones's piazza or Bedford Square on the Southampton estate, but by a number of master builders working on a speculative basis. In the end these men – John Simmons, Benjamin Timbrell, the Barlow family and Edward

Shepherd, builder of Shepherd Market – constructed a pleasing, irregularly skylined composition of four-storey Georgian houses in brownish-red stock brick, surrounding the oval garden with its iron railings. Simmons designed the east side as a symmetrical entity, the houses in the centre and at either end rising to balance the facade of the terrace, but the rest of the square was disparagingly described by the topographer James Ralph in 1734 as 'little better than a collection of whims, and frolics in building, without anything like order or beauty'. The judgement seems unduly harsh. The wide roadway and tree-planted garden gave a tremendous sense of space to the square, whose buildings in contemporary prints sit back modestly with their chimneys etched against a mackerel sky, delicate examples of the builder's art by contrast with the great slabs of thirties neo-Georgian which hem in three sides of the square today, the fourth side being occupied by the modern mass of Saarinen's American Embassy.

The highest price for a new house anywhere on the Grosvenor estate in these early years was £7500, paid in 1730 by the Earl of Thanet for 19 Grosvenor Square. It formed part of a grand pedimented frontage covering the width of three houses and designed to look like a single dwelling, and its interior was partly by Robert Adam. It survived just over two hundred years, its last occupant being the wife of the conductor Sir Thomas Beecham before it was demolished in 1933. Prices elsewhere round the newly built square varied from £1750 for Number 34 on the corner of South Audley Street (close to the fictional site of Dorian Gray's house in the Oscar Wilde story) to £6400, the price asked of Lord Weymouth for Number 7. Weymouth chose not to buy, renting it instead for £396 a year. Rents in the surrounding streets could be astonishingly low: one of the Barlows rented a three-storey house in North Audley Street from Edward Shepherd for a mere £24 a year, and it boasted a garden, a stable behind, and rooms 'wainscotted all round from bottom to top', with chimney-pieces of marble or Portland stone.

Number 4, the largest of the original houses in the square, was sold by the novel method of a raffle in 1739, a device recently re-invented in the United States to achieve the notional market price at a time of recession and sluggish house sales. Number 4 had been built by John Simmons for his own use and was valued at £10,000. To raise the money his widow sold 39,999 raffle tickets at 5s. 3d. each, with a free ticket to anyone who bought two dozen. The draw was held on 8 June 1739 and was won jointly by the wife of a Piccadilly grocer and her lodger. Everyone did well out of the deal. Mrs Simmons got her £10,000 and the winners sold the house to Edward Howard, ninth Duke of Norfolk, who got a bargain at £4725, though he lived in it for less than a year. It then became the town house of two great Anglo-Irish landed families, the Wentworths and the FitzWilliams, who occupied it for nearly two hundred years until it became the Italian Embassy in 1931.

A VERY EXCLUSIVE VILLAGE

4

'STREWN WITH STRAWBERRY LEAVES'

*A*LL the grand London squares attracted the nobility as residents, but until the Second World War no single stretch of the capital drew more dukes, marquesses, earls and viscounts than Grosvenor Square. J. P. Malcolm, author of *Londonium Redivivum*, described it in 1802 as 'the very focus of feudal grandeur, fashion, taste and hospitality'. In the 1730s, when the paint was still fresh in the great formal rooms looking on to the oval garden, they were literally living side by side. On a round of calls in 1735 or 1736 one would have found the Earl of Coventry living at Number 3; Viscount Weymouth, heir to the Marquess of Bath, at Number 7; the Earl of Clinton at Number 11; the Earl of Albemarle at Number 16; the Earl of Buckingham at Number 18; the Earl of Thanet at Number 19, the most expensive house in the square; the Earl of Mountrath at Number 20; Lord Nassau Poulett, heir to the Duke of Bolton, at Number 21 (the fifth Duke shot himself at Number 37 in 1765); the Dowager Duchess of Rutland at Number 22; the Earl of Shaftesbury, great-grandfather of the Victorian philanthropist, at Number 24; the Duke of Manchester at Number 26; the Earl of Scarborough at Number 32; the Earl of Dysart at Number 33; the Marquess of Blandford at Number 40; the Earl of Breadalbane at Number 41; the Duchess of Kendal at Number 43; and Lord North, first Earl of Guilford, at Number 50, then listed as part of Grosvenor Street. (All the houses in the square were renumbered in the late nineteenth century.) The Bishop of Durham resided at Number 6 and nearly all the remaining houses were occupied by lesser lords, knights and MPs.

Grosvenor Square's reputation as a favoured haunt of the rich and aristocratic was to endure for 200 years. At any one time about half its inhabitants were titled, and some member of the Grosvenor family was always in residence from 1755 to 1885. The apogee of its political distinction was in the 1760s, when three current or future prime ministers – lords Rockingham, Grafton and North – had their town houses there. In 1934, when Arthur Dasent described the square's history as 'metaphorically strewn with strawberry leaves and the blue ribbons of Garter Knights', it could still boast a handsome cluster of coronets. Half a dozen houses had been or were about to be demolished, and many more were standing forlornly empty, but the sixth Duke of Portland was at Number 3, the Dowager Duchess of Westminster in part of the sub-divided Number 16, Admiral Earl Beatty, the dashing hero of Jutland, at Number 17, the eleventh Marquess of Huntly, the premier Marquess of Scotland, at Number 24, the fifth Marquess of Bath at Number 29, Lord Leigh of Stoneleigh at Number 31, the Dowager Duchess of Somerset at Number 35, the Dowager Viscountess Tredegar at Number 43 and Lord Illingworth at Number 44. (Number 3 had a special distinction, even in Grosvenor Square, of having up to that time been home to two dukes, two marquesses, six earls, three viscounts, a baron and a baronet in its two centuries of existence: only three of its residents were plain esquires and one was a minister of the Crown).

The streets leading out of Grosvenor Square were also quick to acquire titled exclusivity. Robert Seymour's *Survey of the Cities of London and Westminster* (1735) remarked of Brook Street that it was 'for the most part nobly built and inhabited by People of Quality', and of Grosvenor Street that it was a 'spacious well-built Street, inhabited chiefly by People of Distinction'. In 1736, twenty-two of the seventy-four houses in Grosvenor Street were occupied by members of the aristocracy, including one duke, two future dukes and three earls. Brook Street scored fewer coronets, though William Pitt the Elder, first Earl of Chatham, was an early resident at Number 68. Its lower reaches, between Davies Street and Bond Street, became a magnet for hotelkeepers, to the disapproval of one early Surveyor to the Grosvenor estates who commented in 1805 that this part of Brook Street was no longer 'to be thought an eligible situation for Persons of Rank. . . . The demand for Hotels is every year increasing. . . .' He did add, in mitigation, that the families who, lacking their own town house, required hotel accommodation on seasonal visits to London were 'very respectable persons' and that the establishments themselves – pioneered by James Mivart, the founder of Claridge's – were as 'quiet and respectable in appearance as private Houses'. Where it touched Grosvenor Square, however, Brook Street was as grand as any of the great avenues stretching from Hyde Park to Bond Street; the 'calm retreats', as a writer observed in 1807, 'of nobility and persons of great landed property'.

There were those, too, who sought to do business with the titled and the wealthy. Among the new residents in Grosvenor Street in 1758 were the Adam brother architects from Edinburgh, Robert and James, who were to launch a revolution in architectural design and interior decoration: they perceived the value of a fine London house as their base amid potential clients 'to blind the world,' as Robert Adam said, 'by dazzling their eyesight with vain pomp'. (Their house, renumbered 76, is now part of a 1930s-rebuilt block of three houses forming the offices of the estate agents Hillier, Parker, May and Rowden.)

The Adams became masters of the quintessential Mayfair house, the seasonal *pied-à-terre*, while Parliament was sitting and the great round of society in full swing, for the families who ruled England. Their social life, no mere outcrop of Vanity Fair, formed a substantial part of politics, literature, the arts and the cementing of dynastic relationships, and their houses were designed around these functions. Their grand reception rooms were planned, as Sir John Summerson wrote, for public rather than domestic life:

a life of continual entertaining in drawing-rooms and
ante-rooms and eating-rooms, where conversation
would not be wholly ephemeral, where a sentence might
be delivered which would echo round political England,
where an introduction might mean the beginning of a
career or a deft criticism the dethronement of a policy.

When the Adams prepared their preliminary sketches, key
considerations would include such factors as where dinner
guests would assemble and converse, how they would
proceed to the dining room and where each rank of servant
would carry out their allotted duties with maximum
efficiency and minimum visibility.

No Adam house was unfortunate – or ill-built – enough
to meet the fate of that commissioned by the Duke of Grafton
on Hay Hill. Lady Mary Coke records in her Journal how,
just after the Duke had left on 12 November 1768, it fell
down, burying fourteen or fifteen workmen in the ruins and
killing four. By the 1770s no Mayfair hostess could feel truly
in the fashion without having Robert Adam to remodel her
rooms, though adulation of the brothers was by no means
universal: Lady Mary Coke, for one, much preferred the
work of Jeffrey Wyatt. One of Robert Adam's best clients
was the nineteen-year-old Viscount Stanley, later twelfth
Earl of Derby, who acquired Number 26 Grosvenor Square
in 1771 and turned the interior over to Adam 'without
restriction or limitation of expense', as a newspaper of the
time reported. Angelica Kauffmann and her husband
Antonio Zucchi, who frequently worked on Adam interiors,
contributed murals and Horace Walpole commented acidly
on the cost of it all. Derby House, said to have been Adam's
great London masterpiece, remained in the Stanley family
for more than a century, until it was torn down and rebuilt
in the 1860s.

A lease in the Grosvenor Estate office dated 3 December
1733 and published in the *Survey of London* gives a graphic
profile of a Grosvenor Square house and its fittings a few
years after the square was built. It is Number 45, formerly
40, on the south side, which after three years in the occupation of the Marquess of Blandford and his mother was
leased by Thomas Richmond, a carpenter, at £240 a year to

Philip Dormer Stanhope, the famous fourth Earl of Chester-field. He lived there for fifteen years until his magnificent house by Isaac Ware on the corner of Curzon and South Audley streets, facing Hyde Park, was finished in 1748. The new leaseholder of 45 Grosvenor Square had the use of more than fourteen rooms 'compleatly wainscotted' and fitted with glazed sash windows and marble chimneypieces; a 'Water Closett adjoining to the Garden with a Marble Bason Bosses and Seat compleat a Leaden Cistern on the Top of the same'; three wine vaults and the usual complement of servants' quarters, kitchen, pantries, laundry and stables with standing for twelve horses. The hygiene requirements of the domestic staff were accommodated, not by an expens-ively plumbed water closet but in the garden by a 'Boghouse wainscotted with a Door to the same, a leaden Bason with Bosses and wast pipes and Seat compleat'.

Even minor fittings were solid and handsome. Sashes and shutters on the owner's bedroom floor and in the public rooms were knobbed in brass; the ballcocks in the lead cisterns were also of brass, and the servants' rooms were wainscotted and equipped with closets, Portland stone chimneypieces and firestone hearths. The staircase was painted, with 'Twist Rails & Ballisters carved Brackettes', and the entrance hall was finished off with two Ionic pilasters 'with the Entablature carved around the Hall'.

In such a house, supported by fourteen or fifteen servants, a pillar of the fashionable world would establish himself with his wife and family for the duration of the parliamen-tary sittings which governed the seasonal migrations of the landed classes. The pattern was to endure virtually up to the outbreak of the First World War, reaching its apogee in the middle of the nineteenth century; essentially it was the same in its social framework and assumptions whether in the Mayfair of the Regency or that of the 1870s, pinned so brilliantly by Thackeray and Trollope to the pages of *Vanity Fair* and *The Way We Live Now*.

Some households lived in immense style. Baron Conway, later the Marquess of Hertford, kept twenty-two servants at 16 Grosvenor Street in 1746, and his annual expenses there totalled nearly £3000 – mostly tradesmen's accounts, since the servants cost only £345. Travelling costs from the Hertfords' Warwickshire seat, Ragley Hall, were included in the town house accounts. Lord Ashburnham spent more than £4000 a year on his annual visits to the capital between 1710 and 1716, and the second Duke of Kingston managed to spend £2000 in just two weeks in the summer of 1752. Yet Dr Johnson, lodging with Henry Thrale, a prosperous brewer, and his socially ambitious wife at 37 Grosvenor Square – not far from the Earl of Chesterfield, whose patronage he had sought for the *Dictionary*, with bitter lack of success – considered that £50 a year was 'undoubtedly more than the necessities of life require'. Grosvenor Square, he found, was 'not half so convenient' as Bolt Court off Fleet Street. There is now no trace of Johnson's Mayfair lodgings, the house having disappeared with others in 1937 to make way for a discreetly luxurious neo-Georgian block of service apartments.

The London Season began in the first fogs of November, and throughout the winter months – Christmas being spent at the country seat – the squares and streets of Mayfair and St James's resounded with the rattle and clatter of carriages laden with trunks and household goods as the gentry returned from a summer and autumn spent minding their estates to govern a larger domain from Westminster. *The World* on 15 January 1790 reported that 'London is now almost at the fullest: – every avenue yesterday was crowded with carriages coming into town'. Eighteenth-century parliamentary sessions grew longer as the century wore on, lasting into June or July – sometimes even later. By September, however, the town lay dusty and silent, its great houses given over to squadrons of workmen repairing, re-upholstering, painting and cleaning for the coming season.

While Parliament went about its business the wives and daughters of the legislators pursued an energetic social round. A fascinating portrait of the age emerges from the *Letters and Journals* of Lady Mary Coke, second daughter of the Duke of Argyll and a noted gossip of the period. Her hard-headed marriage to Lord Coke, son of the Earl of Leicester, arranged by her parents for £2500 a year and £500 pin money in exchange for a dowry of £20,000, had ended conveniently in his death after seven years of dislike and contempt on both sides, leaving her a rich widow of twenty-six. Her looks were a matter of debate, some declaring her beautiful, others that her curious albino complexion, lack of eyebrows and fierce gaze gave her the look of a white cat. She had, however, 'fine teeth, an agreeable smile, a handsome neck, well-shapen hands and arms, and a majestic figure', as Lady Louisa Stuart wrote in her memoir of 1827. But by all accounts she was a spoiled, conceited woman with an ungovernable temper to whom nothing, it was said, happened to her as it did to ordinary people. In her egocentric way, she exaggerated even natural phenomena. To quote Lady Louisa again:

> She could not be caught in a shower but it was such rain as never before fell from the skies. The dry-rot that broke out in her house was totally different in its nature from the dry-rot at her next neighbour's [and] all her disorders were something nobody else could judge of, or had ever experienced.

Horace Walpole, at one time an intimate friend of Lady Mary's who dedicated *The Castle of Otranto* to her, constantly made fun of her, apparently without risk of causing offence because, as Lady Louisa remarked, 'she was so cased in self-satisfaction that the keenest raillery, if couched in civil language, would pass upon her for a compliment'. Some thought her downright vulgar: after her death in 1811 one acquaintance complained that 'She said "this here", and "that there", which was extraordinary, as she must always have been in the best circles of society.'

Moving in to town from the suburbs of Sudbrook and Notting Hill, she lived from 1763 to 1775 in a house belonging to Lady Bateman overlooking Green Park, later taking a house in Berkeley Square. She also had houses in Hill Street and, at the time of her death, in Mount Street, though she died in Chiswick. Her account of her daily social round, written as a private newsletter for her sister Anne, Countess of Strafford, was intended, she said, that 'everything that was found in it might be depended upon for truth'. Once ensconced in Mayfair, Lady Mary applied herself with dedication to establishing herself on the fringes of the Court, where the level of her friendship with the

Duke of York was a source of much fascinated gossip around the town.

Her journal probably reflects faithfully enough the life of the aristocratic Mayfair woman of her time; endless rounds of calls and card parties, visits to the Opera and the pleasure gardens of Ranelagh and Vauxhall, keeping up with the latest books and plays and – above all – with who was marrying, divorcing or dallying with whom, with walks in the Park, gardening, attending church (or readiing sermons at home as a substitute), going to auctions and travelling to Spa, the eponymous Belgian watering place, and other staple points on the Grand Tour. Food did not figure prominently in her daily jottings, except when bad: there is one memorably unpleasant incident of peas from Holland being cut open with a knife to reveal an insect in each one. Unproductive it may have been, but the life required a certain stamina: on one particularly busy Saturday evening in May of 1767 Lady Mary began a round of calls at 6.30 p.m. by visiting the Duchess of Norfolk at her mansion in St James's Square, and proceeded from there to make thirty-two more visits, ending at Lady Hertford's, 'where I play'd at Lu till eleven and won eleven guineas'. Lu, or Loo, a card game in which penalties were paid into a common pool, was the craze of the age along with faro, and enormous sums were won and lost by the club members of St James's, reflected on a more domestic scale by their wives in Mayfair. In March 1768 Lady Mary recorded: 'I play'd at Lu and never saw it run so high: the last two stakes were ninety and ninety-five guineas. Lady Ailesbury won one of them.'

Gambling was the curse of the upper classes, and few were immune. Horace Walpole, fourth Earl of Orford, wrote of Almack's, the precursor of Brooks's Club, 'where a thousand meadows and cornfields are staked on every throw, and as many villages lost as in the earthquake that overwhelmed Herculaneum and Pompeii'. Young men, he recorded in 1770, would casually lose five, ten or fifteen thousand pounds in an evening. 'Lord Stavorley, not one-and-twenty, lost eleven thousand last Tuesday, but recovered it by one great hand at hazard. He swore a great oath – "Now, if I had been playing deep, I might have won millions"!' In the following century one of Walpole's own descendants, for whom the title Earl of Orford had been revived after it died with Horace, staked the family house, 11 Berkeley Square, on a game of cards one night and lost it to Henry Baring of the banking family.

Charles James Fox, the heavy-browed Whig politician on whom so many bright hopes were pinned, was repeatedly bankrupted by his gambling debts. He lost £140,000 when still only twenty-four, and had his debts paid by his father, Lord Holland. Once, when out of office and frustrated by political inactivity, he played Colonel Richard Fitzpatrick, the Secretary of State for War and a fellow member of the Devonshire House circle, at faro for eight hours non-stop at Almack's, losing £11,000 in the process. After one of his worst nights at the tables a friend found him calmly reading Herodotus in the Greek. 'What else is there to do when a man has lost everything?' he remarked.

Georgiana, the enchanting young Duchess of Devonshire who held West End society in the palm of her hand throughout the late eighteenth century, used her persuasive charm on Thomas Coutts, founder of the exclusive bank, to help her conceal her enormous gambling debts from her husband, though his fortune was immense enough to have absorbed them without trace. Walpole, the ever-observant gossip, spotted her and her sister Harriet, Lady Duncannon, indulging in the latest craze in 1780, lottery offices which were set up behind the Opera House in Covent Garden. After the performance society ladies would place bets at the booths on numbers to be drawn the following day. If the number failed to come up it cost five guineas, but a winning bet could yield at least forty guineas. In one session at the lottery offices Georgiana won £900, tempting her and Harriet to start trading numbers on their own account. Walpole informed one of his correspondents, Mary Berry, in March 1791: 'Two of our first ladies, sisters, have descended into the *basse cour* of the [Exchange] Alley with Jews and brokers, and waddled out with a large loss of feathers, though not so inconsiderable as was said – yet twenty-three thousand makes a great gap in pin-money.' Harriet was driven to publish a denial in the newspapers, but few believed her.

Gambling apart, society had other obsessions to fill its leisure. There was the Opera – Walpole attended up to five

performances in a week, though Lady Mary Coke observed
tartly that the Duke of Gloucester 'stay'd his usual time, half
an Act' and that the King of Denmark in his box revealed
both boredom and ill breeding: 'He picked his Nose, which
you know is neither graceful or [sic] royal.' There were the
obligatory evening visits to Ranelagh, for an hour or so to
see who was there and with whom, or to pick out a future
partner. Of a society woman known to be planning a
divorce, Lady Mary Coke remarked in June 1769 that 'as She
intends to marry directly, She shall go to Ranalagh [sic] to
look out for a Husband, for She does not think She shall
like Sir Gilbert'. A year later she was noting: 'The Duke of
Gloucester never left Lady Bridget Lane: tis said he is much
attached to her, but some people say She aims at the King.'

Ranelagh was opened in May 1742 at a cost of £16,000.
One paid twelve pence to enter the 'finely gilt, painted and
illuminated' amphitheatre, and twice a week there were
Ridottos, with supper and music, for a guinea. Walpole at
first professed to like Vauxhall better, but in June 1742, a
month after Ranelagh's opening, he was writing to a friend:

> Every night constantly I go to Ranelagh, which has
> constantly beat Vauxhall. Nobody goes anywhere else
> – everybody goes there. My Lord Chesterfield is so fond
> of it, that he says he has ordered all his letters to be
> directed thither. . . . the floor is all of beaten princes . . .
> you can't set your foot without treading on a Prince of
> Wales or Duke of Cumberland. The company is
> universal: there is from his Grace of Grafton down to
> children out of the Foundling Hospital. . . .

In April 1771 society was provided with an additional
pleasure ground, the Pantheon in Oxford Road, described
by Walpole as 'the new winter Ranelagh'. He enthused:

> Imagine Balbec in all its glory! The pillars are of artificial
> *giallo antico*. The ceilings, even of the passages, are of
> the most beautiful stucco in the best taste of grotesque.
> The ceilings of the ball-rooms and the panels painted
> like Raphael's *loggias* in the Vatican. . . . A dome like the
> pantheon, glazed. It is to cost fifty thousand pounds.

Walpole, who enjoyed dual nationality in the worlds of aristocracy and letters, moved easily between them in the dazzling social mix of late Georgian Mayfair. He was born in Arlington Street, where his father Sir Robert Walpole had a house, and later lived there for sixteen years, on the side opposite that favoured by government ministers, before moving to the east side of Berkeley Square. Short and slender, with bright, penetrating eyes and a high, pale forehead, Walpole struck people at first glance as having a boyish appearance, but his hands were swollen with gout and he had an odd, fussy gait, entering a room with affected delicacy, knees bent and on tiptoe 'as if afraid of a wet floor'. His three government sinecures, worth together about £1300 a year, left him ample time for a voluminous correspondence, recording current gossip, books read and plays seen. Of Sheridan's new comedy *The School for Scandal*, generally assumed to be based on the Devonshire House set, he observed that it had 'a great deal of wit and good situations, but it is too long, has two or three bad scenes that might easily be omitted, and seemed to me to want nature and truth of character; but I have not read it, and sat too high to hear it well. It is admirably acted.' Of Laurence Sterne's much-praised picaresque novel *Tristram Shandy* he remarked acidly in a letter in April 1770: 'At present nothing is talked of, nothing admired, but what I cannot help calling a very insipid and tedious performance. . . . it makes one smile two or three times at the beginning, but in recompense makes one yawn for two hours.' Richardson's *Clarissa* and *Sir Charles Grandison* were similarly disposed of as 'deplorably tedious' . . . 'pictures of high life conceived by a bookseller, and romances as they could be spiritualized by a Methodist teacher'.

On society gossip he was equally razor-edged, writing in April 1753:

I hear that my Lord Granville has cut another colt's tooth – in short, they say he is going to be married again; it is to Lady Juliana Collier, a very pretty girl, daughter of Lord Portmore; there are not above two or three-and-forty years difference in their ages, and not above three

bottles difference in their drinking in a day, so it is a
very suitable match!

(The marriage did not take place.)

There was no shortage of gossip of this kind to feed
conversation in the interminable round of social calls. The
early ducal residents of Grosvenor Square provided their
share. The second Duke of Buccleuch, unofficial great-great-
grandson of Charles II, who lived at Number 1, shocked
society when, as a brand-new widower in the 1740s, instead
of courting another well-born lady (his wife had been the
daughter of the Duke of Queensberry) he plunged into a
series of working-class amours, eventually marrying a
washerwoman named Alice Powell at St George's Chapel in
1744. No doubt to the relief of his family, he left no children
by this marriage and according to a contemporary account
was buried 'very meanly' in Eton College Chapel. His heir,
the Earl of Dalkeith, went on to marry the daughter of the
Duke of Argyll. The next tenant of No. 1, the third Duke of
Bolton, also contracted a scandalous second marriage,
setting a pattern for the aristocracy of a later age by wedding
an actress, Lavinia Fenton, the original Polly Peachum in
The Beggar's Opera. By the time of their wedding she had
already been his mistress for twenty-three years. Scandal of
a different kind attended the second Duke of Chandos, who
lived for a while at 37 Berkeley Square and was rumoured
to have bought his second wife, Anne Jefferies, in the market
at Newbury, Berkshire, where her first husband, an ostler
at the Pelican Inn, had put her on sale with a rope halter
around her neck.

Divorce was rife among the dukedom in the eighteenth
century, but still the great families managed to cement their
dynasties with inter-peerage marriages: one of the most
successful ducal mothers in this respect was the Duchess of
Gordon, who married three of her five daughters to dukes
– Richmond, Manchester and Bedford – and one to the
Marquess Cornwallis. One of the most sought-after men of
his time was William Pulteney, the immensely rich Earl of
Bath, whose family owned large tracts of Bath and much of
Mayfair between the Grosvenor estate and Piccadilly. The
London properties later passed by marriage to the Sutton

family, whose estate still owns it today. Lord Bath, whose London home, Bath House on the corner of Bolton Street and Piccadilly, had replaced in 1740 the original built for his ancestor Sir William Pulteney on land adjoining Clarendon House, had been a brilliant political orator in his day – Sir Robert Walpole said he feared his tongue more than another man's sword – but his parliamentary career ended ignominiously when, summoned by George II to form a government in February 1746, he failed to win the necessary allegiances and was dismissed by the irritated monarch after two days. When he became a widower in 1758 there were many society women ready to throw themselves at his feet, despite the fact that he was seventy-four. Lady Isabella Finch played him one night at cards, winning after hours of play the modest sum of half a crown. Bath sent the coin round to her next day with a gallant note saying he wished he could give her a crown, to which Lady Isabella boldly but unsuccessfully replied that he could give her a coronet, and she would willingly accept.

Into this hothouse world of love affairs, gossip and intrigue, political events tended to erupt with the volatility of family passions. The Duchess of Devonshire scandalized fashionable London in 1784 with her uninhibited campaign on behalf of Charles James Fox, dressed in a hat trimmed with foxes' tails and freely bestowing kisses on butchers and stall-holders in Covent Garden in exchange for their votes. Such was the endemic violence of the age – 'one is robbed every hundred yards' complained Walpole in 1774 – that political arguments and even celebrations frequently boiled over into street riots. On one notorious occasion Fox was pulled from his carriage and rolled in the mud. In March 1768, after the election of John Wilkes, the liberal reformer (who lived in Mayfair himself, at 35 Grosvenor Square), a woman in Piccadilly crying 'Wilkes and liberty!' hammered fiercely on the sedan chair in which Lady Mary Coke was being carried home. She had, it appeared, been provoked because the servants carrying the chair had failed to join in the cheering of the mob. 'Why did you not say who you was for?' she demanded, by way of apology.

In 1780 the Gordon Riots, whipped up by Lord George Gordon's inflammatory opposition to a bill advancing Cath-

olic civil rights, reached menacingly into the heart of Mayfair
when the mob, having ransacked and burned the
Bloomsbury Square home of Lord Mansfield with its great
law library, besieged 4 Grosvenor Square, the house of the
second Marquess of Rockingham. Dickens vividly recon-
structed the scene in *Barnaby Rudge*, with guns bristling from
the blockaded houses and the morning sun shining into
'handsome apartments filled with armed men; the furniture
hastily heaped away in corners, and made of little or no
account, in the terror of the time'. An inventory taken at
the time of Lord Rockingham's second premiership in 1782
noted that the porter's room contained 'an Iron Bar taken
from one of the Rioters in June 1780'. The Gordon Riots
caused a hastier than usual exodus of fashionable London
that summer: the Duchess of Devonshire was forced to leave
Devonshire House by a back door and seek refuge on a sofa
in Lord Clermont's house, 44 Berkeley Square, and it was
not considered safe to return to the family mansion on Piccadilly for nearly two months.

Forty years later a house in Grosvenor Square was again
the scene of a political drama, when a latter-day Guy Fawkes
by the name of Arthur Thistlewood hatched a conspiracy to
murder the entire Cabinet as they dined on Wednesday, 23
February 1820 at Number 39 (later 44), the home of Lord
Harrowby, Foreign Secretary and Lord President of the
Council. Thistlewood, who had already served a prison
sentence for threatening the life of the Home Secretary, Lord
Sidmouth, had been meeting with his gang of revolution-
aries off the Gray's Inn Road, waiting for the opportunity
to assassinate the Cabinet, seize the Tower of London and
the Mansion House and set up a provisional government.
He saw his chance when *The Times* on 22 February printed
the announcement of a Cabinet dinner the following evening
at Lord Harrowby's home. The conspirators, about twenty-
five in all, hastily assembled an arsenal of bombs, guns and
other weapons in a loft over a stable in Cato Street, off the
Edgware Road. Among their equipment were two sacks
intended for the heads of Lord Sidmouth and Viscount
Castlereagh, leader of the Commons, which would then be
displayed on pikes on the steps of the Mansion House.

The plan was for one of the gang to call at the house in

Grosvenor Square claiming to have a dispatch box for urgent delivery to Lord Harrowby; once the door was opened they would burst into the hall and up the stairs to the first-floor dining room. One of Thistlewood's confidants, however, leaked the plot to Lord Harrowby; the dinner was cancelled but carriages rolling up to the Archbishop of York's house, two doors away, persuaded the gang's advance men in the square that all was going according to plan. At 8.30 that evening Bow Street officers burst in on the Cato Street loft and caught the conspirators surrounded by their armoury; Thistlewood killed one with his sword and got away but was re-arrested the following day on underworld information. He and four others were hanged outside Newgate on 1 May 1820, Thistlewood defiantly proclaiming on the gallows: 'Albion is still in the chains of slavery. I quit it without regret.'

Lord Harrowby's house was already one of the most celebrated in the square, having been the scene of the first news of Wellington's victory at Waterloo on Midsummer's Day, 1815. Again the occasion was a Cabinet dinner, and as the guests sat down, no one knew what to believe about the rumours that had swept London all that day, Wednesday 21 June. The banker Nathan Rothschild had heard from his courier service of Napoleon's defeat, but there were counter-rumours as well, that the French had been the victors in a decisive battle outside Brussels. Around 10 p.m. there was a great commotion in the square and the diners heard a cheer go up as a chaise and four, with French battle-flags sticking out of its windows, pulled up at Number 39 and out of it sprang a young officer, the Honourable Henry Percy, Wellington's ADC, bearing the famous 'Waterloo Dispatch'. It was addressed to Earl Bathurst, Secretary of State for War, and announced the victory in Wellington's own hand. Lord Harrowby's small daughter Mary witnessed the scene from the staircase and in 1900, her hundredth year, described it to the eight-year-old Dudley Ryder, now sixth Earl of Harrowby.

From then on 44 Grosvenor Square was known as the Waterloo House, but its distinguished history failed to save it from destruction in 1967–8 when, after a series of demolition threats, it was felled with a row of five others to build the Britannia Hotel.

The simplicity, even modesty, of the Georgian aristocrat's town house in the new squares and terraces of London struck many contemporary observers by the contrast with the feudal splendours its owner frequently enjoyed in the country. One remarked how 'many a nobleman, whose proud seat in the country is adorned with all the riches of architecture, porticos and columns . . . is here content with a simple dwelling, convenient within, and unornamental without'. And the magisterial Edward Gibbon noted in his *Autobiography:* 'We should be astonished at our own riches if the labours of architecture, the spoils of Italy and Greece which are now scattered from Inveraray to Wilton, were accumulated in a few streets between Marylebone and Westminster.'

Not that Mayfair lacked its great mansions, true stately homes in the heart of town. By 1725, a mere sixty years after Clarendon House first dazzled the capital, the area could boast at least fifty such successors, with Piccadilly the proud front line of the aristocracy. Great stone houses with a view of Green Park remained the most desirable of town dwellings: in 1759 Horace Walpole, writing to George Montagu, expressed amazement at the transformation of a neighbourhood he remembered as semi-rural and full of livery stables. 'I stared today at Piccadilly, like a country squire. There are twenty new stone houses. At first I concluded that all the grooms that used to live there had got estates and built palaces.'

Those who *were* building palaces on Piccadilly at that time included the Earl of Coventry, who moved there in 1760 from Grosvenor Square, and the Earl of Egremont, whose handsome house by the Norfolk architect Matthew Brettingham was in turn later occupied by the Duke of Cambridge, Viscount Palmerston and, eventually, the Naval and Military Club, the 'In and Out', which took over the premises after Palmerston's death in 1865. Coventry's house at 106 Piccadilly, which became the St James's Club in Victorian times, was built on the site of the Greyhound Inn, much frequented by patrons of the May Fair. Egremont's house was built on a statuary's yard, one of several for which that stretch of Piccadilly was noted in its early days.

When the fourth Earl of Chesterfield built his great mansion at the corner of what is now Curzon and South Audley streets, facing down Stanhope Gate to the Park, the site was so rural that he said he would need a dog to keep him company. In March 1749 the Earl wrote to a friend that he had completed only his boudoir and library: 'The former is the gayest and most cheerful room in England, the latter the best. My garden is now tufted, planted and sown, and will, in two months more, make a scene of verdure and flowers not common in London.'

Chesterfield collected treasures for his house from other great houses – columns and a grand marble staircase from Canons, the seat of the Duke of Chandos; a copper-gilt lantern from Houghton, Sir Robert Walpole's country estate in Norfolk. Of the staircase he said, 'The expense will ruin me, but the enjoyment will please me.'

The greatest in social influence of all the Mayfair mansions, though not the most architecturally distinguished, was Devonshire House. So plain was its exterior that one critic was moved to compare it to an East India Company warehouse, despite the fact that it boasted some of the most splendid public rooms in London, a staircase of marble and alabaster, and galleries thickly hung with Titians, Rubenses and Tintorettos. Before 1897, when the ornamental gates from Chiswick House were installed, the brick wall, a relic of the original Berkeley House, presented a forbiddingly unbroken expanse, and the mansion could only be glimpsed from the top of passing omnibuses. When it was first built a contemporary complained of its

horrid blank of wall, cheerless and unsocial by day, and terrible by night. . . . Would it be credible that any man of taste, fashion and figure would prefer the solitary grandeur of enclosing himself in a jail, to the enjoyment of the first view in Britain, which he might possess by throwing down this execrable brick screen.

Cheerless and unsocial the house may have appeared to the general public (though such fortress-like homes were popular with the wealthy against the lawless mob – Harcourt House in Cavendish Square was another which turned a blank, unscalable wall to the world), but from June 1774 when William Cavendish, fifth Duke of Devonshire, brought his bride Georgiana Spencer there after their Wimbledon wedding, it became the centre of a circle that has been called the 'most brilliant, sophisticated, clever and talented society that England has ever known'.

Georgiana was a rare hostess who drew people into her enchanted circle by a genuine glow of attraction. It warmed them like a coal fire in winter. Not conventionally beautiful – she had reddish fair hair and was so tall that a contemporary remarked that when she entered a room it was as if she were larger than full length – her charm conquered men and women alike. Indeed, the novelist Fanny Burney, who fell under her spell, said the word charming might have been coined to describe her. Georgiana's most recent biographer, Brian Masters, who bestowed the accolade on her circle quoted above, said: 'In an artificial age, she was unstudied, natural and good.' Barely eighteen when she conquered London, Georgiana retained those qualities to the end: on her deathbed, after an agonizing series of 'operations' including the application of leeches to her eyeball, she could remember with pleasure the humble Irishman who once asked if he could light his pipe 'at the fire of your beautiful eyes'.

The stars of the Devonshire House galaxy included three of Georgiana's rival hostesses: Lady Melbourne, the former Elizabeth Milbanke from Yorkshire; Lady Mary Wortley Montagu; and Mrs John Crewe, wife of a rich Cheshire landowner, who presided over a salon in Grosvenor Street during the week and at weekends during the season held house parties at her villa in Hampstead. Mrs Edward Bouverie, an MP's wife, and Lady Diana Spencer (an earlier member of that family to be known as 'Lady Di') who married Topham Beauclerk, great-grandson of the illicit union between Charles II and Nell Gwyn, were all relatives of Georgiana's who joined the circle. The male members spanned an astonishing range of political, literary and social distinction: the Prince of Wales, Sheridan the playwright, Charles James Fox, Horace Walpole, and the shambling, melancholic Samuel Johnson, an odd figure to find in the Devonshire House drawing rooms – Georgiana remarked that he 'ate much and nastily' – but another willing victim of the Duchess's charm. Sheridan based much of *The School for Scandal* on characters he observed in Devonshire House – Lady Teazle was widely assumed to be modelled on Lady Melbourne – and dedicated the play to Mrs Crewe, with whom he was infatuated. After the first night on 8 May 1777 Frances Crewe wrote to Lady Clermont: 'The Farce is charming and the Duchess of Devonshire, Lady Worseley and I cut very good figures in it.'

The atmosphere of Devonshire House at this time was vividly caught by Lord David Cecil in *The Young Melbourne:* 'A dazzling haphazard confusion of routs, balls, card parties, hurried letter-writing, fitful hours of talk and reading.' An earlier historian described it as one of 'high play and dissipation'. It was a hectically nocturnal society. The Duke of Devonshire spent most of his nights gambling at Brooks's club, letting himself in with his latchkey around 5 a.m. after a supper of hot boiled mackerel when in season. The House of Commons often sat all night, members then making their way to St James's to breakfast at their clubs. In Devonshire House breakfast was normally served at 10 or 11 a.m., the afternoon was given over to shopping, and dinner, having moved back from 2 p.m. in Queen Anne's time, was between 6 and 7 p.m. Theatres started at 7 p.m., but it was fashionable to arrive late; then would follow a round of balls, masquerades, gambling and late suppers. No one dared to arrive at an assembly before 11 p.m., said Lady Mary Coke; no man of the world, said Walpole, could appear at Vauxhall before 11 or 11.30.

Eating and drinking were on a gargantuan scale; meals could last up to five hours, with roasts weighing twenty or thirty pounds. One of Boswell's acquaintances, a Dr John Campbell, drank thirteen bottles of port in one evening. No wonder the 'ton' went to spas to relieve their bloated digestions, though the cure was not necessarily achieved, as Lady Mary Wortley Montagu pointed out, by 'the drinking of nasty water, but gallopping [sic] all day, and a moderate glass of champagne at night in good company'.

One of Georgiana's intimates, Lady Sarah Lennox, said of

her hostess that she 'dines at seven . . . goes to bed at three, and lies in bed till four: she has hysteric fits in the morning, and dances in the evening; she bathes, rides, dances for ten days and lies in bed the next ten. . . .' Mrs Sheridan, wife of the playwright, went to bed at her house in Bruton Street at 3 a.m. and breakfasted at 2 p.m. Yet fashionable ladies were expected to cultivate more than bodily enjoyment, their gardens and their gambling instincts. 'Making verses is become almost as common as taking snuff,' sighed Lady Mary Wortley Montagu, to whom the prospect of being offered either in social intercourse was equally abhorrent.

The women of Georgiana's circle talked in a curious, 1920-ish slang, a kind of arch baby-talk. One would 'die' over a popular book or play; lisping was considered attractive and the word 'you' became 'oo', even in correspondence between the Duchess and her taciturn husband, though it is hard to imagine such juvenilities in the company of hard, cynical minds like those of Samuel Johnson and his successor as Devonshire House literary guru, Edward Gibbon. The author of *The Decline and Fall of the Roman Empire* was at the height of his fame in the 1780s; his volumes, priced at a guinea each, were said to sell over the counter like threepenny pamphlets. He lived in Bentinck Street, Marylebone, in what he called 'absolutely the best house in London', and dressed in flowered velvet, with wig and sword, in contrast to Johnson's rusty brown or black worsted. The differences between the two men were memorably encapsulated by a contemporary, George Colman:

> Johnson's style was grand, and Gibbon's elegant; the
> stateliness of the former was somewhat pedantick, and
> the polish of the latter was occasionally finical. Johnson
> marched to kettledrums and trumpets; Gibbon moved
> to flutes and hautboys; Johnson hew'd passages through
> the Alps, while Gibbon levelled walks through paths
> and gardens.

In the last years of the eighteenth century aristocratic refugees from the French Revolution flooded into Mayfair and frequented the drawing rooms of Devonshire House and other society mansions. Madame de Coigny, a leader of Paris society and intimate friend of both Georgiana and her friend Lady Elizabeth Foster, who married the Duke after Georgiana's death, was one of the last to leave before the Terror of 1789: she took a house in Hertford Street and stayed in exile until 1801. The previous year a great ball was thrown at Devonshire House for 800 guests, many of them French emigrés; the cost was more than £1000.

When Georgiana died in 1805 it really did seem the end of an era. In her last hours crowds gathered anxiously in front of the Piccadilly gates, as in a later era they would for much-loved royalty. The Prince of Wales lamented that 'the best natured and best bred woman in England is gone'. The nobility entered the new century in a mood sobered by the awful scenes in Paris, only a few hundred miles distant. In 1830 the Earl of Sefton told the diarist Thomas Creevey: 'I don't believe there will be a king in Europe in two years' time, or that property of any kind is worth five years' purchase.'

5

TRADESMEN'S ENTRANCE

*I*F you were alive and living in London in the closing years of the eighteenth century you would have seen the city growing and changing around you with bewildering speed. A generation earlier, on a January day in 1763, James Boswell and two friends from Scotland had walked from one end of London to the other, starting at Hyde Park Corner – or Turnpike as it was then known – and ending, as he related in his *London Journal*, 'half a mile beyond the turnpike at Whitechapel', where the three men went into a tavern to refresh themselves with 'warm white wine with aromatic spices, pepper and cinnamon'.

By the 1790s such a jaunt would have been virtually impossible. As Horace Walpole wrote to Mary Berry from his 'charming situation' in Berkeley Square in April 1791:

The town cannot hold all its inhabitants; so prodigiously the population is augmented. I have twice been going to stop my coach in Piccadilly, thinking there was a mob; and it was only nymphs and swains sauntering or trudging. T'other morning, i.e. at two o'clock, I went to see Mrs Garrick and Miss Hannah More at the Adelphi, and was stopped five times before I reached Northumberland House; for the tides of coaches, chariots, curricles, phaetons, &c., are endless. Indeed, the town is so extended, that the breed of [sedan] chairs is almost lost; for Hercules and Atlas could not carry anybody from one end of this enormous capital to the other.

A couple of months later he returned to the subject: 'There will soon be one street from London to Brentford; ay, and from London to every village ten miles round! Lord Camden has just let ground at Kentish Town for building fourteen hundred houses. . . .'

The German traveller J. W. Archenholtz wrote three years later, in *A View of the British Constitution and of the Manners and Customs of the People of England*:

Within the space of twenty years, truly a migration from the east end of London to the west, thousands passing from that part of the city, where new buildings are no longer carried on, and to this end, where fertile fields and the most agreeable gardens are daily metamorphosed into houses and streets.

Archenholtz remarked also on the 'astonishing' contrast between London's East End and West End, observing of the latter that 'the houses here are mostly new and elegant; the squares are superb, the streets straight and open. . . . If all London were as well built, there would be nothing in the world to compare with it.'

By this time nearly 1400 houses had been built on the Grosvenor estate, though thirty-eight builders had gone bankrupt in the process and in 1785 the estate itself had been turned over to trustees in order to discharge the debts accumulated by the first Lord Grosvenor. These amounted by 1779 to £150,000, around £4.5 million in today's money. His racing stable at Newmarket alone cost over £7000 a year to run. Although the leasehold system perfected by the family was to enrich future generations enormously as properties reverted to the estate at higher values, it involved more expenditure than return in its early years. At one time in the 1770s Lord Grosvenor contemplated selling all his lands in Middlesex with the exception of the 'Hundred

Acres' in Mayfair and Grosvenor Place in Belgravia, then known as the 'Five Fields'. By the end of the century, however, increasing revenue from rents changed the picture and in 1819 the racing peer's son, Earl Grosvenor, was ranked as one of the four richest men in England. His annual income, the Chancellor of the Exchequer remarked one day to the American envoy in London, was 'beyond £100,000, clear of everything'.

By the end of the eighteenth century Mayfair was becoming recognizably the district we know today. With the removal of the Tyburn gallows in 1783 the north-western corner became socially acceptable as a place to live and shop. From being a rough, unpaved route for the execution processions, Tyburn Road became respectable Oxford Street, a centre for the dress and fashion trades. Breeches-makers, mantua-makers, glove-makers, haberdashers, wig-makers, tailors, linen drapers and perfumers set up along with an array of general stores – ironfounders, provision merchants, chemists, carpet dealers and wine and spirit merchants. Within three years of the gallows going, a foreign lady visitor was writing of 'a street taking half an hour to cover from end to end, with double rows of brightly shining lamps, in the middle of which stands an equally long row of beauti-fully lacquered coaches, and on either side of these there is room for two coaches to pass one another'. The flagstone pavements were deep enough, she reported, for six rows of people to 'gaze at the splendidly lit shop-fronts in comfort. . . . Up to eleven o'clock at night there are as many people along this street as at Frankfurt during the fair.'

Park Lane, the erstwhile Tyburn Lane of dubious repute, though still unevenly paved and patched with left-over materials from its building sites, had improved its social standing with the disappearance of the mobs making their way to the hangings. The first terrace houses built at its northern end, however, still faced discreetly away from the park, on to Park Street. At this time there was not much of a park view anyway, since a high brick wall closed it off from the lane. But individual residents began to take down sections of the wall, with the permission of the government's Department of Woods and Forests, and to erect iron railings at their own expense. Soon the houses were re-designed to take advantage of the green vistas, and their plain brick rear quarters ran riot with charmingly individual Regency bays and balconies. When the wall finally disappeared with Decimus Burton's park improvement scheme of 1825, Park Lane's social ascent was assured. Grosvenor Gate, the entrance to the park which had been a dilapidated structure with a cowshed attached, opposite a busy mews and stables in Culross Street, was moved farther south to the juncture with Upper Grosvenor Street and rebuilt in the Doric style. It became the focal point for the fashionable world to take drives and walks in the park, a pastime made easier by the new road within the railings, and such excursions, particularly 'Church Parade' on Sunday, remained a highlight of Mayfair life until after the First World War.

There was still much street violence about in Regency Mayfair, of an incidence to make late-twentieth-century muggings pale into insignificance. The Prince Regent himself, when Prince of Wales, was robbed on Hay Hill, along with his companion the Duke of York. Grosvenor Square, with its concentration of wealthy and titled inhabitants, was a notoriously risky place, though some victims meted out their own share of violence. Dr Johnson, while lodging at 37 Grosvenor Square, felt his pocket being picked and, turning sharply on the thief, seized him by the collar with both hands, shaking him furiously. He then let him go, slapping the man's face so hard with the flat of his hand that he was sent staggering off the pavement. The Neapolitan Ambassador's carriage, with two strapping footmen on the box, was held up in Grosvenor Square and the Ambassador relieved of his watch and money. Yet Grosvenor Square residents seemed content to put up with the inconveniences and dangers of dim oil lamps and cobbles rather than yield to new-fangled gas lighting and tarmacadam. In 1831 Thomas Moore wrote a verse about it:

> In Grosvenor's lordly Square,
> That last impregnable redoubt,
> Where, guarded with Patrician care,
> Primeval Error still holds out;
> Where never gleam of gas must dare
> 'Gainst ancient Darkness to revolt,

Nor smooth Macadam hope to spare
The dowagers one single jolt.
Where, far too stately and sublime
To profit by the lights of time,
Let intellect march how it will,
They stick to oil and watchmen still.

(Keeping up the tradition of resistance to change, Grosvenor Square was the last part of Mayfair to give up gaslight for electricity.)

Violence apart, Regency Mayfair had a raffish atmosphere of illicit liaisons, high gambling and sexual favours bought and sold. A house on the corner of Bolton Street and Piccadilly was acquired by Jean-Baptiste Watier, the Prince Regent's former chef, to provide cooking of a standard higher than that in White's and Brooks's clubs. It soon became notorious for its gambling and was nicknamed the Dandy's Club; Lord Byron and George 'Beau' Brummell were among the heaviest losers at its high-stake games of macao and whist. 'The play at Watier's is *tremendous*,' wrote Sir Harry Featherstone to Arthur Paget in May 1811. 'Charles Manners has won £3000 or £4000 which he was much in need of.' In 1824 Crockford established his own gambling club at 81 Bolton Street, later moving it to St James's. Crockford's is now back in Mayfair, with a lavish establishment in Curzon Street.

Irish fortune hunters made Mayfair their target. They were furnished with a publication called *The Irish Register*, which Horace Walpole described as 'one of the most impudent things that ever was printed . . . a list of all the unmarried woman of any fashion in England, ranked in order, duchesses-dowager, ladies, widows, misses, &c.' Two Irish sisters, the beautiful Gunnings, scored a female takeover by capturing two English peers, the Duke of Hamilton and the Earl of Coventry. The Duke of Hamilton was one of many eminent clients for the notorious May Fair Chapel 'guinea' marriages, the 'boldest' of the venal practices which flourished among eighteenth-century clergy in the area. Private chapels were run as profitable businesses by several Mayfair landlords, who would hire popular preachers like Sydney Smith for their ability to draw wealthy crowds into the pews of the Grosvenor Chapel and others – pews which could be rented for around £15 a year.

The Grosvenor Chapel, formerly Audley Chapel, is one of the most charming relics of eighteenth-century Mayfair to survive in the vista which Sir Richard Grosvenor planned for it in 1730, facing straight to Hyde Park down what was then Chapel Street and is now Aldford Street. Brick-built with a spire in the plain colonial style copied in countless American towns and hamlets, it was an appropriate place for the US armed forces to worship during the Second World War: in 1945 they placed a plaque there in thanks for the allied victory. Among those buried deep in the Grosvenor Chapel's mysteriously blocked-off vaults are known to be Lady Mary Wortley Montagu, John Wilkes the reformer, and the Earl and Countess of Mornington, parents of the Duke of Wellington.

The most infamous of the Mayfair clerics was Dr William Dodd, who tried to bribe his way into the living of St George's, Hanover Square. He eventually signed his own death warrant by forging the signature of Lord Chesterfield on a bond for £4250. This was a capital offence, and he was hanged at Tyburn in June 1777, a spectacle which drew the biggest crowds ever seen there. Dr Alexander Keith, who ran the May Fair Chapel in Curzon Street, charged a guinea to wed couples who wanted no questions asked, who had no banns or licence or parental agreement. Before the Marriage Act of 1754 such ceremonies were legal if performed by a qualified clergyman, but they were certainly irregular. Dr Keith brought his to a fine commercial art, advertising his services in newspapers, complete with street directions. In 1742 he performed seven hundred such marriages compared with forty properly conducted ones at St George's.

Even from the Fleet Prison, where he died in 1758, Keith continued to run the business through assistants, who set up an alternative 'Little Chapel' across the street. On the day before the Marriage Act came into force Dr Keith's assistants performed sixty-one weddings: in all, the business accounted for seven thousand one-guinea ceremonies.

The Duke of Hamilton met Elizabeth Gunning at Lord Chesterfield's house-warming in 1752 and was immediately taken with her. Two nights later, finding himself alone with her, he impulsively sent for a parson to marry them. The clergyman refused to do so without the proper licence and ring, whereupon, as Walpole recounted: 'The Duke swore he would send for the Archbishop; at last they were married with a ring of the bed curtain, at half past twelve at night at May Fair Chapel.'

Mayfair's most celebrated irregular marriage was that of the Prince Regent, then Prince of Wales, and Mrs Fitzherbert, the attractive and high-principled Catholic whom he first met in 1783 or 1784 when he was twenty-one. She was twenty-seven and already twice widowed. Under the Royal Marriages Act of 1772 no member of the royal family under the age of twenty-five could marry without the monarch's consent, and succession to the throne was blocked if the heir married a Catholic. Nevertheless an Anglican priest named Robert Butt, newly released from debtor's prison, agreed to perform a ceremony under Church of England rites, and it took place on the night of 15 December 1785 in Mrs Fitzherbert's house in Park Street where the Prince had been accustomed to visit her surreptitiously, slipping in through the stables and garden backing on to Tyburn Lane.

Mrs Fitzherbert behaved with impeccable discretion, making no demands on the Prince and keeping their relationship private, but ten years later he was forced into an official marriage with Caroline of Brunswick as the price for George III settling his debts. In 1795 Mrs Fitzherbert bought another house close to Hyde Park, 6 Tilney Street, where she died in 1837. It was pulled down in 1927 for the building of a block of flats called Fitzherbert House, by which time the Park Street house where she and the Prince were clandestinely married had long disappeared.

Already in the closing years of the eighteenth century the social composition of Mayfair was changing, becoming more bourgeois. 'New money' was coming in to join the nobility ensconced in and around Grosvenor, Berkeley and Hanover squares: men grown wealthy on trade like Samuel Whitbread, the brewer, who moved into 17 Grosvenor Street in 1792. A description of its furnishings by Gillow provides a snapshot of prosperous middle-class taste in the last years of George III: striped linen fabrics on the ground floor, yellow with white and gold chairs and cornices in the first-floor drawing room, imitation Turkey fitted carpets in the dining parlour and library, and fitted Brussels on the first floor.

Many of the Mayfair aristocracy rented out their houses while they travelled abroad, stayed in the country or, in the case of Lord North, governed the country from 10 Downing Street. (North always refused to use the title prime minister, saying it was not in the British constitution.) Conscious of the fickle nature of politics, Lord North would never let his house at 50 Grosvenor Square for more than a year at a time. Indeed, his last administration, in the coalition of 1783 with Charles James Fox, lasted only eight months. The house was frequently taken by newly married couples, who found the short let convenient, and in consequence it was nicknamed 'Honeymoon Hall'.

Tenants of Mayfair houses were often more aristocratic than the owners: 52 Grosvenor Street was owned for 130 years by the Pleydell-Bouverie family, who rented it to generations of the Earls of Radnor. Its last private occupant, in 1928, was Lord Peel, who married the revue star Beatrice Lillie.

But the most fascinating characteristic of Mayfair at the start of the nineteenth century was that, socially, it was as mixed as a village while enjoying the sophistication of a metropolitan centre of fashion. Along with the earls, baronets and moneyed gentry with country estates, there were politicians, professional men, civil servants, naval and military officers, composers, craftsmen, writers, architects, doctors, even a chiropodist to the Court – or, as a tax survey of 1790 described him, 'Operator to their Majesties for the Hands and Feet'.

Above all, there was a huge proportion of tradespeople, drawn by the patronage of the wealthy households, most of whose annual expenditure went on tradesmen's bills. A tax collector's survey of 1790 covering the parish of St George's, Hanover Square – which encompassed the Grosvenor estate – reveals that nearly sixty per cent of the inhabitants, including people who had businesses there or who rented houses, were tradespeople and artisans, compared with 8.5 per cent titled residents, 7.5 per cent professional men and 22.5 per cent 'no occupation', which included the leisured category of gentlemen and esquires as well as women of private means. The titled inhabitants included thirty-seven peers, headed by George III's brother the Duke of Gloucester; the professionals included 'placemen' – civil servants and court officials – lawyers, architects, medical men and officers of the armed forces.

Of the seven categories into which Daniel Defoe had classified the English in 1709, the first four were well represented in Mayfair: 'The *great*, who live profusely, the *rich*, who live very plentifully, the *middle sort*, who live well, and the *working trades*, who labour hard but feel no want.'

People earning their living by transport included eight sedan-chair men – one employed by the Duchess of Devonshire, the rest freelance – and workers in the trades connected with horses and carriages. Among these there were twenty-three coach-builders scattered around Mayfair, the equivalent of today's Rolls-Royce and Bentley showrooms, all supporting subsidiary crafts like painters, wheelwrights, carpenters and platers. Among the best-known coach-builders were John Barnard of Park Street, coach-maker to the King, and Joseph Thrupp of Oxford Street, whose firm endured as Thrupp and Maberly to become one of the most celebrated motor-car coach-builders in the years between the two world wars.

In the narrow, cobbled mews behind the main residential streets and squares there were a few private stables attached to the big houses, but many more buildings housed self-employed farriers, blacksmiths, coachmen, saddlers and horse dealers, as well as trades which depended on working-class business; typically, the chandler or general hardware merchant and the corner pub or licensed coffee-house.

Building trades like masons, bricklayers, plasterers, glaziers, plumbers and slaters were concentrated just south of Oxford Street, the last patch of Mayfair to be developed. Upholsterers and cabinet-makers could be found in Mount Street, which was a fashionable centre for furniture showrooms as well as for milliners and peruke-makers. John Linnell, the celebrated cabinet-maker, had a large showroom on the north side of Berkeley Square. Also scattered around the Grosvenor estate were fifteen coal-dealers, twelve apothecaries, a piano-maker, a gunsmith, a printer and a number of stationers, chimney sweeps, 'chinamen' or purveyors of fine china, tobacconists and watchmakers.

Tradesmen dealt from the ground floors of their houses, fitting them with shop windows to display their wares. By the 1760s this practice was becoming so obtrusive at the Bond Street end of Brook and Grosvenor streets, two of the Grosvenor estate's most desirable residential addresses, that Lord Grosvenor's surveyor wrote a new clause into the ground leases, requiring permission to be granted before such windows could be installed. In 1790 most of the fashionable shops were clustered in Mount Street; others could be found in Davies Street, Duke Street, North and South Audley streets, Park Street and the western end of Oxford Street. During the next twenty years shopping fashion moved east to Bond Street, whose commercial success was such by 1811 as to inspire Nash to design the new Regent Street as a great shopping thoroughfare 120 feet wide with a carriage-way 'double the width of that in Bond-street, and where there will be room for all the fashionable shops to be assembled in one Street. . . .' Bond Street's shopkeepers mustered fierce opposition to the Nash scheme, but the parliamentary bill approving it went through in July 1813 and the new, broad boulevard developed rapidly. It did draw some trade away from Bond Street but the outcome was to leave Bond Street a preserve of exclusive speciality shops while Regent and Oxford streets attracted larger emporia and, eventually, department stores.

In 1812 Lord George Cavendish commissioned Samuel Ware to build the Burlington Arcade on Piccadilly; the story goes that it was to stop people throwing oyster shells (oysters were then a cheap convenience food) over the wall of Burlington House into his garden. The arcade cost £30,000 and ownership remained with Cavendish's descendants until 1926, when Lord George's grandson, Lord Chesham, sold it to the Prudential Assurance Co., which still owns it and keeps up Lord Chesham's tradition of recruiting the watchmen or beadles from his old regiment, the 10th Royal Hussars.

Lord George declared the arcade to be 'built for the gratification of the publick, and to give employment to industrious females'. Its seventy-two small shops were let out at £18 a year and one of them, 'a friendly bonnet shop', was known for its extra-mural services as a brothel. Burlington Arcade was a fashionable promenading spot, first for Regency bucks and later, Edwardian mashers, the latter immortalized satirically in two memorable music-hall songs, 'Gilbert the Filbert' and 'Burlington Bertie'. (The nearby Royal Arcade, linking Bond Street and Albemarle Street, was opened in 1879. Queen Victoria bought her riding shirts and vests there at H. W. Brettell, which still possesses an order from Osborne House in 1881: 'Please send for Her Majesty's account 6 men's undershirts with short sleeves like the last . . .')

When the Burlington Arcade was going up, Bond Street was still a mixture of homes and shops, often with lodging rooms let out above them. Laurence Sterne, author of *Tristram Shandy*, lodged in rooms above a silk bag-maker at Number 41 and died there in March 1768, putting up his hand as if to ward off a blow and crying 'Now it is come!' according to an eye-witness account. The following year, in his lodgings at the Piccadilly end of Bond Street, Boswell – who also lived at different times in Conduit and Half Moon streets – gave his celebrated dinner for four of his most gifted contemporaries: Johnson, Reynolds, Garrick and Goldsmith. Nelson spent restless nights at 147 New Bond Street, heavily doped with laudanum after the loss of his arm. Sir Thomas Lawrence, the portrait painter, lived at Number 24 and Byron liked to stay at Stevens' Hotel at Number 18.

Bond Street was the fashionable place to see and be seen: C. J. Fox in his sedan chair, Horace Walpole in his carriage, Sheridan strolling from his Savile Row home to Brooks's Club, Beau Brummell visiting his tailors Schweitzer and Davidson of Cork Street (who were also tailors to the Prince Regent) or Weston and Meyer of Conduit Street. 'To be really elegant you must not be noticed,' was the message Brummell imprinted on the once colourful mode of an English gentleman's dress.

Brummell moved house several times in Mayfair before he exiled himself in France to escape his debtors. He started with lodgings in Chesterfield Street, moving to 18 Bruton Street and 22 South Street before establishing himself in a cosy house at 13 Chapel (now Aldford) Street off Park Lane. His book-lined parlour on the ground floor was a kind of waiting room where the fashionable world crowded in to pay court to the Beau; in the chintz-upholstered first-floor drawing room he entertained close friends and, wearing a muslin dressing-gown, sat in front of a mahogany-framed cheval glass to have his sparse hair waved with curling tongs. When he finally quit England in 1817 his possessions were sold up by James Christie, the St James's auctioneer. Earlier, on the move from Bruton Street, he disposed of some surplus items, including 130 silk cravats, through Phillips's auction house, which set up at 73 New Bond Street in 1797. Harry Phillips, a gregarious man with a keen promotional instinct, used to hold eve-of-sale parties which drew crowds of fashionable people and ensured a steady flow of clients. The Prime Minister, Lord Grey, attended the Brummell sale. The Phillips business continued to occupy the same Georgian house until the summer of 1939, when it was destroyed by fire; the auctioneers then moved to the premises they still own at the corner of Blenheim and Woodstock streets.

Other Bond Street traders used their social contacts to business ends, like Truefitt, the wig-maker to George IV, who established the men's hairdressers Truefitt and Hill, and Thomas Savory, one of the royal apothecaries, who took over an earlier pharmacy on the corner of Bruton Street. Savory and Moore built their success on Seidlitz powders, a laxative named after the Seidlitz springs in Germany, and on digestive lozenges formulated by Dr Jenner, the discoverer of smallpox vaccine. The company prospered by its nearness to Savile Row, then the most fashionable street for doctors' consulting rooms, and retained its royal connections; a medicine chest it made up for William IV is now in the London Museum. Savory and Moore also gained the contract for medical supplies to the British Army in the Crimean War, and in this was greatly helped by Florence Nightingale's exposure of the scandalous hospital conditions there. Miss Nightingale remained a faithful patron of the shop during her long retirement in South Street. Another appreciative female patron was Emma, Lady Hamilton, who gave Thomas Savory a silver loving cup. The shop's original black and gold shop-front still graces 143 New Bond Street although Savory and Moore no longer trade there, a victim like many Bond Street businesses in the 1970s of the steep increase in rents as leases expired.

Another name to survive from the earliest days of Bond Street is Chappell, originally a music publishing business set up by Samuel Chappell in 1811 at 124 New Bond Street. Beethoven remarked in a letter in 1822 that he had heard 'Chappell in Bond Street is now one of the best publishers'. The firm, which moved in the 1830s to Number 50, the site it still occupies, published nearly all the Gilbert and Sullivan Savoy Operas and organized Charles Dickens's readings from his novels, including his tours of America. Dickens was a customer of another early, still surviving Bond Street shop, the hosiers Beale and Inman, founded at 131 New Bond Street by James Beale in 1828. (Their twentieth-century patrons included Winston Churchill.)

The French Huguenot family of Tessier had three jewellery businesses trading in Mayfair by the 1800s, much of their early stock coming from the sale of jewels belonging to refugees from the French Revolution. In mid century they set up a New Bond Street store at Number 26, as specialists in onyx and mourning jewellery; the business still flourishes there, though the family connection ended in 1877.

Another Huguenot family business to endure into the 1980s, still very much in family ownership, is that founded by William Asprey in Mitcham in 1781. His son Charles moved the business to 49 New Bond Street in the 1830s and by 1848 Asprey's fitted dressing-cases were so much in demand that bigger premises had to be found at 166 New Bond Street. Enlarged still further into adjoining shops at the end of the nineteenth century, Asprey's boasts one of London's finest surviving Victorian shop-fronts.

Thomas Agnew, whose Bond Street gallery grew to dominate the world of art collecting in the late nineteenth century, started in Manchester, in partnership with Vittore Zanetti, in 1817 and did not set up in London until 1860, when the firm opened a branch in Waterloo Place, off Pall Mall. In 1875, with business rapidly expanding, Thomas and his son William bought the site of an old coaching yard at 39 (now 43) Old Bond Street and built a spacious, well-lit gallery with red, cut velvet wall coverings, some of which have survived into the 1980s. The move was still in progress when in May 1876, William Agnew bought at auction for 11,000 guineas Gainsborough's portrait of Georgiana, Duchess of Devonshire. It was a painting of striking beauty, showing Georgiana in a large Leghorn straw hat, but its provenance was considered suspect by many experts including the painter Millais, who doubted that Gainsborough had ever come near it.

Agnew put the picture on display at the new gallery, where the most noted collectors of the day flocked to see it, including Junius Morgan, father of Pierpont Morgan, who was considering buying it. On the morning of 26 May the picture frame was found empty, the canvas having been cut out and stolen. The thief was subsequently discovered to have been an international crook known variously as Adam Worth or Wirth and Harry Raymond. His brother was in prison and he planned with accomplices to blackmail Agnew's into putting up a bond for his release.

Agnew's offered a reward of £1,000 for information leading to recovery of the painting, but William Agnew announced that he would never negotiate with the thieves. The theft became an international sensation. A series of ransom letters signed 'New York' arrived at Agnew's stating that the picture was in America and enclosing strips cut from the canvas as proof, but still William Agnew refused to negotiate. In 1901, a quarter of a century later, Pinkerton's, the private detective agency in Chicago, was contacted by the thieves to act as go-between for the return of the painting. Sir William Agnew, who had been made a baronet in 1895, was by now retired, but his son Morland went to Chicago. Then followed the most extraordinary scene. Pinkerton's had hired a suite of three adjoining rooms in the Auditorium Hotel; their men occupied the middle room while those on either side held the art dealer and the thieves. Morland Agnew smoked a cigar to calm his nerves as the appointed hour approached. There was a knock on the door. A messenger stood there carrying a rolled brown paper parcel. 'Mr Agnew?', he inquired. 'Yes', said the British dealer. In silence the man handed over the roll and left. Agnew eagerly cut the string and, as he wrote in his journal, 'there, lightly wrapped in cotton-wool, lay the long-lost Gainsborough. . . . It makes me weep to see how much the canvas has been cut. . . . But the face, which is of wonderful beauty, is unhurt, and, mutilated as it is, the picture is still of immense value and the highest interest.'

The price Agnew's paid to retrieve the Duchess has never been disclosed by the firm, but a history of the family business written by Geoffrey Agnew in 1967 suggested that it might have been as little as £250; that was the amount of a mysterious entry – 'Jewel given to Mrs. Gooden' – put against the expenses of recovering the Gainsborough. Morland Agnew brought the painting home on the SS *Etruria*, resting in a specially padded cupboard in his stateroom. Four days after the ship docked at Liverpool on 8 April, 1901, J. Pierpont Morgan bought the picture his father had been contemplating for his collection in 1876. Still in Morgan ownership, it now hangs in the Metropolitan Museum of New York.

Piccadilly was also a shopping area that served the great houses of Mayfair and St James's. The oldest surviving business of all was founded there in 1707 at Number 181 by William Fortnum, one of Queen Anne's footmen, who developed his trading skills by selling candle-ends from the palace stores to the ladies-in-waiting for their personal use. Out of his partnership with his landlord, Hugh Mason, came the world's most famous speciality grocery store; by the 1790s it was supplying delicacies like boned game in aspic, potted meats, fresh and dried fruits and teas and spices imported through the East India Company. Landed families like the Lascelles of Harewood, with their town house in Hanover Square, kept accounts there for weekly grocery supplies during the London season. The rival provision company, Robert Jackson, was established in 1844 in Egyptian House, 171/172 Piccadilly, as a co-operative venture by several members of the Jackson family who had been trading nearby as hosiers and glovers, tea merchants, warehouse managers and wax and tallow chandlers.

The oldest business within the Mayfair boundaries was Gunter's, set up in 1757 by the Italian pastrycook Dominicus Negri at a shop known then as the sign of the Pineapple in Berkeley Square. When the square was numbered it became

Number 7, a few doors away from Horace Walpole's house. In the 1770s Negri took a partner called Gunter, who by the end of the century had set up on his own and proceeded to become so rich that he bought a magnificent thirty-acre estate in West Kensington, on which he grew fresh fruit for the famous Gunter ices. The estate is remembered today in the street name Gunter Grove. Generations of Mayfair families had accounts with Gunter's to supply food and cooks for their splendid parties and to make their wedding-cakes – celebrated, many-tiered structures, examples of which were displayed in glass cases in the Berkeley Square teashop. The recipe for the exquisite ices remained a Gunter secret, but anyone who ever tasted one claims the flavour has never been equalled: the range of ice creams and sorbets also included some utterly lost varieties like white-currant ice. The custom among the young people of Mayfair was to eat Gunter ices in open carriages under the plane trees of the square gardens, to which waiters would thread their way through the traffic bearing laden trays. In 1937 Gunter's moved to Curzon Street, but its teashop business did not long survive the austerity of the postwar years and it closed in the 1950s.

Out of all the businesses servicing Mayfair in the eight-eenth and nineteenth centuries, one provided its patrons with a unique combination of shop and club, commerce and culture. This was Hatchard's, opened in 1797 at 173 Picca-dilly by the young printer John Hatchard, who recorded in his diary for 30 June of that year: 'This day by the grace of God, the good will of my friends and £5 in my pocket, I have opened my bookshop in Piccadilly.' He paid £40 a year for his shop, plus £31.10s. for 'goodwill'. In 1801 he moved to 190 Piccadilly, buying an initial twenty-four-year lease for a thousand guineas. 'God blessed my industry,' he had inscribed on a plaque in the shop, 'and good men encour-aged it.' Among the latter, an early customer was the statesman George Canning, who lived at 37 Conduit Street and whose mind worked so quickly it was said no one could take dictation from him. On one occasion, the diarist Charles Greville recorded, he dictated simultaneously a dispatch on Greek affairs to George Bentinck and one on South American politics to Howard de Walden, each of his secretaries 'writing as fast as he could'. Canning's orders to Hatchard included works by Johnson and Benjamin Franklin, pamphlets by Burke and 'The Jacobin's lamentation'.

Hatchard brought to the edge of Mayfair the lively cultural tradition of the literary coffee-house, and the writers, artists, politicians and professional men who lived north and west of Piccadilly used his shop as a convivial meeting place, to converse and browse through the daily papers which Hatchard thoughtfully laid out by the fire. In the lamp-lit parlour William Wilberforce planned his anti-slavery bill, passed into law in 1807, and Gladstone and Wellington discussed political strategy. Sydney Smith commented acidly on these gatherings:

> There is a set of well-dressed prosperous gentlemen who assemble daily at Mr Hatchard's shop, clean, civil personages well in with the people in power, delighted with every existing institution and almost with every existing circumstance; and every now and then one of these personages writes a little book, expecting to be praised in their turn for their own little books.

Piccadilly in the early 1800s boasted several large book-shops including Debrett's and Ridgeway's (a Whig 'club' where Hatchard's was Tory). A guidebook of 1816 described London as 'the focus of Literature and the Mart for Books', adding that Nicoll of Pall Mall was 'bookseller to the King, Hatchard to the Queen'. The guide describes the fashionable bookshops as 'lounging shops', furnished with 'all new publications, newspapers, etc.' About 800,000 new books and pamphlets were published each year in London, and the gross annual returns from the printing and selling of these were said to be 'little short of a million sterling', giving employment to nearly two thousand people. By the time John Hatchard died in 1849 his shop alone was selling half a million pounds' worth of books a year.

Hatchard's catalogue for 1814, a fat volume priced at three shillings, contained about seven thousand titles. Byron's *Childe Harold's Pilgrimage*, 'new and neat' with marbled edges, was listed at fifteen to seventeen shillings. Classical authors mingled with Beckford's *Letters*, Cruden's *Concord-*

ance, Marshall on *Gardening, with Hints on Fishponds*, and White's *Natural History of Selborne*.

The shop eventually settled at 187 Piccadilly in 1817, where it remains, recently enlarged. In its archives is a grey-green, faded folder containing orders from eminent customers of Regency, Williamite and Victorian London. Before Rowland Hill introduced the Penny Post, peers and MPs could send their letters for nothing by scribbling their names in a corner of the envelope or folded sheet of paper. A single sheet from the Duke of Wellington dated 19 September 1833 placed an order for three publications: Hamilton's *Men and Manners in the United States*, De Haussey *Sur L'Angleterre*, and 'the Pamphlet Recently Published on the last Session of Parliament'.

Wellington was one of Hatchard's earliest customers. He used to ride to the shop on horseback from Apsley House at Hyde Park Corner – the days when it really lived up to its nickname of 'Number 1, London', the last great mansion before the still rural rides of Knightsbridge and Kensington. In the 1830s Hatchard's customers constituted a roll-call of the aristocracy – the dukes of Richmond and Leeds, the earls of Winchilsea and Anglesey, the marquesses of London-derry and Liverpool, Lord Clancarty, Earl Bathurst, Lord Saye and Sele, Lord Spencer, Lord Willoughby de Broke. A bench was provided for patrons' footmen to wait outside while their masters browsed. Great political figures who bought their books there included Gladstone, Peel, Palmer-ston (who lived just up the road at 94 Piccadilly, now the Naval and Military Club) and Lord Derby. Macaulay, who would stroll across the road from his chambers in Albany, had been encouraged from childhood by his friend Hannah More to patronize the shop. When he was eight she wrote praising an improvement in his letter-writing and saying: 'You have entitled yourself to another book. You must go to Hatchards and choose. I think we have nearly exhausted the epics, what say you to a little good prose, Johnson's *Hebrides*, or Walton's *Lives*, unless you would like a neat edition of Cowper's poems, or *Paradise Lost*, for your own eating. . . .'

The Hatchard family lived for years over the shop at 187 Piccadilly before moving out to the rural delights of

Clapham. Thomas, John's second son, inherited the business in the 1840s. In his blue, velvet-collared dress coat,
yellow waistcoat and brown nankeen trousers he cut a more
dashing figure than his soberly dressed father. When he
died in 1858 the male line of Hatchards died with him,
although a family connection continued. A. L. Humphreys,
who joined the firm in 1881, was fascinated by the shop's
distinguished customers. 'The good and great Lord Shaftes-
bury looked sometimes, so I thought, so downcast because
the wretchedness of the world was almost too much for him
to bear. . . . there were certain folk who would now and
then drive up in state with two powdered footmen in
breeches and white stockings standing up behind.' The sight
of the lovely daughters of Countess Faversham entering his
shop made Humphreys think of a painting by Lord
Leighton, of goddesses 'graciously stepping down from
Olympus [or Mayfair] to ask for a book'.

Another literary 'club' allied to a business flourished at 50
Albemarle Street from 1812, when John Murray, a former
officer in the Royal Marines, moved his publishing house
there from Fleet Street. Curwen's *History of Booksellers*
described the scene:

> His drawing-room at four o'clock became the favourite
> resort of all the talent in literature and art that London
> possessed, and there *were* giants in those days. There it
> was his custom of an afternoon to gather together such
> men as Byron, Scott, Moore, Campbell, Southey,
> Gifford, Hallam, Lockhart, West, Irving and Mrs
> Somerville; and more than this, he invited such artists
> as Lawrence, Wilkie, Phillips, Newton and Pickersgill
> to meet them and paint them, that they might hang for
> ever on his walls. . . .

Other Murray authors included Darwin, Borrow, Crabbe,
Gladstone, Livingstone, Lord Roberts and even Queen
Victoria, when he persuaded her to let him publish her
Leaves from a Journal of Our Life in the Highlands in 1868.
When Murray took over the firm of Smith, Elder, its list was
augmented by some of the greatest names in nineteenth-

century literature including Thackeray, the Brownings and the Brontës.

Murray was a legendary host. Curwen quoted a popular verse about him by Hook:

My friend, John Murray, I see has arrived at the head of
    the table,
And the wonder is, at this time of night, that John Murray
    should be able;
He's an excellent hand at supper, and not a bad hand at
    lunch,
But the devil of John Murray is that he never will pass the
    punch!

James Hogg, 'the Ettrick Shepherd', described one of Murray's dinners as 'such a dinner and such drink as nae words can describe'.

The extraordinary village of all the talents that was Mayfair around this time embraced the fermenting world of science and discovery as well as that of letters. Benjamin Thompson, a New Englander who fought with the British against George Washington and was knighted by George III, founded the Royal Institution in 1799 at 20–21 Albemarle Street for 'diffusing the knowledge and facilitating the general introduction of useful mechanical inventions and improvements, and for teaching by courses of philosophical lectures and experiments the application of science to the common purposes of life'. In 1800 George III granted the institution a royal charter and the year after that Humphry Davy, who had started his career as an apothecary's apprentice in Cornwall, was appointed a lecturer and director of the laboratory, becoming professor of chemistry in 1802. Michael Faraday was engaged as his assistant in 1812 and in the 1830s conducted his experiments in electricity there.

Faraday, the father of electrical engineering, stamped his presence indelibly on the houses in Albemarle Street. His desk and diaries are still there, and brass plates bearing his signature were fixed by him to each piece of furniture. In the basement his laboratory survives alongside rooms devoted to research into lasers and other forms of advanced technology.

Henry Cavendish, the eccentric scientist relative of the Duke of Devonshire who lived in Bloomsbury with a separate house for his books, was responsible for the family's acquisition of Burlington House, which in the 1850s came to house the Royal Academy and a cluster of learned societies. Cavendish, who died in 1810 worth £1 million, had been ostracized by his family. When Georgiana, Duchess of Devonshire, tried to visit him, her husband demurred, saying: 'He is not a gentleman, he works.' Cavendish, a reclusive bachelor, left his fortune to his cousin, Lord George Cavendish, who used part of it to buy Burlington House and to build the Burlington Arcade.

These were years of intellectual giants living within an easy walk of one another. Richard Brinsley Sheridan, the playwright, was one of several writers who favoured Hertford Street as an address; Bulwer Lytton wrote *The Last Days of Pompeii* at Number 36 in a room fitted up like a Roman villa. Sheridan had several changes of address (Great Queen Street and Bruton Street as well), usually just one jump ahead of the bailiffs. At one time they came so close to finding him that provisions had to be lowered to his kitchen by a rope over the area railings. Mrs Sheridan's portrait was redeemed from the pawnbrokers to grace the drawing room for one grand dinner. He was renowned for his beautiful eyes and is supposed to have told a friend on his death bed in 1816: 'Tell Lady Bessborough that my eyes will look up at the coffin-lid as brightly as ever.'

The polymathic Lord Brougham was living at 4 Grafton Street in 1830, the year he was made Lord Chancellor, but later moved to Great Stanhope Street close to Chesterfield House. He founded London University and formed a Society for the Diffusion of Useful Knowledge. Greville, the diarist, quoted a contemporary who was so impressed by Brougham's dazzling powers of intellect and conversation that he remarked: 'This morning Solon, Lycurgus, Demosthenes, Archimedes, Sir Isaac Newton, Lord Chesterfield and a great many more, went away in a post-chaise.' Brougham was, however, not so desirable as a tenant. Lord Grey rented him 48 Berkeley Square from 1830 to 1834. When he moved out, Grey's agent said he had never seen a house left in dirtier condition.

The bedrooms were simply unendurable; and hidden in the handsome satin curtains in the drawing-room he found a kitchen candlestick, and black-lead for the grates. The furniture was nearly all ruined by ill-usage and neglect. . . . it was next to impossible to get him out, and when he went, instead of paying the arbitrated sum – for he had insisted on 'arbitration' as to damages – he sent a cheque short of £15. The cheque was returned and in three days the full amount was sent.

A particular kind of intellectual, with a certain asceticism but a taste for civilized comforts, who liked solitary living at the hub of busy events, was attracted to Mayfair's network of bachelor chambers and apartments. In the early nineteenth century there was one address above all others in the district to which creative men were drawn to write, to sharpen their intellectual weapons and to dream their political dreams in a reclusive, club-like world of its own on the edge of Piccadilly. Its name was Albany.

6

'A COLLEGE LIFE IN LONDON'

*I*N the same year, 1774, that the fifth Duke of Devonshire
brought his bride Georgiana Spencer to the great house on
Piccadilly, inaugurating the reign of the Devonshire House
Circle, Lord and Lady Melbourne – she who was to be the
model for Sheridan's Lady Teazle – moved into their
splendid new home two doors away on the east side of
Burlington House. Built to Melbourne's commission by
William Chambers, it was a magnificent classical mansion
which survives today as the core of Albany, London's first
and still most exclusive apartment house. (The £22 yearly
'fee-farm' rent paid by the first occupier of this site, Sir
Thomas Clarges – after whom Clarges Street was named –
is still paid by the Albany Trustees to the Sir Richard Sutton
estate, successors to the original landowner, Sir William
Pulteney.)

Chambers, who had been knighted by the King of Sweden
and allowed by George III to assume the style of a knight
in England, was at the height of his success in his late forties
and about to be appointed architect of Somerset House. He
considered himself a particular rival of the Adam brothers,
believing that his interpretation of the Italian tradition was
'nearer to the most approved Style of the Ancients', and he
took a keen pleasure, as he wrote to one of his noble clients,

in making sure that the rooms of Melbourne House were decorated in a style 'diametrically opposite' to that of the Adams. Robert Adam, in fact, had been the choice of Lord Holland, owner of the previous house on the site, when he planned to rebuild in 1764, seven years before selling it for £16,500 to the wealthy young Sir Peniston Lamb, the newly ennobled Baron (later Viscount) Melbourne.

Melbourne, an amiable but dull and ill-educated man, already owed much of his social rise to his vivacious and popular wife Elizabeth, a Yorkshire squire's daughter not yet twenty but possessed of ambitions to take fashionable London by storm. She wanted a mansion for entertaining equal to the grandest in the West End, and with Peniston's inherited fortune (in the neighbourhood of a million pounds), and independent wealth of her own, money was no object. It was a dream commission for Chambers and when the building was finished, set back a hundred feet from Piccadilly behind a high wall and a courtyard with coach-houses and stabling for thirteen horses, he brought in another architect, James Paine, to design marble chimney-pieces of grandeur, and instructed Thomas Chippendale to furnish the house. Chambers insisted on being consulted throughout the process of decoration and furnishing, perhaps still feeling the need to establish his credentials over Robert Adam: at one point he wrote to Lord Melbourne, 'I am really a Very pretty Connoisseur in Furniture.' Lady Melbourne, however, was responsible for engaging the celebrated Florentine Giovanni Cipriani to decorate the ceiling of the grand salon, fifty-two feet long.

The Melbournes took up residence early in 1774, but it was another year before the last workman packed up his tools and paint-pots. Melbourne celebrated by opening the house for two public concerts. He professed himself well pleased with his new home, writing to Chambers in February 1774: 'I believe few people have had better reason than myself to be pleased with so large a sum laid out.' Later that year he said Chambers had given 'more satisfaction than all other Architects put together could possibly have done'. A large sum it certainly worked out to be: Melbourne calcu-lated that by the time the house was completely ready, 'so as to sit down in it to dinner', it had cost him nearly

£100,000, and the extravagant social life the couple now embarked upon soon made inroads into even his immense fortune. He also had an expensive liaison with the actress Sophia Baddeley, whom he set up with a companion in a nearby house in St James's, and whose passion for spending money he was in the habit of indulging by leaving two or three hundred pounds at a time in bank notes on her table.

Georgiana Devonshire and Elizabeth Melbourne were now the reigning queens of London society. Elizabeth was not short of lovers to compensate for her husband's infidelities, the most durable being the handsome young Lord Egremont, owner of Petworth estate in Sussex and London's most eligible bachelor. Egremont was fascinated by qualities in Elizabeth Melbourne which men also admired in Georgiana – a naturalness and joy in living, coupled with remarkable beauty, a tall and graceful figure and an astringent wit and intelligence which delighted in male company and conversation. 'She understood the art of getting on with men completely,' as Lord David Cecil wrote in *The Young Melbourne*.

> Level-tempered and rational, she found scenes and caprices as tiresome as they did. After the unaccountable moods of stormier sirens, it was infinitely delightful to find oneself 'laughing away an hour' on the sofa of her sitting-room in Melbourne House. . . . Lady Melbourne, who could be depended upon never to be touchy, or exacting, or shocked, or low-spirited, who did not expect men to be monogamous, and who never asked an awkward question. She seemed to combine the social merits of both sexes, to possess, at the same time, male robustness and feminine tact, a woman's voluptuousness and a man's judgment. Moreover, she had an unusual power of entering into a man's interests. She disliked talking about herself: 'no man is safe with another's secrets, no woman with her own', she once remarked.

Years later Lord Egremont observed to Lord Holland that the ethics of the time, heavily influenced by French philosophy and literature, meant 'There was hardly a young married lady of fashion, who did not think it almost a stain upon her reputation if she was not known as having cuckolded her husband; and the only doubt was, who was to assist her in the operation.' As far as he and Lady Melbourne were concerned, there was little doubt. It was widely assumed that Egremont had fathered the son, William, to whom she gave birth in March 1779, and who became the revered 'Lord M', Prime Minister and mentor to the young Queen Victoria. Egremont remained the most important man in her life and he did not marry for years, despite siring a number of illegitimate children, but Lady Melbourne's most influential conquest was George, Prince of Wales, the future Prince Regent.

'The Prince of Wales is *desperately* in love with Lady Melbourne,' observed Lady Mary Coke in 1784, 'and when she don't sit next to him at supper he is not commonly civil to his neighbours: she *dances* with him, something in the cow stile, but he is in *extase* with admiration at it.' At intervals there would be late-night supper parties for the Prince at Melbourne House, when the classically proportioned reception rooms with their tall windows overlooking gardens at the back fermented with lively political and social talk. Melbourne House gatherings were more characterized by intellectual debate than those of Georgiana Devonshire's circle with their flirtations and gossip.

It was at one such supper in the winter of 1791 that Lord and Lady Melbourne came to their unusual agreement to exchange homes with Frederick, Duke of York and Albany. It seems to have originated in a casual remark by the Duke, who spoke admiringly of Melbourne House and said that he was tired of living in Whitehall. Lady Melbourne obligingly replied that she would enjoy looking out over St James's Park every morning and would willingly exchange the chimes of St James's, Piccadilly, for those of Westminster Abbey. There was evidently a persuasive financial reason as well: as early as 1775 Lord Melbourne had taken out mortgages for £10,000, on which he was still paying the interest, and in 1789 he obtained a further mortgage to Chambers for £3000 still owing to the architect for work completed fourteen years earlier.

The agreement with the Duke gave the Melbournes not

only occupancy of York House in Whitehall (now the Scottish Office) with all its furniture, but enough money to pay off their mortgage debts with £10,000 left over. They continued their glittering social life in Whitehall, while the Piccadilly mansion became known as York House.

The 'Grand Old Duke of York', George III's favourite son, was as extravagant as the Melbournes, a reckless gambler as well as rash in his amorous liaisons: his career as Commander-in-Chief of the army foundered on his affair with Mary Anne Clarke, who took money from ambitious officers to secure promotions for them. When he made the arrangement with Lord Melbourne he was in debt to Thomas Coutts, the banker, for £16,000, and York House was soon re-mortgaged to Coutts for £22,000. At what stage Coutts decided his chances of repayment were slim is not certain, but he was known to be planning schemes for developing the house by 1800, when Thomas Malton's *Picturesque Tour Through London and Westminster* mentioned a plan to pull down York House and build 'a street of handsome houses on the site of the gardens, in a direct line with Saville-row'. Official records of this proposal, which involved the architect Henry Holland and a young builder named Alexander Copley, date from the following year, when the scheme was carefully costed and approved by the Duke of York, but ultimately abandoned. York House was instead to be preserved and converted into what Copland described as 'a magnificent and convenient Hotel in single and double apartments, for the Complete Accommodation of Families for any Length of Time, and of the Subscribers in particular. Also to contain a Coffee Room, Dining Room, extensive Kitchen, wine cellars, etc., to be called The Royal York Hotel.'

Prospectuses were issued in the hope of finding one hundred subscribers prepared to put up £600 each; as soon as forty subscribers had enrolled, a meeting was to select three trustees and a committee of seven who would be responsible for furnishing the hotel and erecting the additional buildings required. But by March 1802, after Copland had formally agreed to purchase the house from the Duke of York for £37,000 in eight instalments spread over three years, a new plan had been devised for 'Dividing and Disposing of the Mansion House and Premises lately occupied by His Royal Highness the Duke of York in Piccadilly'.

It is proposed to make extensive additions to York House and Offices, and to distribute the whole into elegant and convenient Sets of independent Freehold Apartments, appropriating a Part of the Premises for a large Dining-Room, Kitchen, extensive Cellars, Hot and Cold Baths etc., for the exclusive Convenience of the Inhabitants of the Apartments, and also for a Residence for a Maitre d'Hotel. The Dining-Room will be supplied by the Maitre d'Hotel, and great Convenience will be derived to the resident Proprietors from the Facility of obtaining from him every Requisite in their own Apartments.

It was, in essence, a blueprint for London's first service flats, but the hotel part of it was never a success: one John Mollard took over its administration for a rent of £22 a year, providing laundry services as required and undertaking to look after the chambers, clean the staircases and keep the dining room 'well-supplied with good wines and provisions'. In less than a year he was saying that the venture had been 'attended with great loss', and after two more lessees had attempted to make it a success, the hotel was abandoned and its premises converted into two more sets of chambers.

The extension to Melbourne House was designed by Henry Holland and consisted of two long buildings running back from the mansion to Vigo Street on the site of its former garden. A paved and covered path, still known for obscure reasons as the Rope Walk, ran between the cream stucco facades, behind which sets of chambers were arranged on three floors, each equipped with two attic rooms and a cellar for wine and coal. The rooms, in some of which the original pine panelling and built-in bookcases survive to the present day, opened off austere stone staircases in the fashion of an Oxford or Cambridge college, giving the community the donnish, bachelor air it still retains, though in fact women have never formally been excluded. The first woman to own chambers was recorded in 1883, a widow who inherited from her husband, and the first single woman was given formal permission to buy a set in 1889. Nevertheless it was from the beginning overwhelmingly a male enclave, a haven for the gentry with no town residence of their own and, as it gained popularity with men of letters it became more than ever, as Macaulay wrote contentedly from chambers F3 in 1841, like 'a college life in London'.

Each set of chambers designed by Holland consisted of a hall with fireplace, a living room with double doors opening into a bedroom, and a dressing room with water-closet and hip-bath. The bachelor scheme was accentuated by the fact that none had kitchens on the same level: the ground-floor chambers had theirs in the basement, those of the first and second floors were in the attics, in both cases reached by spiral staircases. Meanwhile the main house was divided into twelve sets, some of Lady Melbourne's grand salons being skilfully split and converted, and the outbuildings round the courtyard were turned into apartments as well. The sets were to be sold at prices between £350 and £800, plus an additional rent in some cases of between £20 and £40 a year. Those in the mansion, numbered A1–12, were the first to go. As soon as twenty had been sold, Holland and Copley planned that the freeholders should meet to appoint trustees for administering the property.

By July 1802 eighteen subscribers had registered and were invited to choose their sets, which were still under construction. Thomas Coutts bought several himself as a way of speeding the completion of his investment. Early in 1803 the required number of sales had been completed and on 22 April the first meeting of proprietors was held in a nearby tavern where they elected seven trustees and agreed to draft a set of community rules. The first of these, published in February 1804 when thirty-three sets of chambers had been sold, stipulated that 'the Premises mentioned in the foregoing Articles shall be called Albany'. This style, rather than 'The Albany', remains the accepted 'correct' address among those who live there today, though it was known as 'The Albany' for much of the nineteenth century and Macaulay among others referred to it as such. The stylistic confusion was finally cleared up by the wine writer Cyril Ray, himself an Albany resident, in a letter to the *Manchester Guardian* in 1956. Citing William Stone, the celebrated Albany freeholder who lived to well over one hundred and was known as the Squire of Piccadilly, Ray explained that it was not so much insistence on the original style as the feeling, according to Stone, that 'The Albany' sounded too much like the name of a public house.

The other rules laid down in 1804 have broadly remained in force to this day. They stated that no alterations were to be made without the majority consent of the trustees; repairs were to be made at the direction of the trustees and the expense of the proprietors, and 'in order to exclude improper Inhabitants', there was to be no letting or sale of chambers without the trustees' consent. Furthermore, 'no Profession, Trade or Business' was to be carried on in any of the chambers without a majority of the trustees approving it in writing. But quite early in Albany's history chambers were being used for professional purposes: the architects Sir Robert Smirke and George Basevi were allowed to practise there, Jane Austen's brother Henry had his banking office in the courtyard, and Henry Angelo ran a fencing academy from a house in the courtyard from 1804 to 1809, premises shared at one time by 'Gentleman John' Jackson, the famous boxer. According to Farington's Diary in 1807, 'He has a room in Albany building, Piccadilly, where he gives lessons in Pugilism, and is supposed to make four or five hundred a year.' Byron was later among Albany residents to make use of both these sporting services, Angelo calling on him in his chambers in the main house most days at noon for an hour's swordsmanship at half a guinea a time.

Albany's first residents in 1804 are still on record – a Mr R. Bristow in A4; General Budé in A12; Richard Crofts and Major Mayne, each for a short time, in A8; K. Forster in A11; a Mr White in A9; John Winter in A6; and Captain James in B1. But the house's literary connections were already in bud; it was around this time that Matthew Gregory Lewis, author of the notorious and phenomenally successful Gothic novel *The Monk*, from which he gained his nickname, moved in. He did not, however, buy the lease of K1, the ground-floor set now the home of Cyril Ray, until 1809.

Monk Lewis had been precociously successful even as an undergraduate, pouring out poems, three plays, and four volumes of fiction before reaching his eighteenth birthday. At twenty, while working as a junior attaché in The Hague, he was inspired by the runaway success of Mrs Radcliffe's *The Mysteries of Udolpho* to write his own Gothic novel, *Ambrosio, or The Monk*. It was finished in ten weeks and published anonymously in 1795. At once it was attacked for 'vice' and immorality, ensuring its *succès de scandale*. The attorney-general of the day was asked to take out an injunction against its continued sale; salons buzzed with speculation over the author's identity, and when the secret broke, Lewis was the most sought-after celebrity in London. He continued to write prolifically, mainly ballads and plays, but never again with the impact of his fashionably 'horrid' fantasy. One winter night in 1808, after his new melodrama *Venoni, or the Novice of St Mark's*, starring Mrs Siddons, had been booed off the stage at Drury Lane, Lewis ordered a rehearsal for the next morning, returned late to Albany and, sustaining himself for the rest of the night on strong coffee, wrote a completely new third act which turned the play into a success.

Lewis was an odd-looking little man who remained preternaturally boyish in appearance all his life. Sir Walter Scott, a lifelong friend whose poetry was influenced strongly by Lewis – as was Byron's – wrote of his 'queerish eyes, they projected like those of some insects, and were flattish on the orbit'. His chambers in Albany were cluttered with bric-à-brac and precious objects, especially the seals and jewellery he collected, and there were mirrors everywhere. After attending one of Lewis's all-male supper parties Byron said he was determined not to go again. 'I never will dine with a middle-aged man who fills up his table with young ensigns, and has looking-glass pannels to his bookcases.'

It was probably Lewis who introduced Byron to Albany. The poet had been living in Bennet Street, St James's, and in 1814, three years before he moved into Albany, had announced his intention to 'marry some heiress' in order to settle his soaring debts. In February 1812, just before *Childe Harold's Pilgrimage* sold out in three days and made him an overnight literary sensation, he wrote to Francis Hodgson

that he planned to 'leave England for ever' in the spring of
1813. 'I shall find employment in making myself a good
Oriental scholar. I shall retain a mansion in one of the fairest
islands, and retrace, at intervals, the most interesting
portions of the East.' He thought he would end up with
enough money to buy 'a principality in Turkey'. By April
1813 his disastrous affair with Lady Caroline Lamb was
degenerating into bitterness and threats to 'ruin' him. 'I
thank you, but I have done that for myself already . . .' he
wrote back tartly. Anticipating his twenty-sixth birthday on
22 January 1814 he mourned: 'Is there any thing in the future
that can possibly console us for not being always *twenty-
five?'*

A week before he moved in to A2, Albany, a splendid set
of chambers in the main house dominated by the large bow
window of Lady Melbourne's former library and rented for
seven years from Lord Althorp (an ancestor of the present
Princess of Wales), he wrote jadedly of London life:

> Last night, *party* at Lansdowne House. Tonight, *party* at
> Lady Charlotte Greville's – deplorable waste of time,
> and something of temper. Nothing imparted – nothing
> acquired – talking without ideas . . . Heigho! – and in
> this way half London pass what is called life.

He was sceptical even of the acclaim he enjoyed, telling
Thomas Moore that he thought his 'things' were 'strangely
over-rated' for the time they had taken to write: *The Bride*
had been written in four days, *The Corsair* in ten.

Byron was in the habit of alternating bouts of high living
with the most ascetic regimes, subsisting for days at a time
on tea or soda and dry crackers, and all that last week of
March 1814 he was in abstemious vein, though still
complaining of feeling unwell. On the evening of 27 March
he dined at the Cocoa Tree in St James's with his friend
Scrope Davies, repaying him a debt of £4800 which had been
weighing on his mind. They sat from 6 p.m. until midnight,
drinking between them one bottle of champagne and six of
claret, 'neither of which wines ever affect me', as Byron
noted in his *Journal*:

Offered to take Scrope home in my carriage, but he was
tipsy and pious, and I was obliged to leave him on his
knees praying to I know not what purpose or pagod.
[Byron himself felt] no headach, nor sickness. . . . Got
up, if anything, earlier than usual – sparred with Jackson
ad sudorem, and have been much better in health than
for many days.

That night he moved into Lord Althorp's apartments, noting
with satisfaction that there was 'room for my books and
sabres. . . . Redde a little of many things – shall get in all
my books tomorrow. Luckily this room will hold them.' Ten
days later he wrote to Moore:

Viscount Althorp is about to be married, and I have
gotten his spacious bachelor apartments in Albany. . . .
I have been boxing, for exercise, with Jackson for this
last month daily. I have also been drinking, and, on
one occasion, with three other friends at the Cocoa Tree,
from six till four, yea, until five in the matin. We
clareted and champagned till two – then supped, and
finished with a kind of regency punch composed of
madeira, brandy, and *green* tea, no *real* water being
admitted therein. There was a night for you! . . . I have
also, more or less, been breaking a few of the favourite
commandments; but I mean to pull up and marry, if
any one will have me.

Byron's bachelor days in Albany lasted less than ten
months; he embarked on his disastrous marriage with Annabella Milbanke early in January 1815 and the couple then
moved into 13 Piccadilly Terrace, where they spent one year
together. But the Albany period was fruitful; he wrote *Lara*
during a hectic round of summer balls and parties, returning
home in the small hours to fortify himself with brandy and
write poetry until dawn. He enjoyed the contrast of violent
exercise, sparring with Gentleman Jackson or Henry Angelo
until he was sweating and exhausted (he wrapped himself
in layers of flannel and fur to speed the process), and
languorous evenings at London's great houses, or, even
more congenial to him, 'the company of my lamp and my

utterly confused and tumbled-over library'. On 10 April he recorded in his *Journal* that he had not stirred out of his rooms for four days. 'Today I have boxed an hour – written an ode to Napoleon Buonaparte – copied it – eaten six biscuits – drunk four bottles of soda water – redde away the rest of my time.'

The long table in front of his fireplace was always heaped with books. He kept a macaw, and a small sword lay by his bed; his friend Tom Moore described him plunging it through the bed-hangings before getting up in the mornings. Even more eccentric in his friends' eyes was his loyalty to the 'witch-like' old woman who had looked after him in Bennet Street, Mrs Mule. When Byron moved into the bachelor atmosphere of Albany his friends, according to Moore, hoped he would have 'got rid of this phantom. But no – there she was again – he had actually brought her with him.'

He explained the curious attachment by saying, 'The poor old devil was always so kind to me.' But in his *Journal* he confessed to feeling 'something very softening in the presence of a woman – some strange influence, even if one is not in love with them. . . . I always feel in better humour with myself and everything else, if there is a woman within ken.' With Lady Melbourne, Caroline Lamb's mother-in-law – 'the best friend I ever had in my life, and the cleverest of women' – he kept up a stream of intimate correspondence. 'I am in my and your Albany rooms. I think you should have been included in the lease,' he wrote in one letter to the woman who, now over sixty and growing stout, had captivated fashionable London in those rooms before he was born. He wrote constantly to her of his desire to quit the bachelor life and of his requirements in a wife: 'I wish I were married, and don't care about beauty, nor *subsequent* virtue – nor much about fortune. . . . but I should like – let me see – liveliness, gentleness, cleanliness, and something of comeliness – and *my own* first born. Was ever man more moderate?' And again, three days later in January 1814: 'What I want is a companion – a friend rather than a sentimentalist. I have seen enough of love matches – and of all matches – to make up my mind to the common lot of happy couples. The only misery would be if I fell in love afterwards

– which is not unlikely, for habit has a strange power over my affections. . . .'

Habit also had a power over the affections of his former love, Caroline Lamb, who several times that summer broke into his bachelor retreat, usually when he was out. A night watchman had been engaged that year because the Albany courtyard was becoming a favourite place for prostitutes to transact their business, but Lady Caroline managed to slip past him, probably by using the disguise of a page-boy which she had employed when visiting Byron at his Bennet Street lodgings. On one occasion when she gained access to the Albany rooms she scrawled 'Remember me!' on the fly-leaf of a book lying open on his table. 'You talked to me about keeping her out,' Byron wrote plaintively to Lady Melbourne in June.

> It is impossible; she comes at all times, at any time, and
> the moment the door is open in she walks. I can't throw
> her out of the window: as to getting rid of her, that is
> rational and probable, but *I* will not receive her. . . .
> She has been an adder in my path ever since my return
> to this country; she has often belied and sometimes
> betrayed me; she has crossed me everywhere; she has
> watched and worried and *guessed* and been a curse to
> me and mine. You may show *her* this if you please – or
> to anyone you please; if these were the last words I
> were to write upon earth I would not revoke one letter
> except to make it more legible.

After the episode of 'Remember me!' he wrote the angry verse which so unhinged her after his death:

> Remember thee! Remember thee!
> Till Lethe quench life's burning stream
> Remorse and shame shall cling to thee,
> And haunt thee like a feverish dream!
> Remember thee! Aye, doubt it not,
> Thy husband too shall think of thee;
> By neither shalt thou be forgot,
> Thou *false* to him, thou *fiend* to me!

After Byron's death Caroline claimed that on her last visit to Albany, dressed as a carman, Byron had received her kindly, kissed her and murmured, 'Poor Caro, if everyone hates me, you, I see, will never change – no, not with ill usage.' But she also said that he showed her letters and told her 'things I cannot repeat, & all my attachment went. This was our last parting scene – well I remember it. It had an effect on me not to be conceived – 3 years I had *worshipped* him.' Whether these unmentionable confidences actually happened – perhaps a final attempt to get rid of her by speaking of his relationship with his half-sister Augusta – or whether she made up the whole episode, Byron himself never referred to any such scene, even to his confidante Lady Melbourne.

In September he sent an affectionate though ambiguously worded letter to Lady Melbourne's niece, Annabella Milbanke, with whom he had been corresponding, but whom he had not seen for ten months. She was a serious, academic girl quite unlike any other Byron had paid attention to, and she interpreted it quite clearly as a proposal of marriage, accepting almost by return of post. Somewhat to his surprise, Byron found himself engaged, and on Sunday, 18 September, wrote from Newstead Abbey to Lady Melbourne:

I lose no time in telling you how things are at present. Many circumstances may doubtless occur in this, as in other cases, to prevent its completion, but I will hope otherwise. I shall be in town by Thursday, and beg one line to Albany, to say you will see me at your own day, hour and place. Of course I mean to reform most thoroughly, and become 'a good man and true' in all the various senses of these respective and respectable appellations. Seriously, I will endeavour to make your niece happy; not by 'my deserts, but what I will deserve'. Of my deportment you may reasonably doubt; of her merits you can have none. I need not say that this must be a *secret*. Do let me find a few words from you in Albany. . . .

He seemed in no hurry to leave Albany for the wedding

in Seaham, and confessed in October to being 'horribly low-spirited', brooding in his chambers with his books and macaw for company. 'Never was lover less in haste,' remarked one of his friends. The marriage lasted less than a year, blighted by his financial recklessness and the persistent flaunting of his relationship with his half-sister, which became painfully obvious to Annabella as early as their return from honeymoon in Italy. Soon after their daughter was born, Annabella left to live with her parents in Leicester-shire and Byron never saw his wife or child again.

Twenty years later his old rooms in Albany, A2, were occupied by another writer who had taken fashionable London by storm, entered a doomed marriage and, as a young poet of singular good looks and susceptibility, had experienced a brief infatuation for Byron's old flame Lady Caroline Lamb. Edward Bulwer, later to be Lord Lytton, sought chambers in Albany in 1835 as a retreat from family life in Acton with the wife his mother had all too shrewdly warned him against; Rosina Wheeler, once a famous Irish beauty, spent money faster than he could earn it even with his prolific output of novels and journalism, and lavished most of her affection on a Blenheim spaniel called Fairy, for which she had miniature visiting cards printed.

Bulwer's most durable and successful book, *The Last Days of Pompeii*, had recently come out and *Rienzi* was published late in 1835. In the two years he spent in Albany, Bulwer finished two volumes of a history of Athens, two more novels and a play, as well as carrying out his parliamentary duties as Liberal MP for St Ives. But his tranquillity was rudely interrupted after a year by Rosina, who was convinced that he had a mistress. There were rows, threats of separation, scenes of reconciliation. Bulwer wrote despairingly to his mother that his nerves were shattered and he feared above all that Rosina would intrude on his bachelor haven in some embarrassing fashion like Caroline Lamb with Byron. 'What can I do if she comes to the Albany, throws herself on the ground and declares she won't leave till it is made up? I cannot have scenes in a place like that.'

That was exactly what happened one February night in 1836. When Bulwer, according to Rosina's account, did not turn up for dinner in Acton, she set off for Piccadilly and rang his door bell at 11 p.m. He had been expecting a male friend, Frederick Villiers, who had not arrived, and when Rosina spotted a 'cosy salver with tea for two on it', she drew the conclusion that he was waiting for a woman. She shouted and screamed in the Albany lobby until she was removed, and later made her famous accusation: 'I went to visit my husband in his rooms, which he kept in order to have undisturbed communion with the Muse. I found the Muse in white muslin seated on his knee.' A deed of separation was drawn up, with Bulwer agreeing to pay Rosina £400 a year for life and £50 for each of their two children, but he continued to suffer for his unhappy choice of a bride because Rosina's confidante Mrs Wyndham Lewis (Mary Anne Lewis) proved to be a powerful hindrance to Bulwer's political career when she later married Disraeli. More than twenty years after their separation Bulwer had Rosina certified as insane, but public opinion, whipped along by a press campaign against him, brought about her release. In the end she outlived her husband by nine years.

Meanwhile a contemporary of Bulwer's in Albany had embarked on the longest and most distinguished career in British political history. At the end of 1832 John Gladstone bought the freehold of L2 from the Reverend Francis Brownlow for his son, William Ewart, the newly fledged MP for Newark, a recent double first at Oxford and still only twenty-three years old. The young Gladstone moved into his new chambers in March 1833 and wrote gratefully to his father that he would be able to furnish the rooms 'including plate, within the liberal limits which you allow'. He came to Albany having planned a full programme of reading, eating dinners at Lincoln's Inn, working busily in the Commons and enjoying a hectic social round, sometimes making as many as fourteen calls in an afternoon. The notes he kept for a journal recorded six fruitful years in Albany:

July 21, 1833, Sunday. – Wrote some lines and prose also. Finished Strype. Read Abbott and Sumner aloud. Thought for some hours on my future destiny, and took a solitary walk to and about Kensington Gardens. July 23. – Read L'Allemagne, Rape of the Lock, and finished factory report. . . . July 30. – L'Allemagne. Bulwer's

England. Parnell. Looked at my Plato. Rode. House. July
31. – Hallam breakfasted with me. . . . Committee on
West India Bill finished. . . . German lesson.

He had his first brief taste of government office in 1835,
first as a junior lord of the Treasury in Peel's new administration and then as Under-Secretary of State for the Colonies.
But Peel's government lasted only a few months, and Gladstone had to wait six years before opportunity came again;
by then he was married to Catherine Glynn and had left
Albany in 1839 for 13 Carlton House Terrace. In the interval
he pursued his strenuous private studies, devouring all the
works of St Augustine in twenty-two octavo volumes, and
reading widely in his favourite classical authors, Homer and
Dante. He enjoyed giving breakfast parties in his rooms;
Wordsworth, by then in his sixties and with his greatest
work behind him, was a frequent guest, and they discussed
the merits of contemporary poets. Wordsworth believed that
Shelley had the greatest powers of the age but deplored his
lack of religion. Byron he denounced in the most vehement
terms. Wordsworth was also a frequent guest to dinner,
arriving in a long cloak, thick shoes and coarse grey worsted
stockings which he carefully removed in an ante-room to
reveal black silk ones beneath. A fellow diner once described
him as 'speaking as if he were an old Roman Senator dressed
like an English farmer'.

Gladstone in his twenties – when he was still a Conservative – was a fine-looking young man with a mass of black
hair and penetrating 'falcon's eyes' beneath strong dark
brows. He had a deep and melodious voice which added
immeasurably to his glowing powers of oratory and enjoyed
singing at parties. His physical and mental energy was
already the envy of his contemporaries; it was to carry him
through an extraordinary political career lasting nearly sixty
years and take him four times to the premiership – still
leaving enough vitality to chop trees and walk great
distances in his old age at Hawarden.

There was something about Albany's donnish seclusion
which seemed to inspire prodigious feats of reading and
mental exercise, or perhaps it was simply that the place
attracted men drawn to such activity. In July 1841, just as

Gladstone was entering Peel's second administration and about to embark on his great programme of tariff reform, a new MP moved into E1, on the west side of the Rope Walk. Thomas Babington Macaulay was lately back from a lucrative civil service posting in India which had enabled him to accumulate the money to be independent and enjoy the most desirable bachelor residence London could offer. (Macaulay is still the only Albany resident to be commemorated by a plaque; it is fixed outside E1, although he later moved to the more spacious F3 set.)

As a young man – he was forty-one when he came to Albany – Macaulay had acquired the habit of rigorous working; between twenty-five and thirty he had supported his parents and his two younger sisters by his writing. His pen poured out articles for the influential *Edinburgh Review*, which brought him literary acclaim, invitations from London hostesses and the tribute from the publisher John Murray that 'it would be worth the copyright of *Childe Harold* to have Macaulay on the staff of the *Quarterly*.' Political success came his way early: elected an MP at twenty-nine, he made his name with eloquent speeches on the Reform Bill and became a junior minister while continuing to produce a flood of articles and reviews and dine out almost nightly at the great houses of London.

But his financial circumstances worried him; he longed for a 'competence' to support his family, and he despaired of earning enough by writing while he continued to take an active part in politics. The offer of a post on the newly constituted Supreme Council of India, which carried with it the princely salary of £10,000 a year, seemed the perfect solution. He would be away from England only a few years, could 'live in splendour' in Calcutta on £5000 and save the rest, and his sister Hannah, to whom he was particularly devoted, could go with him. Once in India, however, Hannah married a civil servant named Charles Trevelyan, throwing Macaulay into an emotional trauma. He wrote to his other married sister Margaret: 'At thirty-four I am alone in the world. I have lost everything – and I have only myself to blame. . . . I must bear my punishment as I can. . . .' Tragically, Margaret also was lost to him: she died before his letter arrived.

Macaulay never felt the same intensity of emotion for any other woman, and his celibate temperament found its haven in the collegiate surroundings of Albany. By the summer of 1841 he could afford to take the lease of E1. He was now an opposition MP after a short spell as Melbourne's Secretary for War. On moving in that July, he wrote to his friend Thomas Flower Ellis:

> I have taken a very comfortable little suite of chambers in the Albany; – and hope to lead during some years a sort of life peculiarly to my taste – college life at the West end of London. I have an entrance-hall, two sitting-rooms, a bed-room, a water-closet, a kitchen, cellars and two bed-rooms for servants, all for ninety guineas a year, and this in a situation which no younger son of a Duke need be ashamed to put on his card. Indeed there is a younger son of a Duke on my stair-case. We shall have, I hope, some very pleasant breakfasts there, to say nothing of dinners. My own housekeeper will do very well for a few plain dishes, and the Clarendon is within a hundred yards.

A couple of weeks later he was writing to Mcvey Napier, editor of the *Edinburgh Review:*

> I can truly say that I have not, for many years, been so happy as I am at present. . . . I am free, I am independent. I am in Parliament, as honourably seated as a man may be. My family is comfortably off. I have leisure for literature; yet I am not reduced to the necessity of writing for money. If I had to choose a lot from all that there are in human life, I am not sure that I should prefer any to that which has fallen to me. I am sincerely and thoroughly contented.

He was already planning his *History of England*, a work which he hoped would be so popular as to 'for a few days supersede the last fashionable novel on the tables of young ladies'. It was a bold new approach to the practice of historical writing, but one built on a thick bedrock of research. Fellow writers were awed by his diligence. Thackeray remarked, 'He reads twenty books to write a sentence; he travels a hundred miles to make a line of description.' Every day in Albany he set himself to finish six pages of foolscap, equalling two pages of print. He developed the habit of working for three hours before breakfast, saying, 'A man feels his conscience so light during the day when he has done a good piece of work with a clear head before leaving his bed-room.'

For the third volume of his *History*, he set out the scope of his ambitious research programme:

> I will first set myself to know the whole subject: – to get, by reading and travelling, a full acquaintance with William's reign. I reckon that it will take me eighteen months to do this. I must visit Holland, Belgium, Scotland, Ireland, France. The Dutch archives and French archives must be ransacked. . . . I must see Londonderry, the Boyne, Aghrim, Limerick, Kinsale, Namur again, Landen, Steinkirk. I must turn over hundreds, thousands, of pamphlets. Lambeth, the Bodleian and the other Oxford Libraries, the Devonshire Papers, the British Museum, must be explored, and notes made: and then I shall go to work.

Macaulay's voracious appetite for learning was a legend among his contemporaries; he could get by heart an entire Shakespeare play in an evening, and once replied to a challenge, 'Any fool could say his Archbishops of Canterbury backwards' – and proceeded to do so at a galloping pace until his listeners stopped him at Cranmer. On an overnight boat trip to Ireland, wrapped in a greatcoat on deck with no light to read by, he passed the time by reciting to himself the whole of *Paradise Lost*. Whatever he learned, moreover, he had the compulsion to pass on to others, a trait some found tedious in the extreme. Sydney Smith thought his dinner-table talk 'suffocating' and called him 'a book in breeches'.

But his appetite for knowledge was not always applied in such a daunting fashion. He was fascinated by ballads and popular songs, and on his long striding walks around London would hunt out street stalls and bookshops to snap up every halfpenny song-sheet he could find. During the writing of the first volume of his *History* he experimented with what he called a 'little volume' of poems. This was *The Lays of Ancient Rome*, which owed much to his ear for popular rhythm. They immediately caught the public's imagination and are still part of the mental furniture of most middle-aged people with memories of schoolroom recitations.

It was a pleasant life for a man of letters and politics. Macaulay moved between his three clubs – the Athenaeum, the Reform and Brooks's, the Whig club which attracted so many Albany residents, and still does. He held breakfast parties at which the talk was of Whig politics, literature and history; visited his sister Hannah and her husband, now home from India and settled first at Clapham and later at Westbourne Terrace, and took an active part in the cultural life of London. He was a trustee of the British Museum, a founder trustee of the National Portrait Gallery and a member of the committee supervising the interior decoration for Sir Charles Barry's new Houses of Parliament.

He was Paymaster-General for a year, in 1846–7, during which he moved to a larger set of rooms, F3, on the second floor at the Vigo Street end of the Rope Walk. It had a library twenty-four feet long for his books, which he calculated at one time to number 7000, expecting to have 10,000 by the time his lease expired. His nephew described F3 as

> comfortably, though not very brightly furnished. The ornaments were few, but choice: – half a dozen fine Italian engravings from his favourite great masters; a handsome French clock, provided with a singularly melodious set of chimes, the gift of his friend and publisher, Thomas Longman; and the well-known bronze statuettes of Voltaire and Rousseau (neither of them heroes of his own) which had been presented to him by Lady Holland as a remembrance of her husband.

Lord Carlisle described one of Macaulay's breakfast parties in February 1849, attended by Henry Hallam, Charles Austin, Panizzi and Richard Monckton Milnes.

> The conversation ranged the world; art, ancient and

modern; the Greek tragedians; characters of the orators, – how Philip and Alexander probably felt towards them as we do towards a scurrilous newspaper editor. It is a refreshing break in common-place life. I stayed till past twelve. His rooms at the top of Albany are very liveable and studious-looking.

All this time he was working on the *History*, 'the business and pleasure of my life'. Correcting the proofs of the first two volumes, he worked from seven in the morning to seven at night for ten solid days: when they were published on 7 November 1848 their popular success was all he had hoped for. That morning traffic on Ludgate Hill was brought to a standstill by booksellers' carriages trying to reach Longman's in Paternoster Row. Within three days the first printing of 3000 was nearly sold out, and a meeting near Manchester passed a vote of thanks to 'Mr Macaulay for having written a history which working men can understand'. It was said that every MP had read it, prompting Walter Bagehot to remark that 'a country member . . . hardly reads two volumes per existence'.

By the end of December the second 3000 of the first edition was also sold out, to be followed by further editions of 5000 and 2000 before 1849 was fairly under way. His contract with Longman's, £500 a year for five years on a first edition of 6000 and two-thirds of the profits on subsequent editions, was clearly going to leave him very comfortably off. On 18 November he wrote contentedly:

> I lead a college life in London, with the comforts of domestic life near me; for Hannah and her children are very dear to me. . . . Today I enjoyed my new liberty, after having been most severely worked during three months in finishing my *History* and correcting proofs. I rose at half after nine, read at breakfast Fearon's *Sketches of America*, and then finished Lucian's critique on the bad historians of his time. . . . Ellis came to dinner at seven. I gave him a lobster curry, woodcock and macaroni.

The second two volumes, published in December 1855, had advance orders for 25,000. Macaulay exulted in the fact

that the copies lying at the bookbinder's were insured for
£10,000 and weighed fifty-six tons. 'It seems that no such
edition was ever published of any work of the same bulk.'
Within six months Longman's paid him a cheque for £20,000
– 'a transaction quite unparalleled in the history of the book
trade' Macaulay told Thomas Flower Ellis, adding that he
was investing £19,000 of it to give him 'a certain income' of
£3000 a year. Also unparalleled in the history of the book
trade, though even Macaulay could not foresee it, the work
which he hoped would vie with the latest novel on young
ladies' tables has never been out of print, from its first
publication to the present day.

With the publication of the third and fourth volumes
Macaulay's Albany lease was expiring, and he decided to
move farther west for the sake of his health, 'beyond the
reach of the coalfog and riverfog which, during six months
of the year, make it difficult for me to breathe'. For some
time he had been suffering from asthma and bronchitis: the
long, all-weather walks through the streets and back alleys
of London were now a thing of the past. In 1852 he had
turned down the offer of a Cabinet post from Lord John
Russell on the grounds of his writing commitments and
failing health. Now, he told an American friend, he was
looking for somewhere within easy reach of his clubs, his
sister's house and the British Museum, with 'room for near
ten thousand volumes [and] if possible an acre of green turf
where I can walk up and down among lilacs and laburnums
with a book in my hand'.

He found it in Holly Lodge, Campden Hill, which had
two acres of lawns and flowerbeds and the Duke of Argyll
as a neighbour. But the pangs of leaving Albany were sore.
On 1 May 1856 he noted in his journal:

> After fifteen happy years passed in the Albany I am
> going to leave it, thrice as rich a man as when I entered
> it, and far more famous; with health impaired, but with
> affections as warm and faculties as vigorous as ever. . . .
> I do not at all expect to live fifteen years more. If I do, I
> cannot hope that they will be as happy as the last
> fifteen. The removal makes me sad. . . . The books are
> gone, and the shelves look like a skeleton. Tomorrow

I take final leave of this room where I have spent most of the waking hours of so many years. Already its aspect is changed. It is the corpse of what it was on Sunday. I hate partings. To-day, even while I climbed the endless steps, panting and weary, I thought that it was for the last time, and the tears would come into my eyes. I have been happy at the top of this toilsome stair. Ellis came to dinner; – the last of probably four hundred dinners, or more, that we have had in these chambers. Then to bed. Everything that I do is coloured by the thought that it is for the last time. One day there will come a last in good earnest.

Three years later he was dead.

The late nineteenth century was the golden age of the literary and political review, and of the men of letters who contributed to the vast array of weekly, monthly and quarterly periodicals on the bookstalls. Macaulay, with his long association with the *Edinburgh Review*, would have appreciated the fact that, as he was preparing to leave Albany, in 1855, the set of rooms G1 became the editorial offices of the new *Saturday Review*, and remained so for nearly forty years, until 1893. Douglas Cook, its managing editor and the occupier of G1, put together the magic formula every magazine editor dreams of – a list of distinguished contributors who will write for minuscule fees for the pleasure of being in the company of their peers. Like Harold Ross of the *New Yorker*, Cook was an unintellectual man – it was said that he never opened a book – with the flair for picking brilliant, often polemical writers. During his fifteen-year editorship men of the calibre of Froude, John Morley and Bagehot wrote for the paper, and in the 1860s it established a reputation for abrasive right-wing comment – against trade unions, supporting the Confederacy in the American Civil War, and generally locking horns with liberal spirits of the age like John Bright. Later, names like Edmund Gosse, Andrew Lang and W. E. Henley were added to its contributors.

The *Saturday Review* paid only two or three pounds for an article, none of which were signed. Cook also dropped contributors whom he found to be writing for other publications. Still, to be a Saturday Reviewer (or 'Reviler', as

Bright dubbed its contributors) was a sought-after niche in London's literary life. The editor and his assistant gave luncheons for their writers, attended by a manservant called Wilson who lived in one of the attic rooms, and a brougham called weekly to take the editor and the proofs to the printers and back.

G1 continued to be a focus of London literati in the 1890s, when John Lane, a former railway clerk and antiquarian book enthusiast, took over the remainder of the lease and obtained the trustees' permission to establish a publishing firm there. He converted the dining room into a publisher's office, with an entrance and new bay window facing on to Vigo Street. A black and white drawing of the new entrance decorated the first catalogue of The Bodley Head. Lane was a gifted publisher much liked by his authors, some of whom took advantage of his generosity with accommodation: William Watson was rumoured to have occupied a spare room for twenty-five years.

The Yellow Book focused the attention of the reading public on The Bodley Head and its Albany offices. It launched Aubrey Beardsley – described by Oscar Wilde as having 'a face like a silver hatchet, with grass-green hair' – as a fascinatingly decadent successor to Lord Byron, equally 'mad, bad and dangerous to know'. Among the guests at *The Yellow Book*'s inaugural 'smoke', for which Beardsley designed the invitation card, were Henry James, Edmund Gosse, Wilfrid Meynell, St Loe Strachey, Kenneth Grahame, Lionel Johnson, Ernest Dowson, Arthur Symons, Wilson Steer, Oscar Wilde's intimate Robert Ross, the young H. G. Wells and Walter Sickert.

Beardsley's flame burned out in three years – he died at twenty-five of consumption, and *The Yellow Book* never regained its initial scandalous impact, but G1 continued as a centre of London's literary life, if less louche and fascinating than in the days of Wilde's Café Royal a few steps away across Regent Street. One could meet female celebrities like E. Nesbit and Lady Randolph Churchill at Lane's literary teas; evening parties were predominantly male, a mix of contrasting people who, for one reason or another, Lane found stimulating; in Richard le Gallienne's words, 'not only writers and artists, but generals and literary lords who collected bookplates and old china, and venerable scholars mysteriously learned'. Lane published Zola's *J'Accuse* pamphlet on the Dreyfus case and brought its author from Paris to be entertained at Vigo Street.

The Bodley Head remained in its gentlemanly Albany enclave until 1926, when the 1890s of which it had been, in W. J. Locke's words, 'the Wonder House', seemed to the rest of London as remote as the Regency. Albany continued to be the retreat of novelists and playwrights – Compton Mackenzie, Edward Knoblock, G. B. Stern, Margery Sharp, J. B. Priestley, Graham Greene – and to cast its late-nineteenth-century spell of foggy gaslight, dank stone steps, echoing flagstones and cellars of wine and coal. A living link with the 1890s was maintained into the late 1950s by Albany's leading freeholder, William Stone, 'the Squire of Piccadilly'. A dashing figure who rode daily in Rotten Row and continued to wear a top-hat and frock-coat into the age of rock 'n' roll, Stone died a bachelor in 1958 at the age of 101 and bequeathed his thirty-four sets of chambers to his old Cambridge college, Peterhouse, which still owns them.

Stone belonged to a breed of gentleman-adventurer which had more or less disappeared before the Great War: he had politicked with Lord Randolph Churchill, collected butterflies on the Great Wall of China, sailed to Khartoum up the Nile before General Gordon was killed, and numbered A. E. W. Mason of *The Four Feathers* among his closest friends. In his childhood he had had a nurse whose father had fought at Waterloo. His lifelong hobby was preserving Albany as he had always known it; he first took chambers there in 1893 and he was chairman of the trustees continuously from 1909 until 1952, when he was ninety-five. The journalist and wine writer Cyril Ray secured his first foothold in Albany on a wartime lease from Stone of £100 a year for C6, a set which had once belonged to the eccentric and miserly Marquis of Clanricarde. Stone knew Clanricarde for twenty years and used to swear that in all that time he wore the same pair of patched trousers. 'He had a cloak about fifteen or twenty years old and one tall hat; the grease went gradually up it, higher and higher.' After he died it was said that the fine pictures on the walls of C6 had literally to be chipped away from their beds of dirt. But he left nearly £3 million, most of it to his great-nephew Harry Lascelles, who became sixth Earl of Harewood and husband of the Princess Royal.

Another Albany eccentric was Admiral of the Fleet Sir Harry Keppel, father-in-law of the celebrated Mrs Alice Keppel, mistress of Edward VII. He died in A8 at the age of ninety-five in 1904, having served with Nelson's flag-captain, Hardy, and endured by choice a spartan life of which he was inordinately proud. On hearing one bitterly cold winter that Gladstone was ill he remarked smugly, 'Ah, he is over-nursed. If he would do as I do – climb up eighty steps, have a cold bath every day, and sleep with his window always open – he would never be ill.'

References to Albany are threaded through Victorian novels and plays: Fascination Fledgeby in *Our Mutual Friend* gets a thrashing in his rooms there from Alfred Lammle, 'the meanest cur existing with a single pair of legs'. H. W. Hornung made it the lair of Raffles, the cricketing gentleman burglar, though he invented a side street for getaways that does not exist. Characters in Trollope had rooms there, and a now-forgotten novelist of the 1840s, Marmion Savage, caught the mid-Victorian atmosphere of Albany as

> the haunt of bachelors, or of married men who try to lead bachelors' lives – the dread of suspicious wives, the retreat of superannuated fops, the hospital for incurable oddities, a cluster of solitudes for social hermits, the home of homeless gentlemen, the diner-out and the diner-in, the place for the fashionable thrifty, the luxurious lonely, and the modish morose, the votaries of melancholy and lovers of mutton-chops.

In the year William Stone took up residence, 1893, *The Second Mrs Tanqueray* opened at the St James's Theatre with Pinero's stage directions for Act One, Scene One, reading:

> Aubrey Tanqueray's Chambers in the Albany – a richly and tastefully decorated room, elegantly and luxuriously furnished; on the right a large pair of doors leading into another room, on the left at the further end of the room a small door leading to a bedchamber.

A circular table is laid for a dinner for four persons
which has now reached the stage of dessert and coffee.
Everything in the apartment suggests wealth and
refinement. The fire is burning brightly.

Oscar Wilde's most engaging character had visiting cards
reading 'Mr Ernest Worthing, B4, the Albany'. Wilde might
or might not have agreed with those purist residents of
Albany today, Cyril Ray among them, who consider that
they live in St James's or even on the doorstep of Soho
rather than on the edge of Mayfair, but to a passer-by who
once asked him the way to Curzon Street, Wilde remarked
genially: 'I am pleased that I should be asked to direct you
to so eminently desirable an address. Personally, I am unac-
quainted with any part of London east of Albany.'
Two plays were inspired by an incident in the life of
William Stone, whose valet once impersonated him during
his absence from Albany, robbing him in the process. One,
The Night of the Party, starred its author, Weedon Grossmith,
in the part of the valet, while the other, *The Lackey's Carnival*,
by Henry Arthur Jones, himself an Albany resident, had
Allan Aynesworth in the role.
Maitland, the rich, lonely 'iron dreamer' of John Buchan's
story *Fountainblue*, is described as living in

ugly rooms in the Albany . . . littered like a stable with
odds and ends of belongings . . . you never saw such
a collection of whips and spurs and bits. It smells like a
harness-room, and there you find Maitland, when by
any chance he is at home, working half the night and
up to the eyes in papers.

But of all the literary evocations of Albany, that in
Compton Mackenzie's *Sinister Street* still captures the pecu-
liar time-capsule essence of the place best. Dining there
with his father's friend, Prescott, Michael Fane 'enjoyed the
darkness of the room whose life seemed to radiate from the
gleaming table in the centre . . . and he enjoyed the intense
silence that brooded outside the heavily curtained
windows'. (Cecil Rhodes was attracted by this characteristic:

'I like this place, it's the silence that falls on you,' he said
once.)

Here in the Albany Michael was immeasurably aware of
the life of London that was surging such a little distance
away; but in this modish cloister he felt that the life he
was aware of could never be dated, as if indeed were
he to emerge into Piccadilly and behold suddenly
crinolines or even powdered wigs they would not
greatly surprise him. The Albany seemed to have wrung
the spirit from the noisy years that swept on their
course outside, to have snatched from each its heart and
in the museum of this decorous glass arcade to have
preserved it immortally, exhibiting the frozen
palpitations to a sensitive observer.

7

THE WAY THEY LIVED THEN

*T*HE image of Albany with its panelled peace, masculine self-sufficiency and rooms comfortably cluttered with books remains identified with the nineteenth-century man of letters, but the writer in his bachelor chambers was a familiar feature of other parts of Mayfair as well. The tradition lasted well into the 1920s, when Hugh Walpole took a bachelor flat on the first floor of 90 Piccadilly, on the corner of Half Moon Street. Its dining room and drawing room looked over Green Park and there was a quiet bedroom at the back. Sylvia Lynd wrote an evocative description of the flat which captures the essence of a fashionable novelist's life of the period:

His rooms were so crowded with beautiful things that they gave the impression of a rich background rather than a collection demanding detailed attention. A typical moment in my remembrance of him is finding him one hot summer's day sitting at the pianola in his shirt sleeves playing himself a Beethoven sonata; the purple Persian rug that coloured so much of his writing dominating the room; Gaudier-Brzeska's lovely little green stone fawn snoozing beside him; T'ang horses stepping grandly on the chimney-piece; the white

Utrillo, a new possession, propped on the arms of an
armchair; all sorts of trifles in jade and rose-quartz and
amber giving back the light; the window filled with his
big Epstein bronzes, the Green Park for their background; the whole concourse of London's prosperity
going by outside; and Hugh himself, pearl pin in tie,
about to put on his coat and set out for the Royal Garden
Party across the way.

Popular novelists of an earlier day had lived in even
greater style. Sir Edward Bulwer, later Lord Lytton, had
homes at different times in Hertford Street, Charles Street
and Grosvenor Square, where he spent the last five years
of his life at Number 12 and wrote his final book, *The Coming
Race*. Thomas Raikes, the diarist and man-about-town, also
lived briefly in Grosvenor Square, from which vantage point
he observed the vanities of fashionable London. He was
nicknamed Apollo because he started the day in the east,
spending the early hours at his bank in the City, and ended
it in the West End clubs. Thomas Hughes, author of *Tom
Brown's Schooldays*, lived at 13 Upper Brook Street from 1871
to 1885, after which it was joined together with 80 Park
Street to make a house described by the first Duke of
Westminster as 'hideous and incapable of improvement'.
Hughes had earlier lived at 33 Park Street, one of ten houses
demolished, along with stately Breadalbane House, to
enlarge the Duke of Westminster's garden at Grosvenor
House; next door to Hughes, at Number 31, lived George
Otto Trevelyan, the historian and MP.

Half a century earlier, in 1812, the economist David
Ricardo bought 56 Upper Brook Street from a builder for
£11,550, a sum he considered 'enormous'. He had been
living contentedly in Mile End and blamed his family for
encouraging the extravagant move to Mayfair. Soon after
moving in he found large cracks appearing in the drawing-
room ceiling and other defects elsewhere. 'What must I think
of Mr Cockerell whom I paid to examine it?' he complained
of his architect. 'What compensation can he make to me for
his shameful neglect?' It would cost him 'several thousand
Pounds' he grumbled, and the walls were still unpapered
and unpainted when they moved in. Ricardo worked in a

library at the back of the ground floor overlooking a small garden behind 25 Grosvenor Square, and in 1817 published his most influential work, *Principles of Political Economy*. Despite the expense of the Mayfair house, a year after buying it he was able to purchase a splendid country estate as well, Gatcombe Park in Gloucestershire, now the home of Princess Anne and her husband. (A later inhabitant of Ricardo's home in Upper Brook Street was Clarence Hatry, the City financier whose forging of securities in the 1920s caused a notorious scandal and sent him to jail for fourteen years.)

The most splendid address of any writer or politician – in this case both in the same person – was 1 Grosvenor Gate on Park Lane, the home from 1839 to 1872 of Benjamin Disraeli. An imposing white house with green shutters with an outlook over Hyde Park that was still almost rural (as late as the 1860s Park Lane traffic was liable to be disrupted by herds of cattle being driven along), it had become Disraeli's home on his marriage to Mary Anne Lewis, the widow of Wyndham Lewis. It had large, elegant rooms – Mary Anne Lewis had two drawing rooms of her own for which she worked out a 'cheerful but imposing colour scheme of red, gold and white', and a 'special, grand Blue Room'. It was big enough to give a ball in, which she did in 1827, describing it in a letter to John Wyndham: ' . . . the balustrades of the staircases were entwined with wreaths of flowers, the whole of the balcony, which goes all round the house, was enclosed as if making part of it, a crimson carpet at the bottom, the whole lined with lamp-shades all the way round.'

Disraeli wrote four novels at Grosvenor Gate – *Sybil*, *Coningsby*, *Tancred* and *Lothair*. When he became Prime Minister in 1868 the Disraelis remained there rather than move to 10 Downing Street, which Mary Anne thought dingy and decaying. She was by this time in poor health, and they spent increasing amounts of time at their Buckinghamshire home, Hughenden Manor, but continued to live at Grosvenor Gate until Mary Anne's death in 1872. The house then passed out of Disraeli's hands and he moved to Whitehall Gardens, returning to Mayfair in 1880 when he bought a ten-year lease on 19 Curzon Street with £10,000 earned from the publication of *Endymion*. He died three months after moving in, his last act being to correct a proof for Hansard of a speech he had made in the Lords. 'I will not go down to history speaking bad grammar,' he told a visiting friend.

The Disraelis' marriage was memorably happy and although few records survive of their life at Grosvenor Gate, the few domestic details that do are charming. Mary Anne mentioned 'little notes' passing between Grosvenor Gate and Westminster – on one occasion he asked, 'Will you send me an easy pair of boots and a great coat? It is very cold.' Whatever time he arrived home from a late sitting in the Commons, she would be waiting for him, Mary Anne's biographer recorded, 'with a cheerful smile and a good meal or whatever refreshment was appropriate'. After one particular triumph over Gladstone in a Reform Bill debate, members of his party pressed Dizzy to join them for a celebration supper at the Carlton Club, but he preferred to go home to Mary Anne. 'I had got him a raised pie from Fortnum and Mason's, and a bottle of champagne, and he ate half the pie and drank all the champagne, and then he said, "Well my dear, you are more like a mistress than a wife." '

During the Reform Bill riots of 1866 (when the Duke of Wellington had iron blinds put up against the mob at Apsley House), Mary Anne and Disraeli's new young secretary Montagu Corry (later to be Baron Rowton, the philanthropist who built the Rowton House hostels), watched demonstrators beat down the railings of Hyde Park opposite Grosvenor Gate. Disraeli, at the Commons, was concerned for her safety, but Corry sent him a note that all was well. 'Mrs Disraeli wishes me to add that the people in general seem to be thoroughly enjoying themselves, and I really believe she sympathises with them. At any rate, I am glad to say she is not in the least alarmed.'

When Thackeray was writing *Vanity Fair* the district was still known by the two words May Fair, first recorded as such on voters' rolls in 1749. Its topography is very closely described in the novel, although some streets and squares are given imaginary names. Literary detectives have argued whether Gaunt Square is really Berkeley, Hanover or

Cavendish Square, or an amalgam of all three; Gaunt House, the residence of the Marquis of Steyne, has many resemblances to gloomy Harcourt House with its high, concealing wall facing Cavendish Square. Great Gaunt Street could be either Hill Street or a mixture of Wigmore and Harley streets. Becky Sharp's house at 201 Curzon Street, after her marriage to Rawdon Crawley, is, however, so precisely described as to have been identified as a real house still existing in 1914. W. Beresford Chancellor, writing of Thackeray's London in 1923, says it was probably Number 89 on the south side, painted green in 1914 (the colour of Becky Sharp's eyes). An earlier topographer described it as four and a half storeys high,

> built of blackish brick like its neighbours, with painted sills and portico. Its extreme narrowness, compared with its height, especially distinguishes it: the front door, with drab pilasters and a moulded architrave, is just half its width and only leaves room for one parlour window on the first floor.

Thackeray's Mayfair charted the transition from the Regency to the mid nineteenth century, from the period when eccentric grandees like 'Old Q', the lecherous old Duke of Queensberry, sent his running footmen to pursue ladies who happened to catch his eye from his bow window at 139 Piccadilly. (Old Q was the last employer of running footmen, who travelled at around seven miles an hour and sustained themselves with egg-nog concealed in their silver-topped sticks: the trade is commemorated in the oddly named pub that sits at the corner of Charles Street and Hays Mews: I Am the Only Running Footman.)

In *Vanity Fair*, wrote Chancellor,

> the stage coach still rumbled in and out in all directions. The coaching inns were still a picturesque feature of civic life. The family chariot and the Tilbury, the gig and the buggy crowded Piccadilly on their way to Hyde Park where Decimus Burton's screen had not yet replaced the old insignificant entrance. The Brougham and the Victoria were not. Even the omnibus had not

yet come into existence. Almack's and the Opera were
the resorts of fashion. . . .

(The Tilbury was a gig designed by a coach-builder of that
name. It had a cutaway body perched on two high wheels
and could be drawn by one horse or a pair in tandem. The
Brougham, named after the statesman Lord Brougham, was
a one-horse closed carriage with two or four wheels to carry
two or four passengers, while a Victoria was a light, low-
slung, four-wheeled carriage for two with a collapsible hood.
Almack's, founded by William Almack in 1765, was the
fashionable gambling club in St James's. A box at the Opera
on a twenty-one-year lease cost Lord Grosvenor 5000
guineas in 1821 and a box for the season 180 guineas:
performances lasted up to five hours and always combined
a ballet with the opera. At Drury Lane or the new Haymarket
Theatre, opened in 1821, or the Adelphi, there would be a
triple bill of play, farce and pantomime.)
    In Thackeray's account of George Osborne's carriage drive
from Piccadilly to Fulham to marry Amelia, Apsley House
and St George's Hospital 'wore red jackets still', a reference
to the red brick in which both buildings were constructed
before being rebuilt in Portland stone. The Achilles statue
in Hyde Park was not yet in being (it was put up in 1822),
and there were still oil lamps on the Turnpike (Hyde Park
Corner), superseded by gas in 1825.
    Vanity Fair, published in 1848, offers an intriguing insight
into the interdependence of social classes in mid-century
Mayfair. The Crawleys' 'very small, comfortable house' in
Curzon Street, where they were able to live 'on nothing a
year', was owed to the enterprising Raggles, lately butler to
Miss Harriet Crawley, Rawdon's sister, who lived in 'an
exceedingly snug and well-appointed house in Park Lane'.
Raggles had married the cook, set up a small greengrocery
business in the neighbourhood of Shepherd Market and out
of his savings bought the lease and furniture of 201 Curzon
Street, which he let to the newly weds on nominal terms,
still feeling indebted to the family for giving him his start in
business.
    Writing a quarter of a century after *Vanity Fair*, Trollope
in *The Way We Live Now* observes with exactitude how the

classes impinged on one another in Mayfair: brash newcomers, like Augustus Melmotte with his mansion in Grosvenor Square, impoverished aristocrats like the Marquis of Auld Reekie in Berkeley Square, who wanted his son to marry the heiress Marie Melmotte, and county families like the Longestaffes with their faded Bruton Street town house and Berkshire estate. Here is Trollope's description from 1873 of Madame Melmotte's ball:

> The large house on the south side of Grosvenor Square was all ablaze by ten o'clock. The broad verandah had been turned into a conservatory, had been covered with boards contrived to look like trellis-work, was heated with hot air and filled with exotics at some fabulous price. A covered way had been made from the door, down across the pathway to the road. . . . The house had been so arranged that it was impossible to know where you were, when once in it. The hall was a paradise. The staircase was fairyland. The lobbies were grottoes rich with ferns. Walls had been knocked away and arches had been constructed. The leads behind had been supported and walled in, and covered and carpeted. The ball had possession of the ground floor and first floor, and the house seemed to be endless. 'It's to cost sixty thousand pounds', said the Marchioness of Auld Reekie to her old friend the Countess of Midlothian. . . . The three saloons on the first or drawing-room floor had been prepared for dancing, and here Marie was stationed. . . . There were three or four card-tables in one of the lower rooms. . . .

The great dinner Melmotte proposed to give to the visiting Emperor of China was even grander. It was to be held on a Monday, 8 July, but by the middle of June all London was talking of it, and how the Emperor would be shown by this banquet what 'an English merchant-citizen of London could do . . .'. (Melmotte, a merchant venturer from Middle Europe, had the characteristic urge to appear more English than those born to it.)

On the 20th of June the tradesmen were at work,

throwing up a building behind, knocking down walls, and generally transmuting the house in Grosvenor Square in such a fashion that two hundred guests might be able to sit down to dinner in the dining-room of a British merchant. . . . But who were to be the two hundred? . . . Meetings were held; a committee was appointed; merchant guests were selected, to the number of fifteen with their fifteen wives. . . . The Emperor with his suite was twenty. Royalty had twenty tickets, each ticket for guest and wife. The existing Cabinet was fourteen; but the coming was numbered at about eleven only; each one for self and wife. Five ambassadors and five ambassadresses were to be asked. There were to be fifteen real merchants out of the city. Ten great peers – with their peeresses – were selected by the general committee of management. There were to be three wise men, two poets, three independent members of the House of Commons, two Royal Academicians, three editors of papers, an African traveller who had just come home, and a novelist; – but all these latter gentlemen were expected to come as bachelors. Three tickets were to be kept over for presentation to bores endowed with a power of making themselves absolutely unendurable if not admitted at the last moment, and ten were left for the giver of the feast and his own family and friends. . . . Eight hundred additional tickets were to be issued for Madame Melmotte's evening entertainment. . . .

Before the dinner could take place, however, Melmotte killed himself by poison in the study of Mr Longestaffe's town residence in Bruton Street, which he had rented while the grand house in Grosvenor Square was being remodelled for the imperial visit.

Trollope pins down very precisely how the social boundaries were changing in 1873 and the attitudes of the 'old money' in their draughty, neglected Georgian terraces to recently developed districts like Belgravia where the new rich were making themselves ostentatiously comfortable with expensive architects and furnishings by Gillow. (The second Earl Grosvenor, first Marquess of Westminster, had shrewdly foreseen the potential of the southern portion of his estate when George IV rebuilt Buckingham Palace, and he proceeded to develop Belgravia in 1826: its streets and squares, largely built by Thomas Cubitt, were named after Grosvenor country estates and members of the family, Belgrave being a village in Cheshire from which the Grosvenor eldest son, Viscount Belgrave, took his title.) All this underpins Trollope's description of the Longestaffes' Bruton Street establishment:

> It was not by any means a charming house, having but few of those luxuries and elegancies which have been added of late years to newly-built London residences. It was gloomy and inconvenient, with large drawing-rooms, bad bedrooms, and very little accommodation for servants. But it was the old family town-house, having been inhabited by three or four generations of Longestaffes, and did not savour of that radical newness which prevails, and which was peculiarly distasteful to Mr Longestaffe. Queen's Gate and the quarters around were, according to Mr Longestaffe, devoted to opulent tradesmen. Even Belgrave Square, though its aristocratic properties must be admitted, still smelt of the mortar. Many of those living there and thereabouts had never possessed in their families real family town-houses. The old streets lying between Piccadilly and Oxford Street, with one or two well-known localities to the south and north of these boundaries, were the proper sites for these habitations. When Lady Pomona, instigated by some friend of a high rank but questionable taste, had once suggested a change to Eaton Square, Mr Longstaffe had at once snubbed his wife. If Bruton Street wasn't good enough for her and the girls then they might remain at Caversham. The threat of remaining at Caversham had often been made, for Mr Longestaffe, proud as he was of his town-house, was, from year to year, very anxious to save the expense of the annual migration. The girls' dresses and the girls' horses, his wife's carriage and his own brougham, his dull London dinner-parties, and the one ball which it was always necessary that Lady

Pomona should give, made him look forward to the
end of July with more dread than to any other period.

The first writer to use Mayfair as both setting and syn-
onym for high society in a series of popular novels was Mrs
Catherine Gore, one of the 'Silver Fork' school of novelists
which flourished in the early part of the nineteenth century,
so called from the genteel aspirations of their characters.
Mrs Gore wrote more than sixty three-volume society novels
studded with details of Mayfair life, from the names of
fashionable shops to the opinions of starchy dowagers.
Satirical advice on how to succeed in Mayfair circles was
given by a female character in Thomas Henry Lister's novel
Arlington: 'Mix a great deal of French with one's English and
have the names of singers or dancers and the fashionable
shops quite pat. Then one ought to know a great deal of
scandal and all about the parties that are going on, and all
the marryings that are to be.'
The brittle world of silver-fork Mayfair was captured in
an anonymous poem published in 1827, 'May Fair':

> Dear to my soul art thou, May Fair!
> There greatness breathes her native air:
> There Fashion in her glory sits:
> Sole spot still unprofaned by Cits.
> There all the mushroom, trading tribe
> In vain would bully or would bribe:
> The Rothschilds, Couttses, Goldsmids, Barings
> In other spots must have their parings:
> We fix your bounds, ye rich and silly,
> Along the road by Piccadilly.

> . . . land of *ponch romaine* and plate,
> Of dinners fix'd at half-past eight;
> Of morning lounge, of midnight rout,
> Of debt and dun, of love and gout,
> Of drowsy days, of brilliant nights,
> Of dangerous eyes, of downright frights,
> Of tables where old Sidney shines,
> Of ladies famous for their wines. . . .

'Old Sidney' was the cleric, wit and journalist Sydney
Smith, one of the best-known and most engaging characters
in early-nineteenth-century Mayfair, immediately recognizable with his Falstaffian figure, big Roman nose and loud,
melodious laugh. He took an infectious pleasure in the civilized delights of West End life, making his famous obser-
vation on Mayfair while exiled to a Yorkshire country parish:
'I believe the parallelogram between Oxford Street, Piccadilly, Regent Street and Hyde Park encloses more intelligence and human ability, to say nothing of wealth and
beauty, than the world has ever collected in such a space
before.' He hated being 'transported', as he put it, to livings
in the country. On returning to London after a spell in
Somerset, he wrote to a country-dwelling friend: 'All lives
out of London are mistakes, more or less grievous, but
mistakes.' London brought him fame and prosperity as a
lecturer in moral philosophy at the Royal Institution and as
a fashionable preacher in the private chapels of Mayfair. 'In
three years I have doubled my income. What should I have
ever done if I had been led by the idle love of daisies?' To
another friend he wrote: 'The summer and the country dear
Georgiana have no charms for me. I look forward anxiously
to the return of bad weather, coal fires and good society in
a crowded city.' Rational conversation, he added, was 'only
to be had from the congregation of a million people in one
spot'. More than anything he loved going to great Mayfair
receptions, mounting the staircase in one of those grand
Grosvenor or Berkeley Square houses: his conception of
Paradise, said his biographer Hesketh Pearson, was 'an
immense square full of trees flowering with flambeaux, with
gas for grass and every window illuminated with countless
chandeliers, and voices reiterating for ever and ever *Mr
Sydney Smith coming upstairs*'.

When Earl Grey appointed him a canon of St Paul's in
1831 he took a series of furnished houses and in 1835 bought
33 Charles Street, 'about as big as one of your travelling
trunks', he told Lady Carlisle. In the same year his daughter,
Lady Holland, inherited a 'dear little house' at 6 South
Street, which she described as 'no more than a *closet* and a
cupboard, so small are the rooms.' In 1839 the Smiths moved
to 56 Green Street, a larger, three-storey Georgian house

which he called 'the essence of all that is comfortable' and which was to remain his London home for the rest of his life.

The Smiths loved entertaining as well as being entertained: their Thursday-evening routs at Green Street were famous. The provisions were no doubt supplied by the shop he once memorably extolled: 'I will combat to the death for Fortnum and Mason's, and fall in defence of the sauces of my country.' His breakfast parties were a stimulating mixture, as he expressed it in an invitation to Thomas Moore, of 'muffins and metaphysics, crumpets and contradiction.' He hated to miss a promising social occasion himself, once lamenting to the publisher, Longman, that he was unable to accept an invitation because his house (at that time 20 Savile Row) was 'full of country cousins. I wish they were once removed.' On one unavoidable visit to the country in 1838 he wrote to a London friend: 'You who are revelling in the luxuries of Mayfair may spare a moment of commiseration for diners-out in West Somersetshire.'

His dinner-table technique, as he advised his daughter, was to 'fire across the table'. Most London dinners, he found, 'evaporate in whispers to one's next-door neighbour. I make it a rule never to speak a word to mine. . . .' In 1842, growing infirm and resenting the fact, he told Charles Babbage, the mathematician and grandfather of the computer, 'We are always desirous of coming to your agreeable parties but we are ancient and ailing people, disglued, unscrewed and tumbling to pieces and we are often forced to go to bed when we would be lemonading.' Macaulay, Monckton Milnes and Henry Hallam, father of Tennyson's beloved Arthur, were frequent breakfast and dinner companions: in 1844, having admired Disraeli's novel *Coningsby*, Smith wanted to meet the author, and a friend arranged a dinner at which, besides Disraeli and Mary Anne, the guests included the diarist Charles Greville, Henry Luttrell, Lady Morley and Lord Melbourne. Smith sat next to Disraeli, who was captivated by his warmth and wit.

The Mayfair society over which Sydney Smith reigned for forty years admired wit and learning, beauty and style. Lady Blessington's salons at 8 Seamore Place, off Park Lane, saw nightly gatherings of the brilliant and celebrated from all over Europe. Her library, alternately lined with mirrors and shelves of richly bound books, with its broad windows looking out over Hyde Park, was one of the most favoured places to spend an evening. Another notable scene of routs and gatherings was the home of Paul Beilby Thompson, MP, later first Baron Wenlock, at 29 Berkeley Square. In 1829, describing a ball held there, the *Morning Post* reported:

> The house possesses all the requisites for entertaining a numerous circle, it having *suites* of spacious apartments above and below. The decorations of the walls, their gilding and furniture, may be said to vie with the most far-famed dwellings of the rich and great. . . . There were eight rooms illuminated in the most resplendent style; also the grand staircase, the gallery, or corridor. The inner hall was decorated with shrubs.

Lord Wenlock told Sydney Smith that his ground rent 'cost him five pounds a foot; that is, about the price of a London footman six foot high – thirty guineas per annum'. The house was bought in 1882 by the seventh Duke of Marlborough, who made a number of structural alterations including building a partly enclosed portico with a verandah above, but he died within a year and the new owner was one of Trollope's 'opulent tradesmen', Albert Brassey, son of the railway contractor Thomas Brassey. Albert Brassey's widow continued to occupy 29 Berkeley Square until it was bombed in 1940.

Of all Mayfair's great 'entertaining' houses in the nineteenth century not even Grosvenor House could challenge the far-reaching influence of Londonderry House, or Holdernesse House as it was known until 1872. 'A formidable piece of dullness' in the opinion of Horace Walpole, it was built in 1760 on the corner of Park Lane and Hertford Street for the d'Arcy family, the Earls of Holdernesse, whose title became extinct in 1778. In the eighteenth century it had been a lesser Devonshire House, a meeting place for leading figures in art and literature. In 1822 the house was bought by Charles Stewart, younger brother of the Foreign Secretary, who was still known as Viscount Castlereagh rather than by his newly inherited title of Marquess of

Londonderry. Castlereagh, aged fifty-three, committed suicide that year by cutting his throat, amid ugly rumours of homosexual blackmail. Charles Stewart became the third Marquess of Londonderry. He paid £43,000 for the freehold of Holdernesse House and the adjoining property and a further £200,000 to have the interior rebuilt and redecorated by Benjamin and Philip Wyatt. The money for this work, which included a ballroom, a gallery for paintings and sculpture, a banqueting hall and a magnificent staircase, came from Charles Stewart's rich second wife, Lady Frances Anne Vane-Tempest-Stewart, the heiress to a coal fortune.

In 1825 the new Lady Londonderry opened Holdernesse House with a grand banquet and ball.

Every apartment was illuminated with girandoles or sidelights [ran a newspaper report of the event], except the first which contained an ormolu chandelier of great dimensions. All the interior was illumined with wax candles. At eleven o'clock the company began to arrive: the dancing commenced half an hour after with quadrilles and ended with waltzes. A regular supper was set out in the old banqueting hall at two o'clock. Covers were laid for fifty and the tables replenished six times; on the whole three hundred supped, which was the extent of the party. The dancing was afterwards resumed and kept up till five o'clock.

Later that season Frances Anne gave a fancy-dress ball which was reported as 'a scene unexampled in the annals of the fashionable world since the fifteenth century'. The hostess appeared as Queen Elizabeth, seated on a throne 'gorgeously decorated with crimson velvet and gold'. The whole of the diplomatic corps attended, and three bands played, including that of Lord Londonderry's regiment, the 10th Hussars.

Lady Londonderry became established as the hostess for the Conservative Party and remained so for forty years, handing on the tradition to her twentieth-century successors, Theresa and Edith. The young Disraeli described a party there following a great military review in Hyde Park to mark Queen Victoria's coronation in 1838:

The Londonderrys, after the review, gave the most magnificent banquet at Holdernesse House conceivable. Nothing could be more recherché. There were only 150 asked, and all sat down. Fanny (Frances Anne) was faithful and asked me and I figure in the *Morning Post* accordingly. It was the finest thing of the Season. Londonderry's regiment being reviewed, we had the band of the 10th playing on the staircase: The whole of the said staircase (a double one) being crowded with the most splendid orange trees and Cape Jessamines; the Duke of Nemours, Saoult, all the 'illustrious strangers', the Duke of Wellington and the very flower of fashion being assembled. The banquet was in the gallery of sculpture; it was so magnificent that everybody lost their presence of mind. Sir James Graham said to me that he had never in his life seen anything so gorgeous. This is the *grand seigneur* indeed, he added.

The historian Sir Archibald Alison left a description of the formidable third Lady Londonderry which could well have applied to Theresa, the awesome hostess of Edwardian Londonderry House, or to a lesser extent her successor Edith, known as 'Circe', the charmer of Ramsay MacDonald and terror of 1920s debutantes:

At receptions in her own house her manner was polite and high bred, but stately and frigid, such as invariably inspired awe in those who were introduced to or had occasion to pass her. To such a length did this go that I recollect that once in one of her great assemblies at Holdernesse House, as the Marchioness had taken her seat near one of the doors by which the company were intended to go out to bow to them in passing, the whole people the moment they saw her seated in her grandeur turned about and went back the way they came rather than pass through the perilous straits.

Londonderry House, renamed as such by the fifth Marquess in 1872, remained the centre of glittering political gatherings until the 1930s. The Londonderry family married into many branches of the English aristocracy including the

Dukes of Marlborough; one of Frances Anne's daughters, named after her mother, became the mother of Lord Randolph Churchill and grandmother to Sir Winston.

Grosvenor House, the residence of Mayfair's ruling family, was the other great social focus of the district, especially in the last twenty years of the nineteenth century, when the genial Hugh Lupus Grosvenor, first Duke of Westminster, presided over huge garden parties, dinners and balls during the three summer months of the London Season. 'We always enjoy the entertainments you give at Grosvenor House so much,' wrote the Prince of Wales to the Duke. The house, acquired by the Grosvenor family from the Duke of Gloucester in 1806 and much remodelled by the second Earl Grosvenor to accommodate his magnificent art collection, had grown in grandeur as the family progressed upwards through the peerage. (Sir Richard Grosvenor, the seventh baronet, had been made first Baron Grosvenor in 1761 and in 1784 was created first Earl Grosvenor and Viscount Belgrave. The second Earl was made first Marquess of Westminster in William IV's Coronation honours in 1831, and Hugh Lupus, third Marquess, was created Duke in Gladstone's dissolution honours of 1874. Gladstone's letter of 17 February 1874 ran warmly: 'My dear Westminster, I have received authority from the Queen to place a Dukedom at your disposal and I hope you may accept it, for both you and Lady Westminster will wear it right nobly. With my dying breath, Yours sincerely, W. R. Gladstone.' It was the last Dukedom to be created in England.)

The entrance to Grosvenor House was from Upper Grosvenor Street, through the fine colonnaded screen designed by Thomas Cundy in 1843 and a paved courtyard which was sprinkled with sand to prevent the horses slipping. An outer and inner hall led in turn to two drawing rooms and an ante-room to the picture gallery which was hung, on opposite walls, with Reynolds' painting of 'Mrs Siddons as the Tragic Muse' and Gainsborough's 'Blue Boy'. The great gallery opened on one side through french windows to a wide balcony leading to the garden with its lawns and plane trees. Paintings by Titian, Turner and Velásquez, including the Infante Don Balthazar on his pony, lined the gallery walls; a Rubens Room beyond contained three huge religious paintings done for King Philip IV of Spain, and yet another salon was hung with four Poussins, three Claudes, a fine Rembrandt and the Duke's own favourite painting, a landscape with cows by the English artist Paul Potter. Beyond this again was the dining room, with thirty-one more magnificent paintings including seven Claudes, five Rembrandts, two Gainsboroughs and Van Dyck's self-portrait.

On the first floor of Grosvenor House were the Duke and Duchess's suites; the children's floor above had a school-room, day and night nurseries and six more bedrooms; above that were eight bedrooms for the maids. In the base-ment a battery of stillrooms, china rooms, pantries and scul-leries, kitchens, larders and servants' dining and sitting rooms serviced the indoor staff. Another phalanx of servants was required to run the fleet of vehicles, which ranged from the light phaeton the Duke liked to drive around London, drawn by a pair of Lippizaners, to the state coach with its bewigged coachman and footmen in full livery, used on occasions such as receptions at Buckingham Palace.

Though establishments on this scale were rare, domestic servants bulked large in the Mayfair population. In the census of 1841 they made up more than a third, including the coachmen and grooms who normally lived over the stables in the mews at the back of the big houses. In 1870 the average Grosvenor Square household consisted of thir-teen or fourteen people, of whom ten or eleven were servants. Georgian houses were not built with extensive servants' quarters and in the eighteenth century many senior domestic staff had their own homes near their employers. The porter to Lord Clive's house in Berkeley Square lived in Little Grosvenor Street and the Earl of Powis's cook walked to work in Berkeley Square from a house in Green Street. Four pages in service with the Duke of Gloucester at Gloucester House (which became Grosvenor House) had their own homes within walking distance of Park Lane. One of the Earl of Tankerville's three stewards even ran a sideline business as a coal agent.

This world beneath a world was riddled with corruption and worse. Lord Melbourne's household at 18 South Street, including periods during his premiership when he was not at 10 Downing Street, was run by sixteen servants, 'all thievish and drunk', according to his biographer Lord David Cecil. In May 1840 society was shocked and gruesomely fascinated by the murder at 14 Norfolk (now Dunraven) Street of Lord William Russell by his Swiss valet, Frederic Courvoisier. With an accomplice, the valet had stolen and hidden some of the household silver; he then decided to kill his master and steal whatever else he could. Stripping himself naked, so as not to get his clothes blood-stained, he went to Lord William's bedroom on the night of 6 May and cut his throat with Russell's own razor. In the morning he pretended horror at 'discovering' the crime, but his alibi was short-lived; a neighbour had seen, through a fanlight over the front door, the figure of a naked man creeping down-stairs during the night with a lighted candle in his hand. Courvoisier was duly hanged for the murder.

The most notorious unsolved murder case of the nine-teenth century has been directly linked in recent years with one of Mayfair's most eminent medical men. Sir William Withey Gull, Physician Extraordinary to Queen Victoria and one of England's leading Freemasons, was 'unmasked' as Jack the Ripper in a book by the late Stephen Knight and a television documentary based on it and on a number of earlier TV 'investigations' going back to the early 1970s. Gull, who specialized in the treatment of brain diseases and was the best-known supporter of vivisection in the medical profession, had been given his baronetcy and honorary post in the royal household after curing the Prince of Wales of typhoid in 1871. He lived and practised at 74 Brook Street, an area much favoured by fashionable doctors, from 1870 until his death in 1890, and used to boast that his practice was probably the largest in the West End. He numbered many of Mayfair's most distinguished residents among his patients, including Constance, first wife of the Duke of Westminster. After recommending that she take the air in Bournemouth to recover from a severe chill in the summer of 1880, Gull regularly visited her there at Branksome Towers, the big house on its own cliff which the Duke rented for his wife's convalescence. The treatment failed, however, and the Duchess died shortly before Christmas that year.

Gull had a minor stroke in 1887 and in 1888, the year of

The May Fair of 1716. Originally an agricultural fair, held in the first two weeks of May on what is now part of Shepherd Market, it became notorious for 'vice and impurities not to be mentioned'. It was driven out after the rich built houses nearby.

Berkeley Square in 1865, showing the gardens of Lansdowne House on the left. Some houses in the square were owned by the same families from the 1730s to the 1920s.

Edward Hyde, 1st Earl of Clarendon, whose palace on Piccadilly began society's move westward after the Great Fire of 1666.

Baron de Rothschild's 'new mansion' at 148 Piccadilly, completed in 1836. It adjoined Apsley House (left) and formed part of Piccadilly Terrace, popularly known as 'Rothschild Row'.

First lady of Georgian Mayfair: Georgiana, Duchess of Devonshire, the enchanting hostess seen here painted by Thomas Gainsborough in the portrait stolen from Agnew's of Bond Street in 1876. It was recovered 25 years later in Chicago and is now in the J.P. Morgan collection in New York. (Photograph by permission of Agnew's)

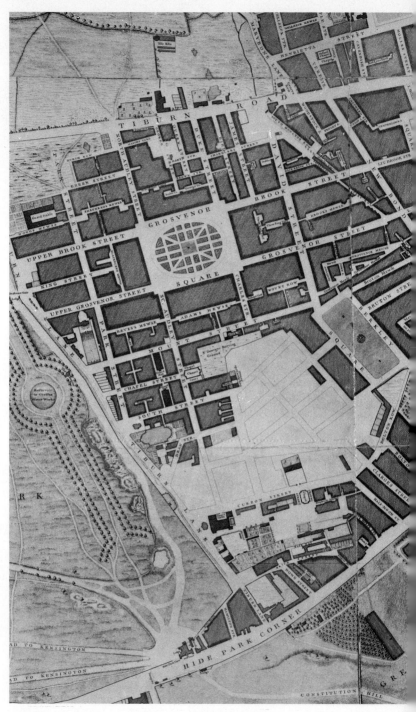

Extract from John Rocque's map of Mayfair, 1746.

Richard Brinsley Sheridan. His greatest play, The School for Scandal, *was based on characters from 18th-century Mayfair society. Sheridan's own home life in Mayfair was a series of escapes from the bailiffs.*

Sydney Smith, preacher, writer and wit who said early 19th-century Mayfair contained more intelligence, ability, wealth and beauty "than the world has ever collected in such a space before".

A College Life in Mayfair: Thomas Babington Macaulay in 1853, working on his History of England *in F3, Albany, rooms described by a visitor as "very liveable and studious-looking".*

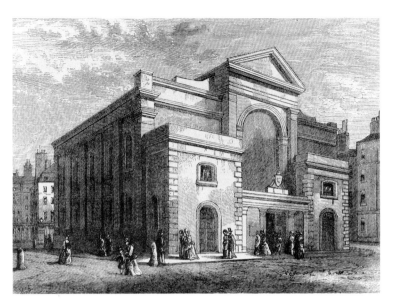

The May Fair Chapel, also known as the Curzon Chapel, where marriages were performed at a guinea a time, no questions asked. It was situated opposite Crewe House in Curzon Street.

Lord Lytton, Edward Bulwer-Lytton. Each of his Mayfair homes featured a room fitted up like a Pompeian villa in celebration of his most successful novel, The Last Days of Pompeii.

The Waterloo House: 44 Grosvenor Square, where the first news of Wellington's victory at Waterloo was received and where the Cato Street conspirators planned to assassinate Lord Liverpool's cabinet in 1820. It was the last private house in Grosvenor Square and was demolished in 1967 with its neighbours to build the Britannia Hotel.

Park Lane in 1910: the central terrace of houses was pulled down in the early 1960s to build the Hilton Hotel. To the right, old Londonderry House, also demolished in the 1960s for an hotel of the same name.

'Daddy Westminster': the philanthropic Hugh Lupus Grosvenor, 1st Duke of Westminster, who built cheap flats for working families among the grand homes. They still provide low-income housing in Mayfair.

Dudley House, 100 Park Lane, in 1890. Home of the Earls of Dudley and their descendants until the 1920s. Dudley House survives today as the head offices of a property company.

The ballroom of Dudley House, one of Mayfair's worst losses from bombing in the Second World War.

A privileged view of the Park: the conservatory of Dudley House in 1890, looking out over Hyde Park.

Park Lane and Mayfair in 1929: This aerial view, first published in The Times, shows the four cliff-like towers of the new Grosvenor House Hotel on Park Lane, and below it, old Dorchester House with its portico and garden, soon to make way for the Dorchester Hotel.

At the foot of the picture, the old mansions still stretch out from Piccadilly to join Apsley House, "No. 1, London". The large expanse of garden in the upper right-hand corner is Grosvenor Square, with Selfridge's department store on Oxford Street above it.

MAYFAIR'S DANCING
YEARS: Rehearsing for a
charity ball in July 1930 at
Lady Cunard's house, 7
Grosvenor Square. Left to
right, Lady Diana Cooper,
Mrs. Baillie-Hamilton,
Lady Cunard.
(Photograph: The Tatler)

The boudoir of Dorchester
House in 1905, replaced in
1930 by the Dorchester
Hotel.

The leafy look of 1930s Mayfair: the top of Park Lane in 1933, still a narrow road with Hyde Park on the right and Brook House on the left.

History up for sale: old Devonshire House in October 1922, looking north up Berkeley Street from Piccadilly. Right, the Berkeley Hotel. Devonshire House, demolished in 1925, was the first Mayfair mansion to fall to developers between the wars. (Photograph by courtesy of the Savoy Hotel)

Old Grosvenor House, London home of the Grosvenor family and the Dukes of Westminster until 1925. This was the carriage entrance on Upper Grosvenor Street.

Gerald Grosvenor, 6th Duke of Westminster, inheritor of 250 years of Mayfair history, whose London home is now in Belgravia. The family estates are now run on thoroughly commercial lines. "One does business to survive," he says.

the Ripper murders in Whitechapel, he was over seventy. Nevertheless, his name has cropped up in several studies of the Ripper case, chiefly because of his connection with the Duke of Clarence, second in line to the throne and another frequently mentioned 'suspect'. The finger was first pointed directly at Gull in the BBC's drama-documentary of 1973, *Jack the Ripper*, in which all known facts of the case were freshly 'investigated' by the fictional police detectives Barlow and Watt. The accuser, who appeared in the programme, was Joseph Sickert, son of the painter Walter Sickert. Gull's motive was said to have been to find and get rid of Mary Kelly, the last prostitute killed by the Ripper: she had been the witness at a secret and illegal marriage ceremony between Clarence and a Catholic shop assistant from the sleazy Cleveland Street area, had subsequently drifted into prostitution in the East End and begun to gossip dangerously and dabble in blackmail. Years later, Walter Sickert had married a girl he claimed was the child of this liaison between Clarence and Elizabeth Crook, and by her had his son Joseph.

After further researching the theory, Stephen Knight in *Jack the Ripper: the Final Solution* (1976) suggested that Gull committed the murders, following Masonic ritual, inside a closed carriage driven by a coachman named John Netley. The use of a carriage would explain the curious lack of blood at the scenes where the bodies were found in alleys and backyards, and would have provided a convenient escape route for Gull back to his private mews stables at the rear of 74 Brook Street. As Ripper theories go, it has perhaps more convincing credentials than most, though Knight's network of conspirators in the plot to hush up Mary Kelly reaches improbably high, including the Commissioner of Police, Sir Charles Warren, and even the Prime Minister, Lord Salisbury.

Prostitutes of a very different kind from the doomed creatures of Whitechapel have flourished in Mayfair since the time of the lewd Fair itself – and noticeably in the same area, around Shepherd Market and Curzon Street. The most celebrated of the breed in Victorian times, however, lived in respectable style at 15 South Street, 'the last great Victorian courtesan', as a plaque put up in 1974 describes her. She was Catherine Walters, known as Skittles from a remark she once made to some young Guards officers that she would knock them down like ninepins if they didn't stop drinking. She lived in the tall, narrow, four-storey house on the corner of Rex Place from 1872 to 1920 under a variety of names, generally Mrs Baillie, Bailie or Bailey, and by one of those piquant ironies of London life, her near neighbour for thirty-five years was that most proper of eminent Victorians, Florence Nightingale.

Miss Nightingale was doubtless spared the sight of Skittles and the comings and goings of her clients, who included Gladstone, the Marquess of Hartington ('Harty-Tarty') and the Prince of Wales, because almost as soon as she moved into 10 South Street in 1865 she took to her bed and stayed there for the next forty-five years until her death in 1910. Before moving to South Street she had lived briefly in a furnished house in Chesterfield Street ('a fashionable old maid's house in a fashionable quarter', as she described it), and even more briefly in Park Street, where she found herself 'perfectly sleepless' from the traffic noise.

The South Street house was taken for her by her parents on a twenty-one-year lease for £7000. It was described by her biographer Cecil Woodham-Smith as 'central, manageable, and backing on to the gardens of Dorchester House. . . . she was able to enjoy fresh air, sunlight and trees, and to observe the birds of which she was passionately fond.' Her second-floor bedroom was at the back of the house, with french windows opening on to a balcony. There were blinds instead of curtains, the walls were painted white and the furniture was unpretentious. A vase of fresh flowers always stood by her bedside reading lamp, supplied each week from the country estate of her admirer Lady Ashburton. The room was invariably 'bathed in light [and] conveyed an exquisite and fastidious freshness. Flowers were never faded, vases sparkled like crystal, the pillows and sheets of Miss Nightingale's bed were spotless and without a crease. . . .'

Here the Crimean heroine lived severely alone, except for servants and a large number of cats, until 1901 when her eyesight failed and she employed a companion-secretary to live in. She used to invite nurses and probationers for a

'Saturday to Monday in bed' to give them a good rest; they would be given a cake to take away. But visitors never saw her except by appointment, even if they were staying in the house. She always ate alone, organizing her meals with a beady eye on quality and many fussy notes to her butcher and housekeeper. 'Why was the glue-pot used?' she wrote against one day's menu order of stewed cutlets. A favourite meal was a couple of oyster patties, or some broth, followed by a fried sole.

In 1876, when she was in her middle fifties, Florence Nightingale applied to the Duke of Westminster to renew her lease for 'as long as possible'. The Duke not only agreed but extended it for life, a concession he also gave in 1880 to her eighty-year-old neighbour at 12 South Street. By another irony, this was the Earl of Lucan who had ordered the disastrous charge of the Light Brigade at Balaclava. At first the Duke wanted to charge a much higher rent, £400 a year, for the renewal of the lease, but he reduced this to £150 after Florence Nightingale's brother-in-law, Sir Harry Verney, protested that such a sum would force her out to 'Onslow Gardens or South Kensington, which would be a Public injury. . . .'

After her death in 1910 the house was inspected by the Grosvenor Estate and ironically was found to be far below the standards of sanitation and hygiene on which her reputation had been founded in the Crimea. Grosvenor Board minutes record that 'all the drainage was bad' and the lavatories and hot-water system inadequate. There were no bathrooms at all. Her successor in the house, after improvements had been made, was the Lord Chief Justice, Sir Alfred Lawrence, later Baron Trevithin; it was demolished in 1929.

The streets adjacent to Park Lane such as South Street, Green Street, Park Street and Norfolk Street (renamed Dunraven Street in 1939 after a member of the London County Council who lived there, the Earl of Dunraven and Mount-Earl) had become more fashionable as the nineteenth century progressed and Park Lane shook off the last lingering shadows of the Tyburn Tree. Despite the proximity of the gallows, the northern end of Tyburn Lane had some fine houses as early as 1766, when Somerset House was built for Viscount Bateman and Breadalbane House for the

Marquess of Breadalbane. When the last owner of Somerset House left in 1914, shortly before its demolition, she reported that there were 'vaults with chains in them' – supposedly used to detain prisoners on the way to Tyburn – but the estate surveyor, Edmund Wimperis, found no trace of them.

In 1773 Camelford House was built even closer to the gallows corner, as the home of Thomas Pitt, MP, first Baron Camelford. Its sprawling stables and outbuildings gave a countrified air to the corner of Park Lane and Oxford Street as late as 1913, when it was torn down and replaced by the Pavilion Cinema. Breadalbane House, which adjoined Grosvenor House, was famous for its medieval-style 'Baronial Hall', complete with a gorgeously coloured and gilded hammerbeam roof, inlaid floor of oak and cherrywood and windows of stained glass. Astonishingly, even by the flamboyant standards of mid-Victorian wealth, the hall had been put up as a 'temporary' dancing salon in the gardens of 30 Upper Grosvenor Street; in fact it lasted nine years, from 1854 to 1863. Sir Edward Bulwer-Lytton and Lady Palmerston briefly owned Breadalbane House before it was demolished in 1876 to extend the Duke of Westminster's garden.

By 1845 the spaces between these great houses along Park Lane had been filled in with attractive villas and Regency terraces. The owner of a house for sale on the corner of Upper Grosvenor Street about this time described its location as 'one of the most recherché in London, enjoying the Varied Scenery of the Park, the distant Hills of Surrey, and the salubrious Air therefrom, while at the same time it is placed in the Centre of Fashion'.

Even in the last decades of the century the area retained its free, country atmosphere. Lady Mabel Lindsay, daughter of the Earl of Crawford and Balcarres, looked back in the 1930s to her childhood in the 1870s in Grosvenor Square:

> It was a very friendly Square in my childhood. On the
> east side lived the Fitzwilliams and the Homes – and
> old Mr Cunliffe Brooks, tenant of Glentannar, and Lord
> Wilton at the corner of Upper Brook Street; on the south
> side at the corner House into Charles Street (now Carlos
> Place) lived the Amhersts; and in an angle house

corresponding to ours on the north lived the Leicesters. It used to be a standing joke seeing the carriages of the Fitzwilliams and the Lindsays standing waiting in the shade of the trees. My grandfather every day entered his brougham and drove for miles with a pair of fast bay horses – always alone, and if the sun was low, with a large umbrella up inside the shut carriage. Many saddle-horses always waited at the doors of the various big houses for the fashionable midday gallop in the Row.

The high-spirited Margot Tennant, later to marry Herbert Asquith, created a minor sensation one day in 1885, the year of her coming-out, by riding her bay horse Tatts, named after Tattersall's sale ring, up the steps of her father's house at 40 Grosvenor Square. The footmen obligingly held the double doors into the hall open for her. Tatts negotiated the steps cautiously enough but then unluckily caught a glimpse of his reflection in one of the hall mirrors. As she recounted it in her *Autobiography:*

> At this he instantly stood erect upon his hind legs, crashing my tall hat into the crystal chandelier. His four legs all gave way on the polished floor and down we went with a noise like thunder, the pony on top of me, the chandelier on top of him and my father and the footmen helpless spectators. I was up and on Tatts' head in a moment, but not before he had kicked a fine old English chest into a jelly. This misadventure upset my father's temper and my pony's nerve, as well as preventing me from dancing for several days.

The 1870s, however, brought considerable social change. Grosvenor Square saw an influx of 'opulent tradesmen', including the brewer Sir Henry Meux, the engineer-ship-builder Sir Charles Palmer, inventor of the marine turbine, and the shipowner Charles Wilson, later Lord Nunburnholme. High prices were paid for long leases; £50,000 for 33 Grosvenor Square, £60,000 for Number 10 and £65,000 for Number 27. This period also saw the start of wholesale rebuilding on the Grosvenor Estate, a process that had begun in mid century with the rebuilding of about one quarter of Grosvenor Square in white brick or stucco facings.

Private remodelling now began to be fashionable, a vogue prefigured in Trollope's novels and which was to reach its apogee in the extravagant Edwardian years. Derby House, 26 Grosvenor Square, was pulled down and rebuilt in 1861–2 and twenty years after that was extensively remodelled inside by W. E. Nesfield, the country-house architect, for Arthur Heywood-Lonsdale. It was given elaborate plaster-work ceilings, rich panelling and embellishments in oak and marble. The neighbouring house, Number 27, was the subject of some alterations by the seventh Earl of Shaftes-bury, the philanthropist commemorated by the Eros statue in Piccadilly Circus. But when it was suggested that he should rebuild completely, he objected that he could foresee the redistribution of wealth and property 'and what then, in a subdivision, will a Palace be worth?' (The house was, however, twice rebuilt in later years, once in 1886 for the first Marquess of Aberdeen and again in 1912–14 for the banker Robert Fleming. Like Derby House and five other adjoining houses, it was demolished in 1957.)

Any large-scale rebuilding of Mayfair by its chief land-lords, the Grosvenor Estate, was always inhibited by the leasehold system, which in other respects was a landlord's dream, creating a steady income from rents and culminating in the reversion of the freehold property, maintained in good order by the tenant, at the end of the lease. For the purpose of redevelopment, however, it was very rarely that all the leases on a block of houses would fall in at the same time. The second Marquess of Westminster, who inherited in 1845, started to tackle this by granting only short leases, enabling eight on neighbouring houses in Upper Brook Street to expire at roughly the same time in 1886 or 1887. In 1865 the journal *Building News* said it was well known that the Marquess was 'determined to pull down and rebuild on his estates whenever he has an opportunity', but develop-ment remained mostly piecemeal.

The second Marquess did commission Thomas Cundy II to design a new look for about a dozen houses in Grosvenor Square along with others in the streets leading off it. The plain Georgian frontages were converted to stucco, balustrades and Doric porches similar to those in South Kensington. Tenants were sometimes involved in considerable expense as ground rents were raised to pay for the work: a Miss Mary-Anne Talbot, living at 24 Grosvenor Square in the mid 1850s, found hers increased from £13 to £460 a year when the lease was renewed for a much shorter period. Yet most seem to have acquiesced in the cost of architectural fashion: only one, a Mrs Gwynne Holford of 36 Grosvenor Square, refused to comply and forfeited £300 of the £1000 bond she had signed for the alterations to be done to her property.

The second Marquess established the condition, still in force, that the Grosvenor Estate office must approve any change in the frontages of property on its land. Staff there were kept busy in the thirty-odd years from 1880 when American millionaires, South African mining tycoons and various other 'opulent tradesmen' were vying with each other to demonstrate their worldly success in terms of balconies, balustrades and Portland stone porticos. One of the more attractive changes was wrought by Lady Bouch, widow of the architect of the disastrous Tay Bridge, Sir Thomas Bouch. In 1889, ten years after the death of her disgraced husband, she bought 128 Park Lane and put in a verandah with awning overlooking the park as well as spending £9000 on the interior. In 1903 the art dealer Joseph Duveen gave the rooms an elegant French character they still retain today. Less successful, and a victim of the estate's disapproval, was Viscount Goschen's attempt to build a conservatory on to his house at the corner of Park Lane and Mount Street.

Lord Grosvenor's surveyor also firmly refused to grant permission to Colonel Augustus Meyrick to keep a cow at his house in Grosvenor Street in 1865. In vain his lawyers argued that 'some gentlemen like to keep a cow in London'. Also forbidden by the estate office was any demolition or rebuilding work during the sacred three months of the Season: important people were then in residence, and as *The Building News* commented in 1865, the second Marquess was 'determined to have none but tip-top people on his estates'.

It was left to the third Marquess and first Duke of

Westminster to embark on the largest rebuilding programme
to be carried out on any of the privately owned London
estates. Between 1869 and 1899, when he died, the whole
of Mount Street, Duke Street, Aldford Street, most of South
and North Audley streets, half Green Street, much of South
Street, Park Street, Carlos Place (formerly Charles Street)
and Davies Street were rebuilt, predominantly in Queen
Anne style red brick and terracotta. The Duke loved the
effect of these materials: 'The more red brick, the better', he
commented shortly before his death, referring to a
rebuilding proposal in Davies Street. He even had the stucco
work at his estate office there painted orange. Thomas
Cundy III, who succeeded his father as estate surveyor in
1867, was in turn succeeded in 1890 by Eustace Balfour,
brother of the subsequent Prime Minister, Arthur Balfour.
It was Balfour who presided over the flush of red-brick
rebuilding, in the course of which Sydney Smith's old house
at 56 Green Street, 'the essence of all that is comfortable',
was demolished with others to make way for a florid late-
Victorian terrace.

In Mount Street and South Audley Street, the prime shopping centres, the cost of rebuilding was often undertaken
by shopkeepers forming themselves into consortia and
apparently happy to pay to be in the latest architectural
style. Some commentators, however, saw the whole thing
as monstrously unjust. In *The Great Landlords of London*, a
polemical series of newspaper articles published as a book
in 1888, Frank Banfield claimed that the wholesale rebuilding
of Mount Street, 'rich in all the ornament which the artistic
skill of Messrs Doulton can command', was done at the
expense of the existing tenants. 'They constructed this
massive pile no more willingly than the children of Israel,
some thousands of years ago, expended their energies in
deference to the task-masters of Pharaoh.'

Each of the new buildings, containing smart shops at
ground level and residential chambers above, cost on
average £7000, Banfield claimed: 'In certain instances, the
occupier has found his outlay run up to £9000, and has had
no choice in the matter. . . . If he consents to build in this
way he is granted a lease, the ground rent varying from £3
to £6 a foot, and as much as £6.10s. a foot has been asked.'

Ultimately, Banfield noted, the premises would revert to the descendants of the Duke 'without one pennyworth of compensation to the descendants of the man who staked his capital and ventured his credit that they might stand a monument to the Duke's taste in architecture'.

Banfield was heavily critical of the leasehold system in general and of the Duke of Westminster and his powerful agent, Henry Trelawney Boodle, for allowing tenants to go within three months of their leasehold expiry date without knowing whether they were to be granted a building lease or not. Some tenants, however, were entrepreneurial about it. James Purdey, the celebrated gunmaker of whose products it was said in Edwardian times that no crowned head in Europe was without his set of Purdeys, persuaded neighbours in South Audley Street to sell their leases to him rather than undertake the cost of rebuilding themselves. In 1881 he took the choice Mount Street corner for a new shop and built residential chambers above it on a speculative venture which paid off. Thomas Goode, the china merchant, was another who chose to rebuild his premises in grand style: the shop today ranks as probably the best commercial example of the Queen Anne revival on the Grosvenor estate.

In spite of Banfield's strictures, the first Duke of Westminster was generally regarded by his tenants as a model landlord. He was also a respected public figure. chiefly known as a successful and popular racehorse owner, and had a personality which, as his *Times* obituary recorded, enabled him to 'pass from the racecourse to a missionary meeting without incurring the censure of even the strictest'. Known in the family as 'Daddy Westminster', he had fifteen children by two wives, the second of whom was his son-in-law's sister. He was intensely philanthropic and devoted to certain causes, among them animal welfare and temperance; the latter accounts for the comparative scarcity of public houses on the Grosvenor estate in Mayfair. Between 1869 and 1891 he reduced the number from forty-seven to eight; today there are five. He also controlled drinking hours through careful wording on his public-house leases, and insisted that when they were rebuilt they should look like private residences. The architect Thomas Verity had his first designs for a pub at the corner of Mount Street and South

Audley Street returned with the comment: 'His Grace thinks that the elevation . . . is too gin-palacey in Mount Street.'

The Duke was also prompted, well before the campaigns of the 1880s for better housing for the poor of London, to build blocks of flats for artisans on his Mayfair estate. Several had been built privately in his predecessor's time, such as St George's Buildings and Grosvenor Buildings in Bourdon Street, but the Duke went into it in a larger way, in joint undertakings first with the Metropolitan Association for Improving the Dwellings of the Industrious Classes and later with Sir Sydney Waterlow's Improved Industrial Dwellings Company. The latter was employed by the Duke in 1871 to build Clarendon Flats on George Street (now Balderton Street); this development was described ten years later by the vicar of St Mark's, North Audley Street, as 'of itself a great civilizer, and [sic] has exercised a very marked influence for good in the Parish'.

Most of the Grosvenor Estate's working-class developments had been concentrated in Pimlico, but the area of north Mayfair between Grosvenor Square and Oxford Street had a large working-class population servicing the big houses, and between 1886 and 1892 the estate and the Improved Industrial Dwellings Company together built nine blocks of flats there. Along with Clarendon Flats, they provided accommodation in all for 2000 people, and the Duke also paid for a garden to be laid out in the centre: it is now a raised, paved area in Brown Hart Gardens. As a result of this philanthropic scheme his total rental income for that area fell from £2193 to £502 a year.

Rents in these buildings averaged two shillings a week per room, and the flats, which were built to an improved design with scullery and flush toilet off the hall, ranged in size from two to five rooms. Their tenants were envisaged as 'mechanics and others earning from 30s. to 35s. a week for the three and four-room lettings, and earning 25s. a week for the two-room lettings'. The buildings were all six storeys high, built in the Duke's favourite red brick (though he was told this would cost £2500 more than London stock brick), with gabled roofs. The Duke had wanted a cocoa– or coffee-house to be part of the development, but nobody could be found to run it. Needless to say, there was no pub.

Mount Street changed its character entirely as a result of its rebuilding under the first Duke of Westminster. In 1880 over fifty different trades were represented there including a cow-keeper, a music engraver, a vet and many dress-makers and lodging-house keepers. There had even been a parish workhouse at Number 103. Within twenty years the shops had risen in status to antique dealers, picture restorers and art metal-workers – much the same kind of business as today. Virtually the only people to retain their occupation unchanged in the street were the Jesuits, whose Church of the Immaculate Conception had been built on the Berkeley estate in Farm Street in 1844–9, and who had taken 114 Mount Street at the same time for residential accommo-dation, obtaining the Duke of Westminster's permission in 1885 to build a presbytery and sodality chapel next door.

At the foot of Mount Street a new road curving round to link Berkeley and Grosvenor squares was completed in 1892. It replaced Charles Street and was renamed Carlos Place to avoid confusion with the other Charles Street nearby.

Sumptuous private houses built by Trollope lined it, featuring Jacobean-style panelling and genuine mid-Geor-gian fireplaces. Also rebuilt was the Coburg Hotel, originally an offshoot of Grillon's Hotel in Albemarle Street, which had occupied a pair of modest early Georgian houses in the former Charles Street. In 1892 the Coburg's owner, August Scorrier, was granted permission to rebuild his hotel provided that he did not include a bar in it: Scorrier wanted to borrow money on his building contract and the Grosvenor Estate feared he might mortgage his lease to his solicitors, who also acted for a firm of brewers and distillers; it might therefore become 'a large public house instead of a quiet hotel'.

The new red-brick building was finished by 1896, offering apartments from six shillings a night for a single bedroom, ten shillings for a double, and hot or cold baths either 'in Bathroom, or Hip Bath in Bedroom', price one shilling. A charge of a shilling was also made for an electric reading lamp. In 1917 the Coburg became the Connaught in response to the same tide of prejudice against Germanic names that changed the family style of the Saxe-Coburg-

Gothas to Windsor and that of the Battenbergs to Mountbatten.

Mount Street always had more lodging-houses than anywhere else in Mayfair: before the coming of comfortable and respectable hotels they were much patronized by middle-class or professional people from the country with no town houses of their own, like Archdeacon Grantly in Trollope's *Framley Parsonage*. Early Mayfair hotels were rather seedy, gloomy places frequented by hard-drinking sportsmen and squires up from the country, like Limmer's on the corner of Conduit Street and Hanover Square. Its head waiter, John Collins, invented the refreshing long gin-based drink which bears his name, and it had a secret passage through the back into Bond Street by which embarrassed patrons could flee the bailiffs. Both Limmer's and Long's of New Bond Street were more like sporting clubs than hotels; Long's was a favourite of Sir Walter Scott's and its smoking room was a popular meeting place for young blades. It was famous for its devilled soles and its whisky and soda mixed by the head waiter William to a secret formula of his own. The Clarendon, also in New Bond Street – where Cartier's now stands – was regarded earlier in the century as the best in London. It housed a literary society founded by Sir Joshua Reynolds and Dr Johnson and during the Napoleonic Wars was the only place in town to find a 'genuine' French dinner, albeit at the enormous cost of three or four pounds a head, with champagne at a guinea a bottle.

Pulteney's at 105 Piccadilly (now the home of the Arts Council) was also fashionable. It was visited by the Tsar of Russia and his sister in 1814, while Grillon's in Albemarle Street claimed the patronage of Louis XVIII of France. The best of the hotels in Albemarle Street, half of whose buildings were occupied by hotels at one time, was the Albemarle itself, on the corner of Piccadilly. Its distinctive rose-pink brick exterior is still there, now housing suites of modern offices. Several old coaching inns in Piccadilly survived into the nineteenth century, like Hatchett's, whose name lingers on as a restaurant and nightclub, and the Old Gloucester Coffee-House and Hotel between Dover Street and Berkeley Street. This was the starting point for the mail coach run to the West Country, and the inn where Thackeray's

Pendennis stopped after being rusticated from Oxford. Hazlitt wrote about the Gloucester Stage roaring down Piccadilly, and Dickens stayed at the hotel in 1869, when it became known as the St James. In 1898 it was rebuilt as the Berkeley.

The Berkeley, overlooking on one side Devonshire House and its tree-filled gardens, became popular with the county set and with the growing number of American visitors coming to London, although it had fewer private bathrooms and lifts than some of its rivals. The Savoy, opened in 1889, had introduced London's first 'ascending rooms' – worked by the hotel's own hydraulic power – while the new Claridge's, opened in November 1898, boasted so many advanced features that the management printed a reassurance to patrons that 'the spirit of modernism . . . would not in the least interfere with their comfort and privacy'. The Berkeley's trump card was its managing director, George Reeves-Smith from Scarborough, who was said to have the best knowledge of food, wine and cigars in the whole of Europe. Such was his reputation in the hotel business that Richard D'Oyly Carte, having failed to tempt him to the Savoy, bought the Berkeley in 1901 just to acquire his talents: it has remained part of the Savoy Group ever since.

The Savoy had already bought Claridge's in 1895, and with it a venerable slice of Mayfair history. Claridge's had begun life in 1815 as two houses in Brook Street run by James Mivart (sometimes known as Jacques, though he was born in the parish of St James's, Piccadilly). The Prince Regent had a hand in the hotel's founding and kept a permanent suite of rooms there. In the 1850s it was taken over by a hotelkeeper called William Claridge, who continued to advertise it as 'late Mivart's' long after changing its name. Claridge was described as a born courtier, so skilled in the nuances of royal protocol that it was said he gave bows of a different depth to a Serene Highness and a Royal Highness. His hotel became virtually an annexe to Buckingham Palace, and established a connection with foreign royalty which lingers on today. In 1853 a correspondent in *The Times* noted only three first-class hotels in London; Mivart's, the Clarendon and Thomas's, at 25 Berkeley Square. In the late 1890s Claridge's was completely rebuilt to designs by C. W.

Stephens, the architect of Harrods' department store, after the Duke of Westminster had given permission with the proviso that he did not want 'anything like a repetition of the Savoy in Brook Street'. Much of the gracious late-Victorian interior, with its French or Adam styling, remains basically unchanged. More public rooms, including a ballroom, were added in the 1900s when the hotel felt itself under severe competition from the new Ritz on Piccadilly.

Brown's Hotel, another discreet Mayfair establishment frequently patronized by foreign royalty, was opened by James Brown at 23 Dover Street in 1837, the year of Queen Victoria's accession. Dover Street was then occupied by fine town houses and Brown's first neighbours included eight peers, three baronets, the Bishop of Ely and the Russian Ambassador. Under a later ownership in the 1880s the hotel was extended back in depth with the acquisition of St George's Hotel fronting Albemarle Street: both names still show on a blue and gold plaque by Brown's Albemarle Street entrance.

A small piece of scientific history was made in Brown's in 1876 when one of the hotel's guests, the young Alexander Graham Bell, arrived carrying a large bag with a collection of instruments and wires in it. He told the hotel owner's son it was his new invention for transmitting the human voice over long distances by means of a pair of wires: he had come to London from New York to try to interest the British Government in it. Before demonstrating it officially, however, he wanted to experiment once more in private, and by good fortune the Ford family who owned Brown's had a private telegraph line between the hotel and their home in Ravenscourt Park, about four miles away in west London. After an abortive first attempt when telegraph traffic was cluttering up the line, they tried again in the quiet small hours of the morning and made the first successful telephone call in Britain.

Mayfair hotels such as Brown's and the Connaught cultivated an elegant club-like atmosphere and still do, to an extent – particularly the Connaught (now also part of the Savoy Group), which publishes no tariff and exudes a subtle impression that guests are somehow selected to fit in with the discreet, country-house air of the place. Elizabeth Taylor and her retinue once found it impossible to get in: press conferences and TV camera crews simply do not go with the Connaught's polished panelling and velvet sofas.

Of clubs proper, those all-male establishments whose heyday stretched from the Regency until the Second World War, Mayfair has had comparatively few within its boundaries, notable exceptions being the Savile, which bought the ill-starred Viscount Harcourt's home in Brook Street in 1927, and the Guards' club nearby, which in the nineteenth century had been Buckland's Hotel, and which flourished through the worst of the Blitz. 'The Germans have got to go a long way before they starve this country out,' remarked the US Military Attaché, General Raymond E. Lee, in November 1940 after lunching there on lobster mayonnaise, roast beef, Yorkshire pudding and apple tart with cheese (all for three shillings). In 1946 the premises at 41–43 Brook Street became the Bath Club until it, too, fell on hard times and amalgamated its membership with others in the late 1970s.

Piccadilly, however, the southern border of Mayfair, was dominated by clubs in the closing years of the nineteenth century. There were the Junior Constitutional, the St James's, the Isthmian, the Savile (until 1927), the Junior Athenaeum, the Piccadilly, the Cavalry, the Royal Thames Yacht Club and the imposing Naval and Military, always known as the 'In and Out' from the lettering on its driveway pillars. The premises of the Naval and Military at 94 Piccadilly had been a private mansion for more than a century before the club took it over in 1866. Built by Matthew Brettingham for the Earl of Egremont, it was known as Egremont House until the Duke of Cambridge acquired it and renamed it Cambridge House in 1756. After a spell in the ownership of Sir Richard Sutton, the West Country landowner whose estate still owns the freehold of this and much other property on the southern fringe of Mayfair, it was occupied by Lord Palmerston, the Foreign Secretary, for ten years until his death in 1865.

The Naval and Military, founded in 1862 by officers of the Buffs stationed at the Tower of London, had been looking for larger quarters than their early premises in Clifford Street and Hanover Square. In 1866 the club took a sixty-year lease on 94 Piccadilly from the Sutton Estate, later greatly extended. Of the house as Palmerston knew it, only the club's public rooms remain more or less as they were before 1866; much has been built on or remodelled, or damaged in the Second World War. One side of the courtyard, where a carriage drive once led through to the stables (Palmerston was the last British minister to ride on horseback to the Commons), has become a broad, built-in passageway linking the entrance lobby to the club dining room. The original courtyard remains, now a pretty alfresco spot to take coffee after lunch, and so does the famous old plane tree, supposedly planted in line with the avenue in Green Park, under which A. E. W. Mason is said to have written the opening chapters of *The Four Feathers*, the action of which begins in the club.

On the first floor is an octagonal reception room looking over the Green Park which the club secretary, Major W. Ellery Anderson, calls 'the ghost room': Lady Palmerston is said to have attempted suicide there and Anderson, a bluff ex-prison officer, finds it a place he would not linger in alone after dark. There is no truth, however, in another legend of the In and Out – that an underground passage links it with Buckingham Palace across Green Park. There *is* part of a subterranean passage, but it ends in a blind wall and probably forms part of the drainage system.

The St James's Club, a near neighbour at 106 Piccadilly, was founded for members of the diplomatic service by Lord Granville and his Italian friend the Marquis d'Azeglio, a fashionable Mayfair figure who lived in Albany. Established first in St James's in 1858, it moved to Piccadilly in 1869, occupying the mansion formerly known as Coventry House. The St James's Club was said to have the most splendid lavatory of any club in London. It had many aristocratic young members in the early twentieth century: Viscount Lascelles, on leave from the trenches in 1916, had a fateful meeting there with his eccentric great-uncle, the Marquis of Clanricarde, and as a result inherited his fortune of £3 million and became a successful suitor for Princess Mary, the daughter of George V. In the 1920s Viscount Castlerosse, the gossip columnist, was writing endlessly about it, and a latter-day member was the notorious Lord Lucan, who belonged to a club-within-a-club known as the Dilettanti

Society; its membership together with that of the St James's merged with Brooks's Club in 1975.

Two rather more sociable Mayfair clubs which welcomed women within their doors were, oddly enough, the Bachelors' at 8 Hamilton Place, next door to Apsley House, and the Albemarle, scene of the Marquis of Queensberry's fatal provocation to Oscar Wilde. The Bachelors', which fined its members £25 on marriage, is supposed to have been the model for P. G. Wodehouse's Drones' Club. (Wodehouse lived in Mayfair from 1924 to 1934 at 34 Green Street.) It was at the Bachelors' in the summer of 1889 that young George Curzon, not yet the 'most superior person' who became Viceroy of India, held a dinner for a group of friends including Margot Tennant (later Asquith), George Wyndham and Harry Cust – each of whom was known as the handsomest man in England. The occasion was later looked back on as the founding of the Souls, that influential group of intellectuals, politicians, sportsmen and hostesses which flourished until the First World War.

The Albemarle, established in 1875, was at 13 Albemarle Street, next to the Royal Arcade. In the 1920s it housed the night club Uncle's in its basement. It survived until 1963, when its members included leading cricketers like Richie Benaud, Peter May and Sir Len Hutton as well as the Labour politician George Brown and the Conservative MP Dame Patricia Hornsby-Smith. The Albemarle was the first Victorian club to admit as members 'both ladies and gentlemen'. In February 1895 its most distinguished literary member was Oscar Wilde. On the day before *The Importance of Being Earnest* opened to rapturous reviews at the St James's Theatre, Wilde and his gilded young companion Lord Alfred 'Bosie' Douglas had visited Hatchard's bookshop together and bought a new translation of Aristotle's *Poetics*. Three afternoons later, at 4.30 p.m. on 18 February, the hall porter at the Albemarle was startled to be handed a visiting card from the enraged Lord Queensberry, Lord Alfred's father. On the back was a scrawled, mis-spelled message: 'To Oscar Wilde posing as a somdomite.' As Queensberry had hoped, it provoked Wilde to sue for libel, and the evidence that emerged in court led to the playwright's ruin.

For single men with private means, the 1890s in Mayfair

were a golden age, even if one multiplies prices by more than thirty to account for inflation. George Cornwallis-West, briefly the youthful stepfather of Winston Churchill, gave a flavour of the life in his autobiography, quoted in Angela Lambert's *Unquiet Souls:*

> A bachelor in London with a thousand a year was comparatively well off. He could get a very good flat in Mayfair, to hold himself and his servant, for a hundred and fifty pounds per annum. Dinner at his club cost him about four shillings, and any good restaurant would have been prepared to provide an excellent dinner, if he chose to give one to his friends, at ten and sixpence a head. The best tailor in Savile Row would make a suit of evening clothes for eleven guineas, and a morning suit for about eight guineas; dress shirts could be bought for ten and sixpence.

The farthest cab fare listed in the Coburg Hotel's brochure for guests was five shillings: that would take you all the way from Carlos Place to Bow Church in the East End. Thirty-three theatres and music-halls provided entertainment, you could hire a one-horse carriage with coachman for a day in town or a trip to Kew or Richmond, for £1.4s. And to round off the day with a spot of culture, there was the Grosvenor Gallery at 135–7 New Bond Street, with its grand, glass-roofed interior in marble and multi-coloured brickwork, approached through a marble doorway flanked by columns from a church in Venice. It was James McNeill Whistler's painting *The Falling Rocket*, shown in the opening exhibition on 1 May 1877, which provoked Ruskin to explode that he 'never expected to hear a coxcomb ask two hundred guineas for flinging a pot of paint in the public's face', causing Whistler to launch a disastrous libel suit.

The gallery's founder, Sir Coutts Lindsay, intended it to provide art for a popular taste, bridging the gap between the Royal Academy's straitlaced conservatism and modern art. The opening day attracted 7000 visitors at a shilling a head and the gallery was celebrated by W. S. Gilbert in *Patience* in a skit on the Aesthetic Movement: 'A greenery-yallery, Grosvenor Gallery, Foot-in-the-grave Young Man.'

But it failed to make money and in 1903 was taken over by a New York pianola company and became the Aeolian Hall, later managed by the BBC from 1939 to 1975.

The 1880s and 1890s had transformed the look of Mayfair and brought a new ease and comfort to its social life, with houses made cosier and more convenient, and lavishly appointed hotels and restaurants replacing the old inns and chop-houses. But the explosion of wealth was only just beginning.

LONDON'S PRIDE

8

EDWARDIAN EXCESS

'*THERE* are lots of vulgar people live in Grosvenor Square,' observed the Duchess of Berwick, acidly and ungrammatically, in *Lady Windermere's Fan*. When Oscar Wilde was writing his play in 1892 much of Georgian Mayfair was in the process of being floridly rebuilt; its new red brick, terracotta and heavy pediments and porches expressed the change from a village community where artists and artisans mingled with aristocrats to a society of moneyed achievers. Trollope's Augustus Melmottes had arrived in force, not entirely displacing the Dukes of Omnium but looking them levelly in the eye from addresses in Green Street, South Street, Grosvenor Street, Brook Street, North and South Audley streets, the new mansion flats in Mount Street and, above all, from the opulent monuments to self-made wealth rising along Park Lane.

Here, rubbing shoulders with the great hereditary mansions of Grosvenors, Dudleys and Londonderrys, was above all where the new millionaires wanted to establish their social credentials. The town houses of the aristocracy were at the peak of their glory in Edwardian London. In 1907 Lansdowne House in Berkeley Square, residence of the sixth Marquess of Lansdowne, was described as 'among the half-dozen finest private palaces of London'. Sixty years earlier the poet Matthew Arnold had worked there as secretary to the third Marquess, who was Lord President of the Council in Lord John Russell's Government. It was then a 'backstanding lordly mansion' frequented by Whig ministers whose carriages rolled up and down the gravel forecourt behind the row of lilacs and the lawn, carpeted in spring with crocuses, which separated it from the square and the gardens of Devonshire House. Inside, Lansdowne House had a magnificent suite of inter-connecting salons by Robert Adam on the ground and first floors, and its dining room was probably the most elaborate example of Adam's style to be seen anywhere. The third Marquess was as noted for his literary parties and collection of Old Masters as for his political gatherings. He did not, as a contemporary said, 'extend a haughty or condescending patronage to men of talent or genius. He claimed brotherhood with them.'

Londonderry House was famous for the sheer size of its grand political and diplomatic receptions. Lady Londonderry wanted as many people as possible at her soirées, and on the King's birthday in 1903 Sir Almeric Fitzroy, one of the guests, remarked:

> The crowd at Londonderry House was the densest I had ever seen at a London party. . . . A large section of the company had to remain in the hall, and a still larger body was collected in Park Lane and never entered the house. On his return from conducting Princess Christian to her carriage, Lord Londonderry was very nearly torn in pieces, and the struggle to get out of the house was one of superhuman difficulty. One girl fainted in the street and had to be laid out on the pavement, and one or two others collapsed inside the building.

Edward VII and Queen Alexandra were entertained eight times in thirteen years at Londonderry House and the family's country estate, Wynyard. At Edward's request Kaiser Wilhelm II was entertained at Londonderry House when he paid his first state visit to England in the 1890s. Theresa, the wife of the sixth Marquess, and the model for Lady Roehampton in Vita Sackville-West's novel *The Edwardians*, was said by a close friend to be 'deeply interested in the love affairs of her friends and very disappointed if they did not take advantage of the opportunities she put in their way' – opportunities which, in the country, extended to allocating conveniently sited bedrooms according to the interests of her female friends and their current paramours.

Outside, Londonderry House was a plain, rather dour building – Horace Walpole's 'formidable piece of dullness'. The same could certainly not be said of Brook House, which the doyen of the new millionaires, Edward VII's friend and financial adviser Sir Ernest Cassel, bought from Lord Tweedmouth in 1908. It was an awkwardly tall, red-brick building with white Portland stone dressings and a profusion of white and coloured marble inside. The residents of Brook House, as the popular drawing-room ballad went, really did 'dwell in marble halls'. Cassel secured the approval of the Duke of Westminster to add the adjoining, smaller house at 27 Upper Brook Street, where he installed even more marble, 800 tons of it in blue and white, imported from quarries in Canada and Italy. This was to decorate a two-storey-high entrance hall, later to be nicknamed 'the Giant's Lavatory' by debutantes of the 1920s. The hall had pillars of lapis lazuli and four Van Dycks on the walls. Even the kitchens were panelled in marble.

Cassel was typical of the new, socially acceptable plutocrat: sociable, generous, Jewish and cosmopolitan. Less acceptable, rougher round the edges and with fortunes dubiously acquired in the brawling gold and diamond fields of South Africa, were the 'Randlords' who began muscling in on London society in the years immediately preceding the Boer War. The first to invade Park Lane was the notorious Sir Joseph Robinson, hated even by his fellow freebooters on the Rand. When Lloyd George offered him a peerage in 1922, there was such uproar in the House of Lords that Robinson felt obliged to cancel his acceptance. His obituary in the *Cape Times* in October 1929 has probably never been equalled in its vituperation: 'Those who in the future may acquire great wealth in this country will shudder lest their memories should come within possible risk of rivalling the loathsomeness of the thing that is the memory of Sir Joseph Robinson.'

In 1895 Robinson bought a lease on Dudley House, 100 Park Lane, from the second Earl of Dudley, whose father, appropriately enough, had paid £30,000 for the first great diamond to come out of Kimberley, the Star of Africa. Built in the 1820s for the first Earl of Dudley, and remodelled in the 1850s, Dudley House had a famous ballroom connected to an eighty-foot-long picture gallery with white marble pillars and crystal gasoliers. The Dudley art collection had been sold at auction before Robinson moved in, but he brought with him his own fine works of art, including paintings by Frans Hals, Constable, Rembrandt and Gainsborough. His biographer Leo Weinthal, one of the few to record a good word about Robinson (who, after all, paid him to write the book), observed: 'It could never be said of Robinson, as it was of another magnate who also bought himself a house in Park Lane, that the only pictures it contained were photographs of himself, and the only book was *Ruff's Guide to the Turf'*.

Alfred Beit and Barney Barnato, rival diamond millionaires from Hamburg and the East End of London respectively, had arrived simultaneously on the Kimberley fields in 1873 and later formed, in partnership with Cecil Rhodes, the great De Beers monopoly. Twenty years on, in the 1890s, they were vying with each other for adjoining Park Lane sites on which to build grandiose houses as a passport to British society. The sites were between Chapel (now Aldford) Street and South Street, in a block of houses due for rebuilding after expiry of their leases. Barnato, who had been born Barnett Isaacs over his father's shop in Aldgate, was already an habitué of Mayfair, having lived in Curzon Street and in a suite at the St James's Hotel. But his repeated applications for building permission on Park Lane were rejected by the Duke of Westminster on the grounds that 'he does not stand in a high position in South Africa, and he is a land speculator'.

Beit, a shy and socially awkward bachelor with a passion for art, proved more acceptable to the Duke, and succeeded in acquiring a lease on the northern of the two plots, 26 Park Lane, for £13,000 in 1897. Despite Beit's reputation as one of the richest men in the world, the Duke was worried that the house the diamond tycoon proposed to build might not be up to the standard he required of a neighbour to his own town residence, Grosvenor House. On the day before the lease was to be signed he sent a note round to Beit stipulating that the house must cost at least £10,000. Beit replied that he intended spending that much on the stables.

Beit further allayed the Duke's fears by engaging as one of his architects the Grosvenor Estate's own surveyor, Eustace Balfour. The finished design, built by George Trollope and Sons, was unkindly described as a cross between a glorified bungalow and a dwarf Tudor grange, though to a modern eye it would appear fairly conservative in a solid, late Victorian way, with a rough-cut Portland stone exterior and a heavily arched entrance on Park Street supported by columns of dark Alloa granite. The most exotic touch was provided by three gable ends filled with elaborate stone carving by Henry Pegram. After building had begun, Beit acquired the southern plot as well, the one sought by Barnato, and laid it out as a garden into which an extension was built housing a vaulted billiard room with brocaded silk walls and a winter garden, a dim oasis of palms, rockeries and fountains set in a tesselated pavement. Two panelled, Regency-style drawing rooms and a panelled and inlaid library formed the backdrop for Beit's collection of paintings and Italian Renaissance bronzes.

The building was named Aldford House and six years after Beit died in 1906, aged fifty-three, it was bought for £30,000 by a wealthy MP, Captain Frederick Guest of the Welsh iron-founding family, and his American wife Amy, who altered the interior to the style of Louis XVI. When Mrs Guest sold it in 1929 it was pulled down and rebuilt as the block of shops and flats which bears the name Aldford House today.

Barney Barnato, after his rejection by the Duke of Westminster, found himself a more expensive site a little farther south on Park Lane and off the Grosvenor estate, at the junction with Stanhope Gate. Later renumbered as 45 Park Lane, it became in the 1960s the home of the Playboy Club. Here Barnato proceeded to commission a flamboyant imitation French chateau, its roof bristling with gargoyles. It stood just across the street from the mock-medieval mansion being built for R. W. Hudson, the soap manufacturer, on the site of a dignified Queen Anne house which had belonged to the Earls of Lanesborough. Hudson's astonishing edifice, all stone curlicues and leaded Gothic windows, is the sole survivor today of Park Lane's era of plutocratic fantasy: it now houses the Park Lane branch of Barclay's Bank along with Middle Eastern and other company offices. The 'frippery and extravagance' of these nouveau-riche palaces caused the *Architectural Review* in 1901 to complain that the old, elegant Park Lane was becoming another Fifth Avenue.

Barnato's high-flying life, accumulating gold companies in Johannesburg, backing plays in London, spending £10,000 a year on the English turf and renting Spencer House in St James's while his Park Lane chateau was being built, did not last to see him fulfil his ultimate goals. The failure of his Rand banking house and a mounting pile of debt had already brought on a kind of breakdown; he was found by his lady companion trying to claw diamonds out of the wallpaper in his Johannesburg home. The MP and magazine editor Henry Labouchere remarked, driving down Park Lane one day, that the contorted statues on Barnato's roof must represent his creditors, turned to stone while waiting to be paid. Still only forty-four, Barnato had planned a huge house-warming party for 22 June 1897, the day of Queen Victoria's Diamond Jubilee, and he sailed for England on the SS *Scot*, whose passenger list was studded with Cape dignitaries visiting London for the Jubilee. As the ship approached Madeira he fell or jumped overboard; an officer dived in after him but the sea was choppy and Barnato was already dead, floating head down, by the time a lifeboat reached him. The coroner's verdict was death by drowning 'while temporarily insane'. Barnato's Park Lane palace was bought by Sir Edward Sassoon, the banker and art collector, who got rid of the gargoyles (two of them now grace the rose-garden pool in Brighton's Preston Park) and filled the house with eighteenth-century paintings and furniture.

Cecil Rhodes was probably the only leading Randlord who never aspired to a Mayfair address, though he confessed he was attracted by the deep silence of Albany. But he gave Hatchard's, the Piccadilly bookshop, one of its most ambitious commissions, asking for a collection to be assembled for his Cape house, Groote Schuur, of all the authorities used by Edward Gibbon in writing *The Decline and Fall of the Roman Empire*. Everything had to be in English, which meant Hatchard's hiring a team of classical translators. One copy of each work was to be typed on the best paper and uniformly bound in red Levant morocco. When the texts – Greek, Latin, Byzantine – were eventually put together, they filled an entire room. Rhodes came to his senses when Hatchard's bill came to £8000 for 150 volumes of translations, though at one stage he grandly told the booksellers: 'If you want more money you can always get it from Wernher, Beit and Co.'

Hatchard's was *the* source for Edwardian grandees to furnish their libraries; Lord Dudley of Dudley House and Lady Warwick, Edward VII's favourite, were just two who consulted the omniscient Mr Humphreys. In 1900 the Prime Minister, Lord Rosebery, who had been collecting books about Napoleon, summoned the bookseller to his home in Berkeley Square and handed him a short manuscript which he proposed to have privately printed. Humphreys told him it merited commercial publication and, after work on it, Rosebery found himself the author of a minor best-seller; *Napoleon – the Last Phase* sold 25,000 copies in a few weeks. Hatchard's was always willing to take a commercial risk: in 1918 it filled an entire window with copies of Marie Stopes' *Married Love*.

During the twenty years before the Great War about two dozen South African mining magnates established residences in Mayfair and Belgravia while collecting their knighthoods and entries in *Who's Who*. Lionel Phillips lived in Grosvenor Square, Friedrich Eckstein at 15 Park Lane, George Farrar at 54 Old Bond Street, Julius Wernher at Bath House (the former home of 'Old Q', the Duke of Queensberry), and Sigismund Neumann at 146 Piccadilly in the grand terrace of houses running up to Apsley House and known as 'Rothschild Row' from the several members of that family who lived there. (Alice de Rothschild lived at Number 142, Baron Ferdinand de Rothschild at Number 143, Baron Albert de Rothschild at Number 145 and Baron Lionel de Rothschild at Numbers 147 and 149, which actually adjoined Apsley House.)

American wealth was also well represented with Astors and Pierpont Morgans. Waldorf Astor rented 54 Berkeley Square during 1894 for $25,000, then equivalent to £5000; he was followed into the house by his countryman Gordon

Selfridge, who fitted it up lavishly and lived there while his new department store was being built on Oxford Street. John Pierpont Morgan Junior lived from 1902 to 1943 in Lord Lytton's former home at 12 Grosvenor Square, where the dining room had been decorated by Lytton in Pompeian style in honour of *The Last Days of Pompeii*, a habit he indulged in all his Mayfair homes. (The house was demolished in 1961 along with three of its neighbours to make way for the Europa Hotel, now the London Marriott; some of its panelling survives in the Park Lane Hotel's Louis Restaurant.) Ava Astor, the first wife of John Jacob Astor, Waldorf's cousin, took 18 Grosvenor Square in 1912, the year J. J. Astor drowned on the *Titanic*.

Several New York financiers were responsible for grandiose rebuilding schemes in Mayfair's most exclusive streets. Walter Hayes Burns, brother-in-law and business partner of Pierpont Morgan Senior, converted 69 and 71 Brook Street into a single extravagant dwelling with a sprung maple ballroom floor, a branching, carved staircase like a set from *Der Rosenkavalier*, and mauve marble pillars. Sir Edgar Speyer, whose merchant bank Speyer Brothers helped to finance the building of several early tube railways in London, bought 46 Grosvenor Street in 1899; ten years later he had added Number 44 to it and hired the Grosvenor Estate's architect Detmar Blow along with Fernand Billerey to join the two beneath a new skin of Portland stone. Before approving the scheme, the Duke of Westminster insisted that the two houses should be capable of being separated again, although this never happened. The result was that two staircases were installed, one in carved Gothic style, the other an oak copy of the Scala dei Giganti in the Doge's Palace in Venice. (Number 46 was already a composite of two former houses which had been joined by their owner in 1820.)

Speyer reputedly spent £250,000 on the house, installing a silver bath and a special cellar for wine and fruit. Richard Strauss and Debussy gave recitals of their works there at Lady Speyer's famous musical soirées, but the Speyers were not to enjoy it for long. In 1917, at the height of public hostility to prominent men with German names, Speyer was forced to leave Britain and the Grosvenor Street house was taken over by the government. It subsequently became the American Women's Club and is now the Japanese Embassy.

Clara Huntington, a Detroit heiress who had married a German diplomat and become the Princess Hatzfeldt – her husband won the Grand National of 1906 – spent another fortune on 33 Grosvenor Street, into which she moved as a widow in 1912. Much of the house had just been redecorated in imitation of German medieval style by its previous owner, a stockbroker named Auguste Lichtenstadt. Princess Hatz-feldt had the Gothic woodwork ripped out and replaced by French panelling of the early nineteenth century, installed carvings after the style of Grinling Gibbons in the front reception rooms and re-fronted the entire house in Portland stone.

The American magnates of Mayfair imported continental antiques and fittings into their houses as extravagantly as their contemporaries were shipping them over the Atlantic to mansions on New York's Fifth Avenue and San Francisco's Nob Hill. Robert Emmet, a New York banker who bought 66 Grosvenor Street in 1913 from an English owner who could not afford to maintain it, filled it with genuine Louis XV and XVI panelling from historic buildings in Paris, rooms which have survived almost intact into the house's present-day use as a hairdressing and beauty training centre. (The last private owner was Victor Cazalet, the MP who died in the wartime plane crash with the Polish leader General Sikorski.)

Grosvenor Street and, to a lesser extent Brook Street, attracted most of the lavish Edwardian remodelling. Lord Edward Spencer-Churchill, a younger son of the Duke of Marlborough, had 28 Grosvenor Street rebuilt by C. W. Stephens, the architect of Harrods and Claridge's, as a four-storey red-brick house with white stone dressings; his widow lived there from 1911 to 1940. The chairman of the Westminster Bank and the *Yorkshire Post*, Rupert Beckett, had Number 34 expensively remodelled in 1909. Ralph Lambton, a banker who lived at Number 59 from 1909 to 1914, built a racquets court out into the mews and added a fourth storey and decorative balconies. Seven houses in Grosvenor Street had storeys added between 1905 and 1912. Number 75, before its rebuilding in 1912–14, was the home of Sir Henry Hozier, secretary of Lloyd's from 1886 to 1892. His daughter Clementine, who was to marry Winston Churchill, was born there on 1 April 1875. Number 50 was remodelled by Walter Spencer Morgan Burns, a nephew of Pierpont Morgan; Number 58 by the Marquess of Aberdeen, Governor-General of Canada, who spent £10,000 on the alterations between 1900 and 1908 and then sold the house to Sir Herbert Samuelson, chairman of University College Hospital, who put in a new staircase, a lift and a ballroom.

Upper Brook Street had always, from its beginnings in 1721, been more free from the intrusions of commerce than Brook Street to the east of Grosvenor Square, and therefore more fashionable. In 1760 it had fourteen titled residents among its fifty-seven houses, half of them women. Professional people, mainly doctors, moved in during the nineteenth century, but the Edwardian years saw an incursion of trade in the form of fortunes made from commerce. The rich merchants who now rubbed shoulders with the peers, admirals and MPs and would continue to do so through the first half of the century (Sir Edmund Vestey of the meat-packing dynasty lived at Number 5 from 1924 until 1941) spent lavishly on rebuilding. Between 1905 and 1915 fourteen houses in the street were remodelled, most of them by Edmund Wimperis. Arthur W. Davis, a merchant who lived at Number 19, spent £20,000 in 1903–4 converting its interior to Empire style and then was succeeded by Solly Joel of the Rand mining family, Barney Barnato's nephew. His elder brother, Jack Barnato Joel, chairman of Johannesburg Consolidated Investment Co. ('Johnnies') in London, lived at 34 Grosvenor Square (rebuilt by an earlier occupant in red brick and red terracotta in the 1880s) from 1903 to 1940; his next-door neighbour in the 1900s was Sir Lionel Phillips, the Witwatersrand gold millionaire.

New staircases, lifts and ballrooms were typical installations made by the plutocrats of Edward's reign, and the furnishings they favoured were those of the eighteenth-century French courts. In this respect wealthy taste of the time was perfectly epitomized by the new Ritz Hotel which arose on Mayfair's doorstep in 1905. The architects Charles Mewès, a Frenchman from Alsace, and Arthur J. Davis, were both schooled in the Beaux-Arts movement and designed houses for several important Mayfair clients in the years before 1914. Among their works were 16 Charles Street for Mrs Ronald Greville, the well-known hostess, and 88 Brook Street (8 Grosvenor Square) for Henry Coventry, younger son of the ninth Earl of Coventry. This was an extravagant rebuilding project in 1909–10 which culminated in a roof garden opening out from a top-floor dining room.

For the London counterpart of the immensely successful Paris Ritz, which Alfred Beit had helped to finance in 1898, Mewès and Davis designed London's first steel-framed building, a concept first developed in Chicago in the aftermath of the great fire of 1879. Cesar Ritz himself, who had originally come to London to manage the Savoy and was by this time an ailing man, had no part in the London company, known as the Blackpool Building and Vendor Co., which in 1902 bought two prime adjoining sites facing Piccadilly and Green Park. They already had hotel buildings on them, the old Bath Hotel and a red-brick block of mansion flats known as the Walsingham Hotel. These were demolished in 1904 and the revolutionary new structure put up, a steel skeleton on which was hung a veneer of Norwegian granite and Portland stone. The design expressed the style of the Rue de Rivoli, with an arcade over the Piccadilly pavement and a mansard roofline. Inside it was all Louis XVI; a third of the cost of £345,227 was spent on the furnishings, supplied by Waring and Gillow.

Several elderly residents of Berkeley Square were annoyed by the new building, which impeded their view over the Park; some even thought it might affect their health by blocking the flow of fresh air. But from the inaugural dinner on 24 May 1906 – an eleven-course Edwardian feast featuring saddle of lamb, quail, asparagus, champagne and 1878 claret – the Ritz became the focus of a new, gayer society than that of Victoria's London. The embassies of Germany and Austria each reserved a permanent table for every meal. One could dine in the same room as Melba, Caruso, Rodin, Diaghilev and Pavlova, French and English dukes. Lady Violet Bonham-Carter, as a young socialite before the Great War, used to dance in the underground ballroom to Cassano's orchestra and go upstairs to dine on cold consommé, quail with grapes and ice cream. It was the first West End hotel, Lady Diana Cooper recalled, to which young unmarried women were allowed to go unchaperoned. Its Winter Garden, later known as the Palm Court, and its pretty, painted dining room overlooking Green Park, breathed Parisian elegance and luxury, and its prices were the highest in London: a guinea a night for a single room with bath, twice the rate at Claridge's and the Savoy and three times that of the Carlton on the Haymarket. Norman Shaw's Piccadilly Hotel at the other end of the street, also built in 1905, could not compete for sheer glamour.

Edwardian society was openly enjoying its wealth (Cartier's, the jewellers, opened its Bond Street store in 1909), and some members of it were not only accepting men who made their wealth in trade, like Julius Wernher and Thomas Lipton, but were going into it themselves. Most of the women who took tea in the Ritz Winter Garden or danced in its ballroom patronized the leading dressmaker of the day, Lucile. In private life she was married to the Scottish baronet Sir Cosmo Duff Gordon and was the sister of Elinor Glyn, the novelist whose torrid romance *Three Weeks* sold two million copies in the nine years following its publication in 1907. Lucile, born Lucy Sutherland, had begun her dressmaking business in a house in Davies Street, Mayfair, moved to Old Burlington Street and subsequently took a lease on Sir George Dashwood's house at 17 Hanover Square. In its magnificent Adam salons with carved chimneypieces and Angelica Kauffmann ceilings, she showed clothes that became the talk of London: tea gowns and ball dresses, debutante frocks and sophisticated models that looked, in her own words, like 'the last word in wickedness'. When the Dashwood lease expired she moved to an equally splendid house at 23 Hanover Square, with a big ballroom that proved an ideal showroom.

Lucile revolutionized Edwardian ideas of fashion. In her memoirs she recalled: 'I loosed upon a startled London . . . of flannel underclothes, woollen stockings and voluminous petticoats a cascade of chiffons, of draperies as lovely as those of Ancient Greece. . . .' For the first time her clothes revealed the natural shape of a woman, her breasts and legs, hitherto known disapprovingly as 'limbs'. Lucile introduced the brassiere in place of the stiff, whaleboned corset, and draped her skirts in such a way that they parted to reveal the legs. She also introduced the daring Paris custom of showing clothes to the customer on a real-life mannequin instead of the stuffed lay figure with a wax face which used to stand about in dressmakers' salons in London. Even in Paris, however, the mannequins had worn shiny black satin garments with high necks under the dresses they modelled: Lucile changed all that, actually allowing flesh to be shown above the décolletage, and her shows, though condemned by some dowagers as immoral, were attended by all society from Princess Alice through Margot Asquith to Lillie Langtry.

By 1900 her fame was such that Hanover Square was lined with carriages every morning and afternoon. She had dressed her sister Elinor for her fashionable marriage in 1892 to Clayton Glyn; she designed the costumes for *The Merry Widow* in 1907, including the famous Merry Widow hat worn by the star, Lily Elsie, in the London production at Daly's. By 1909 Maison Lucile was turning over £40,000 a year and had branches in Paris and New York. The latter, designed by Elsie de Wolfe in a large brownstone house on West 36th Street, became an immense success with New York society. In 1912 Lucile had to make hurried arrangements to visit it, and the booking clerk at the shipping office told her the only berths available were on the new White Star liner *Titanic*, making its maiden voyage on 10 April. 'Oh, I should not care to cross on a new ship,' she said. The clerk assured her there was no need to worry, the ship was unsinkable. 'This first voyage,' he said, 'is going to make history in ocean travel.'

Sir Cosmo Duff Gordon offered to travel with her to calm her nerves about the trip. They enjoyed the first days of the crossing, meeting friends and rich American clients of Maison Lucile, including Jack Thayer, president of the Pennsylvania Railroad, and his wife. Lady Duff Gordon was delighted to find strawberries on her breakfast tray in April. But her unease persisted, and each night when she retired to bed in her pretty cabin with its lace quilt and pink cushions she remained fully dressed, keeping a warm wrap and her jewel case close at hand. When, on the fourth night out, the iceberg struck – as if, she thought 'some giant hand had been playing bowls, rolling the balls along' – she looked around at the flower-filled room, 'so homely and pretty, just like a bedroom on land', and could not believe the danger until a vase of flowers on the washstand slid off suddenly and fell with a crash on the floor.

Duff Gordon was one of the few male survivors of the wreck, but his escape ruined his life. He asked an officer's permission for them both to get into boat Number 1, being lowered away only partly full from a part of the deck which for some reason was almost deserted. As they watched the *Titanic* go under, a seaman rowing the lifeboat remarked bitterly that he and his mate could not afford to buy new kit, as their pay stopped from the moment the ship went down. Duff Gordon offered the men five pounds each to help buy new clothes and on the rescue ship *Carpathia* made good his promise by writing out cheques drawn on Coutts' Bank on half-sheets of ship's writing paper. The *Carpathia*'s purser supplied the necessary stamps and the ship's doctor took a photograph of the little ceremony. This well-meaning but naive act was to prove fatal; on arrival in New York one of the recipients of Sir Cosmo's cheques claimed sensationally that he had bribed them to row away from drowning people, for fear the lifeboat would be swamped.

The 'Duff Gordon Scandal', the newspaper headlines about the 'cowardly baronet' and 'Sir Cosmo Duff Gordon safe and sound while women go down', resulted in a gruelling two hours on the witness stand at the official inquiry into the disaster presided over by Lord Mersey in London. The Duff Gordons were finally exonerated of any blame, but as Lucile recalled twenty years later,

> the real charge we had to face was a moral one. We could have incurred no legal penalties, but the real issue at stake was to both of us infinitely more serious. . . . A great deal of the mud which was flung stuck to us both. For years afterwards I was quite used to hearing people who did not know me whisper, 'That is Lady Duff Gordon, the woman who rowed away from the drowning.' For myself I did not mind . . . but I minded very much for Cosmo's sake. To the end of his life he grieved at the slur which had been cast on his honour.

The *Titanic* cast a long shadow over people like the Duff Gordons on both sides of the Atlantic, but the style of life it represented continued in Mayfair even throughout the First World War. In 1914 the Duke of Westminster's income was put at £1000 a day: the average working wage was about 30 shillings a week.

Harold Macmillan, who was to marry the Duke of Devonshire's daughter after the war, went to France with the Grenadier Guards and enjoyed a two-hour luncheon served by waiters from the Ritz, a treat arranged by the wealthy commanding officer of Number 1 company. Lady Randolph Churchill, living then at 72 Brook Street, replaced her footmen as they were called up with 'footgirls'. She dressed them in footmen's livery re-cut for female wear; black jacket with shiny buttons, black tie, long black skirt and large apron. An advertisement in *The Times* of 10 September 1914 advised 'West End men' – employees of West End businesses and shops – who 'might wish to serve side by side in a regiment of the Line' to register at an enrolling office in the estate agents, Knight, Frank and Rutley in Hanover Square.

The great houses were turned over to government use for the duration of the war. Crewe House, home of the Marquess of Crewe, housed the Ministry of Propaganda under the direction of Lord Northcliffe. Devonshire House, in prewar times presided over by the famous 'Double Duchess' (of Manchester as well as Devonshire through her two marriages) had its picture-lined ballroom protected by boarding nine feet high. Lady Freda Valentine, then Lady Freda Danvers-Butler, daughter of the ninth Earl of Lanesborough, remembers working there in some department of the food ministry known as 'fish control'. Grosvenor House, where the picture gallery was also heavily buttressed, and Londonderry House were both hospitals for officers, and Londonderry House was also the headquarters of the Women's Legion, founded by Edith, wife of the seventh Marquess, who had succeeded in 1915. For this service she was created a Dame of the British Empire in 1917.

The niceties of the London Season persisted through most of the war: Church Parade in Hyde Park, at which the fashionable world used to gather between Grosvenor Gate and Stanhope Gate each Sunday morning ('rather like a drinks party without the drinks', said Loelia, Duchess of Westminster, in her memoirs) now had a sort of evening extension in summer. This was entrancing for young society women newly liberated by the war's loosening up of conventional behaviour. Lady Freda Valentine, who had been presented at court in 1913 in a ceremony of stuffy formality, made worse for her by the after-effects of diphtheria, recalled how 'if you wanted a partner for a dance you went and sat at Stanhope Gate at 6 o'clock and you saw everybody'. Loelia Westminster, now Lady Lindsay, remembers one 'always used to be meeting people in the Park'. The favoured ground stretched from Hyde Park Corner to the Dell, and at one penny for a green-painted wooden folding chair it was 'a wonderfully cheap entertainment'.

Among things that disappeared after 1918, Loelia recalled in her autobiography, were ladies taking the air in their carriages in the Park; straw in the street outside the home of an invalid; and whistles blown to attract taxis – 'this used to be a most characteristic Mayfair noise and was given up because of the wartime hospitals'.

Francis Meynell wrote in the *Daily Herald* in November 1917 of 'How they starve at the Ritz'. Meals there, he reported, consisted of hors d'oeuvres, rich soups, sole and lobster, half a chicken per person, three rashers of bacon and three tomatoes, fruit salad and coffee. Cream was everywhere – on the soup, in the fish sauce, on the fruit salad. The bill for two, including a bottle of the cheaper champagne at fourteen shillings, came to three pounds. In Poplar, in London's East End, sixpence bought a meal of vegetable soup, fish pie and baked rice. Food hoarders were prosecuted and people adjured to 'eat slowly – you will need less food', but full rationing was not introduced until almost the end of the war; ration books were issued in the middle of 1918 for meat, bacon, fats and sugar. Coal, however, was rationed in late 1917 – two hundredweight weekly for a dwelling of three to five rooms, four hundredweight for six to seven rooms. In affluent areas people hired taxis to collect their coal rations, because so many coalmen had been called up.

From 1915 onwards, when the Zeppelin raids began, baths

were filled nightly with water in the houses of Mayfair as a precaution against incendiary bombs. A total blackout descended on London; the streets were lit only by the weak flicker of torches as pedestrians hurried about. Few enemy aircraft did come over the West End, though Lady Freda Valentine remembers seeing a cluster of seven Zeppelins over the East End one day. Prewar class hierarchies were eroded as basement kitchens became a communal air-raid shelter for 'upstairs' family and 'downstairs' staff. Sonia Keppel remembered her mother Alice, the intimate friend of Edward VII, repairing to the basement of 16 Grosvenor Street during raids, ordering Rolfe the butler to bring champagne from the cellar and leading a spirited sing-song with 'Tipperary' and popular revue numbers like 'You're Here and I'm Here'. Sonia, then aged fifteen, and her older sister Violet (who was to marry Denys Trefusis and be seduced by Vita Sackville-West), were moved down to the drawing room to sleep, their camp beds mingling oddly with the Louis XV consoles and tapestry, the Chippendale looking-glasses and Persian rugs.

Colonel George Keppel had bought the lease of 16 Grosvenor Street in 1909 from Collard and Collard, the piano manufacturers, who had been there since 1860. The house's first occupant in 1725–38 was Sir Robert Walpole's son, the second Earl of Orford, and it had a history of being tenanted by dukes and marquesses. The Keppels had it remodelled inside, installing a new 'branching staircase' and a 'Dutch room'. Edward VII, who used to take tea daily with Alice Keppel and was known familiarly as 'Kingy' to the Keppel daughters, approved the plans for the remodelling but died before he could see the results. The spacious ground- and first-floor salons which had been used as piano showrooms gave Alice Keppel an ideal setting in which to display her cultivated, well-travelled taste; porcelain and Coromandel screens from a visit to China; pictures, English china, and cut-glass chandeliers. Many of her finest pieces came from the royal furniture stores, including two porcelain pagodas that once graced the Prince Regent's Brighton Pavilion. Her first-floor bedroom opened into a boudoir with eighteenth-century Chinese painted silk wall-hangings and Chippendale Chinoiserie furniture. Colonel Keppel had an identical suite, furnished in heavier style, on the floor above. The dining room could seat seventy.

Violet marked her coming-out year, 1913, by converting a housemaid's closet into an exotic den influenced by Bakst's designs for the Russian Ballet. Her sister Sonia recalled:

Heavy gold lamé curtains shut out the daylight, and the electric light bulbs were dimmed to obscurity behind opaque shades. The room glowed redly, as though it were smoulderingly on fire. . . . Gorgeous Persian jackets lay about on the divans, ready for Violet's guests to put on when they entered. On top of the cushions, casually lay a huge, feathered turban. Probably to counteract homely smells of Sunlight soap and Brasso, now incense hung heavily on the air. The minute Violet's guests arrived, quickly she shut the door on them. Much to my disgust, as I wanted to know whether Lord Haldane or George Moore wore the turban.

The Keppels lived in Grosvenor Street from 1912 to 1924, when the egregious Mrs James Corrigan from Cleveland, Ohio took it over. In the 1930s it was rebuilt as premises for a dressmaking firm and is now occupied by a property company.

During the First World War the house was a temporary haven for the displaced Herbert Asquith and his wife Margot when he resigned office as Prime Minister in 1916. Alice Keppel gave up her bedroom to Mrs Asquith and moved in with her husband on the floor above; the ex-premier went into the Keppels' spare room and their fourteen-year-old son, Anthony, known as 'Puffin', was accommodated in a vacant maid's room.

Most of Mrs Asquith's tremendous correspondence was maintained at night, and for this ordeal she asked to be fortified with sandwiches [wrote Sonia Keppel in her memoirs, *Edwardian Daughter*]. These she would pick at and frequently forget to consume. But even so, they meant butter, and butter was scarce.

Eventually, Fortnum and Mason solved the problem with some sort of composite filling which Mrs Asquith

absorbed quite happily. . . . In the day-time, Mr Asquith
looked tired and ill and probably had not slept much,
but he made great conversational efforts, and so did
Puffin. (Puffin had the best manners of any schoolboy
I had met.) Mrs Asquith was outspoken against her
husband's critics, but about them he was silent. He
seemed to have lost interest in the present and to have
slipped back into the past.

During the summer of 1915 Mrs Keppel gave luncheon
once or twice a week to a varied gathering of politicians,
service chiefs, diplomats, soldiers home on leave and war
correspondents, leavened with as many of her women
friends and Violet's contemporaries as were available to
entertain them:

The big and small tables in the dining-room were again
in session; with a sharp demarcation line of intellect
between the two.
   Mama dominated the big table, where usually it was
tacitly understood that the conversation should remain
on a light level with the darker shades of war excluded
from it. But occasionally Mr Asquith, or Winston
Churchill, or some leading soldier like Sir John Cowans,
would be present, and then, for a second, the animated
chatter would cease, and the company would sit
respectfully listening, suddenly reduced to the same
student level as myself.

Some of the women at these luncheons, Sonia Keppel
recorded, were 'as remarkable as the men. Mrs Asquith
and Winston's mother Lady Randolph Churchill, both were
seeded players in any conversational contest . . .'
   It was, to a large extent, still the self-confident ruling
society of late Victorian and Edwardian England. Walter H.
Page, the American Ambassador who arrived in 1913, was
an impressed observer during his first few months in
London. He put up at the Coburg Hotel while his Chancery
premises were being moved from the 'dark and dingy'
rooms at 123 Victoria Street to 6 Grosvenor Square.

To his brother, Robert N. Page of Aberdeen, North Caro-
lina, he described his new residence in December, 1913:

> We have a splendid, big old house – not in any way
> pretentious – a commonplace house in fact for
> fashionable London and the least showy and costly of
> the Embassies. But it does very well – it's big and
> elegantly plain and dignified. We have fifteen servants
> in the house. They do just about what seven good ones
> would do in the United States, but they do it a great deal
> better. They pretty nearly run themselves and the place.
> The servant question is admirably solved here. They
> divide the work according to a fixed and unchangeable
> system and they do it remarkably well – in their own
> slow English way. Katharine simply tells the butler that
> we'll have twenty-four people to dinner tomorrow night
> and gives him a list of them. As they come in, the men
> at the door address every one correctly – Your Lordship
> or Your Grace, or what not. When they are all in, the
> butler comes to the reception room and announces
> dinner. We do the rest. As every man goes out, the
> butler asks him if he'll have a glass of water or of grog
> or a cigar; he calls his car, puts him in it, and that's the
> end of it. Bully good plan. But in the United States that
> butler, whose wages are less than the ramshackle nigger
> I had at Garden City to keep the place neat, would have
> a business of his own. But here he is a sort of duke
> downstairs. He sits at the head of the servants' table and
> orders them around and that's worth more than money
> to an Old World servile mind.

In May 1914 Page wrote to President Woodrow Wilson an
illuminating personal report on the English establishment
as he saw it. He commented on the centuries-old habit of
putting pots of herbs on court officials' desks to ward off
the plague; on the fact that a special guard still stood watch
at the Bank of England because of an attempted break-
in several hundred years before – and this practice was
maintained although the Bank was now housed in a building
'that would withstand a siege'; that King Charles's statue in
Trafalgar Square was still hung with flowers on the anniver-

saty of his execution; that books appeared every month about

> the mistresses of old kings – as if they, too, were of more than usual interest . . . serious, historical books.
> Nothing is ever abolished, nothing ever changed. . . . In every house too (to show how nothing ever changes), the towels are folded in the same particular way. In every grate in the kingdom the coal is laid in precisely the same way. There is not a salesman in any shop on Piccadilly who does not, in the season, wear a long-tail coat. . . . In this hot debate about Ulster a frequent phrase used is, 'Let us see if we can't find the right formula to solve the difficulty'; their whole lives are formulas.

Nevertheless Page sensed a strength he admired in this old, slow-moving civilization. Contrary to much opinion in the United States, he found England and her people neither effete nor decadent. In a letter to Herbert S. Houston in August 1913 he wrote:

> The world never saw a finer lot of men than the best of their ruling class. You may search the world and you may search history for finer men than Lord Morley, Sir Edward Grey, Mr Harcourt and other members of the present Cabinet. And I meet such men everywhere – gently bred, high-minded, physically fit, intellectually cultivated, patriotic. . . . I can't see that the race is breaking down or giving out.

Above all, Page admired the English for what he called

> their high art of living. When they make their money they stop money-making and cultivate their minds and their gardens and entertain their friends and do all the high arts of living – to perfection. . . . I guess they really believe that the earth belongs to them.

9

AFTER THE DELUGE

IN the first few years of the 1920s Mayfair still appeared a haven of gracious residential living and almost rural seclusion amid the gathering pace of industrial and social change that was transforming London. Berkeley Street, with the gardens of Devonshire House running up its western side to join those of Lansdowne House, was leafy and tree-lined. 'It was like a garden all the way from Piccadilly to Berkeley Square,' recalled a former Duchess of Westminster who, as the Honourable Loelia Ponsonby, daughter of the King's assistant private secretary, then lived nearby in grace and favour lodgings in St James's Palace. The Mayfair mews were still largely inhabited by horses, though some mews were being turned into garages, and one cab in ten, as Barbara Cartland recalled in her memoirs, was still horse-drawn. The smell of the West End streets in summer was of manure, leather harness, flowers, straw and dust, 'with a whiff of salt from the wind blowing up the Thames', and only the occasional hint of petrol fumes. Straw was still occasionally put down in the road in Park Lane and the Mayfair squares to quieten the noise of wheels for sick residents. (The last recorded instance of this happening in London was in 1931 when Arnold Bennett lay dying of typhoid in his flat in Chiltern Court, Baker Street.)

As the 1920s opened, most of the big Mayfair mansions were still inhabited, if intermittently, by their titled owners.

The Duke of Devonshire had just moved out of Devonshire House, and the Duke of Westminster preferred Bourdon House in Davies Street to Grosvenor House on Park Lane, but the Marquess of Londonderry lived at Londonderry House; Sir John Ward, brother of the second Earl of Dudley, was at Dudley House; Sir Ernest Cassel at Brook House; the Marquess of Crewe at Crewe House; the Marquess of Lansdowne at Lansdowne House. Colonel Sir George Holford, a former equerry to King Edward VII, had been renting out Dorchester House for years, but the splendid Italianate palace facing Hyde Park which Holford's father had built in 1852 was still in family ownership. Recently one of Mayfair's most stately mansions, Chesterfield House on South Audley Street, had been bought by Viscount Lascelles, heir to the fifth Earl of Harewood, who lived there when in London with his bride, the Princess Royal.

In the year of their marriage, 1922, the London Season resumed its prewar glamour with Court presentations and extravagant balls; there was no shortage of money, it seemed, for elaborate entertaining. In a few weeks of one season, the young Loelia Ponsonby went to balls in five grand houses in Park Lane alone. From north to south these were Brook House, on the corner of Brook Street; Dudley House at 100 Park Lane with its mirrored ballroom; Grosvenor House with its gardens backing on to Park Lane and pillared courtyard facing Upper Grosvenor Street: Dorchester House with its grand marble staircase leading to an arcaded picture gallery, and finally, Londonderry House, renowned for its political soirées but the least popular for dances among the younger generation.

Loelia Ponsonby, who was to marry Bendor, second Duke of Westminster in 1930, remembers its vast staircase, with Lady Londonderry standing at the top 'bristling with jewels' to receive her guests. 'Parties there were never any fun, it's hard to tell why. They used to have the best bands, but we girls loathed going there. Some balls were gay and amusing, some were simply stiff.' The ballrooms of these great houses were always on the first floor, approached by a sweeping staircase; in Dudley House, Loelia, now Lady Lindsay, recalls, there were two rooms for dancing, awkwardly linked by 'a tiny little passage with a door at each end, just wide enough for one person'. In the smaller Mayfair houses dances would be held in the first-floor drawing room and back drawing room, which were usually linked by double doors and could be turned into one L-shaped room for parties. Suppers invariably consisted of cold chicken smothered in white sauce, asparagus and salmon, with champagne, lemonade and ices. The most popular band in the early 1920s, according to Lady Lindsay, was that of Clifford Essex, whose pianist was famous for a flashy rendering of 'Kitten on the Keys'. Dances were still numbered in the Edwardian manner, might last as long as twenty minutes and were supposed to be distributed among a number of different partners. To dance with the same person twice running was regarded as 'rather compromising'. Often there would be two or three balls taking place on the same evening and enthusiastic dancers would go from one to another, meeting different parties of friends.

The coming of the night-club era overlapped for a while with the last of the old formal private entertaining, and it was regarded as dashing to slip away from a boring ball and spend the rest of the evening at the Embassy Club in Old Bond Street. Parents disapproved intensely, which added spice to the whole thing. 'I can't think why,' remarked Lady Lindsay. 'If you were going to get into trouble you were much more likely to do so at a ball in a private house, where you might have got into one of the bedrooms, than at the Embassy where everybody was in one well-lit room'. Before the night-club era really got under way, the popular place to go out dancing was the Grafton Galleries in Grafton Street. It was literally a picture gallery in a large basement, with a dance floor and a black jazz band which played one-steps like 'I'm Just Wild about Harry'. It was, Barbara Cartland recalled in her memoirs, 'extremely respectable, so much so that when there was an exhibition of nude drawings they were covered at night with pieces of tissue paper'. According to her no alcohol was served with the sandwiches and iced cakes supplied by Gunter's – only iced coffee and a bright pink fruit punch known as 'Turk's Blood' – but others who went there say that you could get a drink if you wanted one. The Prince of Wales, already a trend-setter of his generation, was a member, and the Grafton Galleries was the focus of West End night life at the beginning of the 1920s, until eclipsed by the rise of more glamorous clubs and restaurants like the Embassy, the Café de Paris, the Ambassador and the Kit-Cat.

Young men short of money might dine alone at their clubs before taking a girl out dancing, but a stylish social life did not depend upon expensive meals or drinks. Champagne cocktails at the Ritz were only a shilling, the basic price of a taxi ride in 1925, and if you were known at the Berkeley Hotel you could dance from 9 p.m. until well after midnight without having to order anything stronger than beer or orangeade. The accepted way to end an evening was to call at the Hyde Park Corner coffee stall in the early hours, opposite St George's Hospital, where couples could sit cosily in the rows of taxis, sipping milky coffee out of thick cups while the drivers waited discreetly in a green wooden hut until dawn broke and it was time to go home.

But if life was sweet, elegant and inexpensive for the privileged young, it was becoming much less so for their elders. Lloyd George's 1919 Budget, with its heavy new death duties aimed at the great landed estates, permanently changed the long hegemony of hereditary wealth in Britain and, together with the nearly fourfold increase in income tax occasioned by the war, brought about a flood of property sales. By the end of 1921 the *Estates Gazette* reported that a quarter of England had changed hands. Most sales were of land – between six and eight million acres in the three years since the Armistice – but the new order also spelled the end of Mayfair's great houses.

Devonshire House was the first to go, though its death was a lingering one. The house and its site were sold in September 1919 by the ninth Duke to the building contractors Holland and Hannen and Cubitts Ltd for a sum reported by *The Times* to be in excess of £1 million. The Devonshires moved to a lesser mansion in Carlton Gardens, the Duchess remarking 'It's interesting to see what the pictures look like in a small house.' In May 1920 Holland, Hannen and Cubitts sold out for a profit of a further half-million to a Liverpool shipowner, Laurence Harrison, and a London businessman, Shurmer Sibthorp, whose interest was immediately acquired by Harrison and a new partner, City financier H. E. Barley.

Harrison and Barley, it was reported, planned to turn the great house on Piccadilly into a cinema with a restaurant and 'dancing room' attached. Nothing came of this, or a variety of other proposals for the old mansion with its great white marble and glass staircase installed by the sixth Duke in 1846, and the house languished for another four years 'emptily awaiting its destiny', as Michael Arlen described it in one of his Mayfair novels.

Demolition, when it came at the end of 1924 – the wreckers moving in almost as the last costumed guests at a charity ball departed – was a shock to Londoners. Artists came to record the destruction of the house and its wooded garden and soon the new twelve-storey Devonshire House, clad in Portland stone and housing motor showrooms and offices, was rising alongside Piccadilly and a widened and thoroughly urbanized Berkeley Street. A new street, Mayfair Place, was driven through to link Stratton and Berkeley streets and more offices and shops covered the site of the old house and gardens back to the end of Stratton Street, which was extended right to link up again with Berkeley Street in a one-way traffic system. Stratton Street, a hitherto quiet and dignified residential address distinguished at Number 1 by the big Georgian town house of the Baroness Burdett-Coutts, was also permanently altered in character by the wholesale development of 1925. The Burdett-Coutts mansion was torn down and replaced by Stratton House, another office building, and the street took on an increasingly commercial role.

The size of the original Devonshire House site with its gardens can be gauged today by walking back from Mayfair Place to Stratton Street where it joins Berkeley Street and following the bulk of the May Fair Hotel as far as Lansdowne Passage, which originally separated the grounds of Devonshire House from those of Lansdowne House. The May Fair was built for Gordon Hotels, then the leading hotel group in London (they owned the Grand in Northumberland Avenue and were to operate the Dorchester until financial difficulties put them out of business) and had the rare distinction for a commercial building of being visited by the King and Queen on its opening in 1927. Like the Park Lane Hotel, opened the same year, the May Fair was designed for the American

market; the boom years of transatlantic travel after the Great
War were to shape the first profound change from residential to commercial life in Mayfair, particularly in the fate of
its great houses.

Lansdowne House escaped demolition by finding a
wealthy tenant in the figure of Gordon Selfridge, the Amer-
ican-born department store magnate, who gave it over to
his protégées, the Hungarian cabaret artists known as the
Dolly Sisters. Selfridge paid a rent of £5000 a year for
Lansdowne House, which became the scene of famous
dancing parties in the 1920s at which the Dolly Sisters gave
demonstrations of the Black Bottom and the Charleston.
The last big social event of the old order was the wedding
reception on 21 April 1920 of the Duke of Devonshire's
daughter, Lady Dorothy Cavendish, and the young Harold
Macmillan, MP. Since Devonshire House next door had
gone to developers, the bride's grandfather, the Marquess
of Lansdowne, lent his house with its adjoining garden
stretching along the south side of Berkeley Square. Queen
Alexandra, the young Duke of York – later King George VI
– and the aged Thomas Hardy were among the wedding
guests. Lord Lansdowne moved his town residence to 65
Brook Street and the Adam mansion remained intact until
1935 when its two wings were demolished for the extension
of Curzon Street into Berkeley Square – never carried out as
planned – and the core of the house was turned into the
Lansdowne Club.

The demolition of Grosvenor House and its rebuilding as
an American-style hotel and service apartments provoked
much criticism of the Duke of Westminster, though elsewhere he resisted the tide of development more than other
Mayfair landlords and hated the idea of the district becoming
commercialized. Grosvenor House was not built for the
Grosvenors, coming into their hands only in 1806. Its first
owner in 1732 was Viscount Chetwynd, and it was
subsequently occupied by three Dukes – Beaufort, Cumber-
land and Gloucester. William Henry, Duke of Gloucester,
was a brother of George III, and during its forty years as a
royal residence the house was known as Gloucester House.
When Robert, second Earl Grosvenor, acquired it in 1806 for
£20,000, his surveyor was not impressed. The house was

'very dirty', he reported, and 'not so chearful as the situation would lead one to expect'. He advised his employer to have the interior whitewashed and furnished by Gillow's. It was remodelled several times in the nineteenth century, substantially so by Thomas Cundy and his son in the 1820s and 1840s, and magnificent galleries were added to house the Grosvenor art collection. The first Duke installed electricity in the Park Lane mansion in 1889, only eight years after its first appearance in London streets, enthusing to his daughter-in-law that 'Edison's electric lighting is the best thing out . . . all perfectly safe, you may lay hold of the wires with perfect immunity – *delightful*.'

The first Duke's son died before he could inherit, and the grandson, Hugh Richard Grosvenor, always known as 'Bendor' after a famous Derby winner owned by his grandfather, came into the title and vast estates when he was not yet twenty-one, and on his way to serve in the South African War. Bendor kept up Grosvenor House until the First World War, when it was used as a hospital for officers. He lived there periodically with his first wife Shelagh Cornwallis-West, although his liaisons with other women, including the musical comedy star Gertie Millar, were already becoming notorious, and even when in London he was frequently absent from home. On the occasions when he was elsewhere a brougham was dispatched to Grosvenor House to collect his letters each morning. The first marriage broke up in 1919 and in the following year he married the divorced Violet Rowley, by which time he had decided to use Bourdon House in Davies Street as his London residence and was looking for a tenant or buyer for Grosvenor House. The Duke of Sutherland expressed interest and offered £6000 a year, twice as much as the outgoings on the house, but for some reason the deal fell through and the Duke of Sutherland took Hampden House in Green Street instead.

Year by year the overheads on Grosvenor House mounted, and the Duke of Westminster's fortune, though large, was at that time nowhere near its size at his death (he had multiplied it tenfold, mainly by land acquisitions overseas, by the time it passed to his heirs in 1953). In 1921 he sold a number of pictures from the Grosvenor House galleries, among them Gainsborough's celebrated 'Blue Boy', a sale engineered by the international art dealer Joseph Duveen on board the Cunard liner *Aquitania*. Duveen was in the habit of using Atlantic crossings to find potential customers and on this occasion wangled an invitation to dine with the railroad millionaire Henry E. Huntington, a collector of English eighteenth-century pictures, who was occupying the liner's Gainsborough suite. Glancing round the walls, which were hung with reproductions of Gainsborough's most famous paintings, Huntington said, 'Joe, who's the boy in the blue suit?' Duveen told him. 'Where's the original?' Huntington wanted to know. 'It belongs to the Duke of Westminster and hangs in his collection in Grosvenor House, in London,' replied the art dealer. 'How much is it?' asked Huntington bluntly. Duveen made a tactical retreat. 'It can probably not be had for any price,' he demurred. Then, after a pause, he added, 'It is the greatest work of England's greatest master and would be the crown of any collection of English pictures.' Huntington duly fell into the trap and asked Duveen for an estimate of the price, should the picture ever be sold. Duveen made a show of hesitation and suggested around $600,000. 'I might see my way clear to paying that much,' said Huntington.

On arrival Duveen rushed to London and called on the Duke of Westminster. Not only was he willing to sell 'The Blue Boy', but other pictures as well. Duveen also secured Gainsborough's 'The Cottage Door' and Sir Joshua Reynolds's 'Sarah Siddons as the Tragic Muse', all three for little more than the price he had quoted Huntington for 'The Blue Boy'. In the end he sold 'The Blue Boy' to Huntington for £620,000, following it up after a discreet interval with the two others. The sale of 'The Blue Boy' caused the first big outcry over a national art treasure departing for foreign shores. Ninety thousand people came to a farewell exhibition staged by Duveen at the National Gallery, and the painting's arrival in New York, encased in three waterproof and fireproof boxes, made headline news across the country. Cole Porter wrote a topical number, 'The Blue Boy Blues', for the Cochran revue *Mayfair and Montmartre:*

> For I'm the Blue Boy, the beautiful Blue Boy,
> And I'm forced to admit I'm feeling a bit depressed.

A silver dollar took me and my collar
To show the slow cowboys just how boys
In England used to be dressed.
I don't know what I shall do
So far from Mayfair;
If Mister Gainsborough knew,
I know he'd frown.
As days grow fewer,
I'm bluer and bluer,
For I'm saying goodbye to London town.

By the middle of 1924 the Duke of Westminster was looking for at least £10,000 a year for Grosvenor House, but
there was no likely tenant in view. It was clear that it would
have to be sold for redevelopment. Then Lord Leverhulme,
the recently ennobled soap manufacturer, came forward
with a plan for a public art gallery on the site. One alternative proposal was for an opera house. They agreed terms,
£20,000 a year with an option to purchase for £400,000, but
Leverhulme died in 1925 and his executors assigned the
purchase option to a speculator, the architect and builder
Alfred Octavius Edwards, who had been involved in the
plans for the May Fair Hotel. Edwards was in no doubt that
the site should be used for an hotel aimed at the American
market and he brought in as his architects the eminent firm
of Wimperis, Simpson and Guthrie. Edmund Wimperis had
originally been the surveyor to the Grosvenor Estate, and to
add the final imprimatur to the scheme, Edwards proposed a
collaboration with the most distinguished architect of the
day, Sir Edwin Lutyens.

Lutyens was excited by the concept of building as high as
the London County Council would allow: 'What fun we are
going to have!' he told Edwards. But the Manhattan-style
twin towers of self-contained flats serviced by the adjoining
hotel were much criticized as they rose starkly above the
surviving Edwardian town houses of Park Street and the
leafy glades of the Park. The towers were the first part of
the hotel to be completed: severe brown brick structures
with unrelieved rows of windows. Lutyens's main contribution was to the Park Lane frontage of the hotel, in which
he incorporated a graceful classical colonnade echoing

Thomas Cundy's courtyard screen of 1843 for the original house. (The Cundy screen was bought by the Phyllis Court Club in Henley-on-Thames but has since disappeared.) Only Sir William Orpen, the society painter, had a good word to say for the Grosvenor House towers; he would rather look at them, he said, than at St Paul's Cathedral.

A New York office was set up to take bookings for the apartments, which were advertised as 'the best that New York can give and that Paris can offer'. Tenants were assured of a range of business services on the premises, from instant life insurance to the latest stock-market prices. An even greater novelty in the main hotel was the huge ice rink in the basement; it was advertised grandly as 'The Murren of London' and became a popular meeting place for young socialites until its attractions were rivalled by the opening of the Queen's Ice Club in Bayswater. It was dismantled in the late 1930s and became the Great Room, the largest hotel public room in Europe. (The labyrinth of piping for the ice rink is still there beneath it.)

The apartments were unlucky in the timing of their opening; the Wall Street crash took away their main market and the prices were reduced in the first couple of years. But by 1931 most of the 160 flats were taken and they are still very much in demand today at rents ranging from £20,000 a year for a one-bedroom apartment (originally £520 a year) to more than £73,500 for a five-bedroom, four-bathroom spread. Margaret, Duchess of Argyll, is one of a dozen or so permanent private residents, but 70 per cent of the flats are let to companies.

The other Park Lane mansion to fall to hotel developers in the late 1920s was Dorchester House. Like Clarendon House, as the Mayfair chronicler Reginald Colby has noted, it was destined to be built and swept away within one lifetime. In its day it had been the most splendid of the great houses facing Hyde Park, owing its name to the Earls of Dorchester, who once lived on the site, the freehold of which had been bought from Westminster Abbey by a Victorian speculator named Robert Stayner Holford. He had inherited a million, made a further fortune on the stock market and was also romantically reputed to have benefited from a hoard of bullion buried on the Isle of Wight to escape a

Napoleonic invasion. Holford spent lavishly on the house, which was designed by Lewis Vulliamy in 1852 with a facade modelled on that of the Villa Farnese in Rome and decorated inside by Alfred Stevens, sculptor of the Wellington monument in St Paul's.

Building occupied nearly twenty years; the dining room alone took fifteen years to complete and cost £8000. By 1863 Holford had already met bills of £138,000, of which £30,000 went to pay for the marble staircase. The house also contained magnificent works by Titian, Velásquez and Van Dyck. Holford died in 1892 and his son, Sir George Holford, increasingly found himself unable to maintain both Dorchester House and Westonbirt House at Tetbury, Gloucestershire, which his father had also commissioned from Vulliamy, in this case in Elizabethan style. Holford let Dorchester House to a series of distinguished foreign visitors, beginning with the Shah of Persia in 1895 and ending with Theodore Roosevelt's Ambassador Whitelaw Reid, who used it as a more dignified official address than the actual US Embassy at 123 Victoria Street, housed dingily 'between two cheap stores,' as Reid's successor Walter Page remarked. Reid was much criticized by political opponents for his extravagant way of life in London, but he paid the annual rent of 4500 guineas for Dorchester House out of his own pocket. His last flamboyant gesture was to install a marble eagle with a six-foot wingspan over the front door before he died there in 1912.

For all its magnificence, however, old Dorchester House with its forty bedrooms, vast salons for entertaining and four-foot-thick external walls, was singularly lacking in creature comforts. When the Dorchester Hotel was built upon the site it had 275 bathrooms, one to every bedroom: the old house had in all its acreage just one bathroom for guests and one for staff. Sir George Holford died in 1926 and the house passed to his nephew the Earl of Morley. Two years later he sold it for £500,000 to Gordon Hotels and the building firm of Sir Robert McAlpine and Sons. The Gordon group, it was announced, planned to build an hotel 'which shall rank as the finest in Europe', but after a few years, it was unable to meet the mortgage requirements and McAlpine's operated the hotel themselves for the next half-century.

The fittings of the house were auctioned on 13 August 1929, and crowds of sightseers thronged through the rooms to take a last look before demolition began. A giant crane was already being moved into position to lift the massive marble staircase out through the roof. But the bidding fell far short of expectations, in all raising little more than four thousand pounds. The staircase which had cost R. S. Holford £30,000 fetched only £273: removed from the house in four sections, it went to a Scottish buyer and ended up in 1965 in the home of a Dallas businessman called Paul Knight. The Portland stone balustrade facing Park Lane and the double entrance gates each went for 105 guineas; stretches of oak flooring were knocked down for a few guineas and for most of the ornamental tiling there was no bidding at all. The fittings were evidently too monumental to attract private buyers; several ended up in the Walker Art Gallery in Liverpool and the famous dining-room fireplace by Alfred Stevens with its marble caryatids went to the Victoria and Albert Museum. Much of the lovely old panelling, as in other great Park Lane houses, simply went to feed the demolition fires. 'Dorchester House is dead, and it is better so. The present age is not attuned to it,' lamented *The Times* in a fourth leader of the day after the sale.

In other respects, however, the demolition of Dorchester House was a model of what would now be called recycling. Individual bricks had their surrounding mortar chipped away and were sold to builders throughout London. The steelwork was cut into two-hundredweight pieces and ended up in railways, ships and cars. Even broken bricks, building rubble and old mortar were ground down to be mixed with sand and cement. About twenty thousand tons of material were dismantled and marketed within seven weeks, and construction of the new building set a record; the first floor was completed in September 1930 and thereafter the hotel went up at the rate of a floor a week, the roof being put in place in November. Mechanical excavators removed 40,000 tons of earth from below Park Lane to make room for the underground part of the hotel, the garages, kitchens and Turkish baths, which covered an area equal to one-third of the building visible above ground. The construction throughout was remarkably in advance of its time. The ground floor had a solid reinforced concrete roof three feet thick, giving great spans fifty-six by forty feet over the public rooms. The entire structure was interlaced with steel rods embedded in concrete and the outside walls finished off with crushed and polished marble mixed into the concrete. Inside walls were lined with cork two inches thick to insulate the bedrooms from noise and external changes in temperature, added silence being provided by lining floors and ceilings with compressed seaweed.

On the Dorchester Hotel's opening in 1931 Sir Francis Towle, chairman of Gordon Hotels, described it as 'of such strength that it might be held to be bomb-proof, earthquake-proof and fireproof', and in the Blitz it was undoubtedly one of the safest public buildings in central London, with the ground-floor grill room under that concrete umbrella a popular place for those who could afford to spend an evening there. Most of Churchill's War Cabinet had rooms in the Dorchester, as did socialites like Lady Cunard and the former Margaret Whigham, then Mrs Charles Sweeny. In 1938, when a new bar was being built, barman Harry Craddock mixed three popular cocktails of the day, Martini, Manhattan and White Lady, and buried them in phials in the wall; the bar was rebuilt in 1979 and when the wall was demolished the cocktails were found to be in perfect condition.

If one had taken a series of aerial trips over Mayfair between 1925 and 1935 the scale and speed of the changes in its streets and squares would have seemed unimaginable to the residents of a few years earlier. The character of whole thoroughfares changed in that decade; none more so than Park Lane, as smoke rose from the rubble of its old mansions and cliff-like blocks of apartments, hotels and offices rose in their place. In 1925 Brook House with its twenty-four bedrooms, nine or ten bathrooms and dozen reception rooms had become the property of Sir Ernest Cassel's granddaughter Edwina, Lady Louis Mountbatten, who lived there in a large third-floor apartment. Seven years later the Mountbattens sold its sixty-four year lease to Coutts' Bank. They leased it to a building firm which demolished it and put up a neo-Georgian block of luxury apartments, one to a floor. The Mountbattens retained the right to the two-storey penthouse, surrounded by its own terraced garden. They rented it for £4,200 a year. Aldford House, once the home of the mining magnate Sir Alfred Beit, also went about this time, rebuilt as offices, shops and flats.

The last great Mayfair mansion to be demolished in the 1930s was one of the earliest in the area, Chesterfield House, built by Isaac Ware for the fourth Earl of Chesterfield in 1748. Viscount Lascelles, its owner since 1919, succeeded his father as sixth Earl of Harewood in 1929 and in 1932 he and his wife, the Princess Royal, sold Chesterfield House and its contents and moved to a more convenient London home at 32 Green Street. Five years later Isaac Ware's glorious rooms with their rococo plasterwork fell to the wreckers and yet another cliff-like block of flats, still known as Chesterfield House, was put up on the site.

On Mayfair's eastern boundary, during most of the 1920s, the whole of Regent Street was being rebuilt in the interests of twentieth-century commerce. Nash's small-scale shops and arcaded pavements were swept away and monumental department stores put up. The comprehensive redevelopment, at its height in 1923, prompted one cartoonist to joke that American visitors would think the area had been raided by Zeppelins in the Great War. By the summer of 1927 the rebuilt street was ready for the royal opening by King George V and Queen Mary, who drove down in in an open carriage on the afternoon of 23 June. The King observed to the Mayor of Westminster that he was 'very pleased with the new Regent Street', and it proved equally popular with the shopping public.

Even before the demolition of Devonshire House signalled the first great redevelopment of Mayfair's southern edge, Londoners had become accustomed to a strange-looking structure in the dip between Devonshire House and Hyde Park Corner. Known as 'the Birdcage', it was the giant skeleton of a building destined to be an hotel before the First World War, for which a row of houses had been pulled down in 1912. Funds ran out and the project was abandoned in 1915. The steel cage stood nakedly on Piccadilly until 1924, when a Yorkshire businessman named Bracewell

Smith raised the money to complete it as the Park Lane Hotel. Apart from the Edwardian panelling in its Louis Room restaurant, acquired from Pierpont Morgan's old house in Grosvenor Square, it has a striking art-deco interior, recently refurbished by its owners (still the family of Bracewell Smith) and part of it was used as locations for the Atlantic liner scenes in the television version of *Brideshead Revisited*.

While all this demolition and rebuilding was going on around the outer rim of Mayfair, the remaining eighteenth-century squares and terraces in its heart were also being raided, progressively more noticeably after 1935. In the late 1920s the Duke of Westminster had been persuaded that development of Grosvenor Square was necessary because of increased motor traffic around it and the lack of a market for the big Georgian family houses. In 1925–7 rebuilding began with a block of flats on the south-east corner. The Duke was reluctant to see the square rebuilt; as Loelia, his third wife, recalls, he was, for all his playboy image, essentially an Edwardian and a man who 'hated change'. But at least it was intended to be an elegant and homogeneous composition of buildings, designed by the French architect Fernand Billerey in Beaux-Arts style. Unfortunately the pattern of leases made it impossible to rebuild in more than a patchy way, and although most of it was redeveloped by the outbreak of war – in neo-Georgian rather than Beaux-Arts – the western side lingered on until filled by the giant American Embassy in the late 1950s. Berkeley Square did not have the advantage of a single landlord and its brutal rebuilding in the late 1930s was an aesthetic disaster. In 1930 twenty historic houses along its eastern flank, including that of Horace Walpole, were sold together with a block in Bruton Street by Lord Bearsted, founder of Shell Transport and Trading, to the Canadian Pacific Railway for a giant hotel development. The slump intervened and the site remained empty until Berkeley Square was built in 1937–8. Among the houses lost in Bruton Street was Number 17, the elegant double-fronted Georgian building where the Queen was born in April 1926. The south side of Berkeley Square was also redeveloped in wholesale fashion in the mid 1930s when Lansdowne House was turned into the Lansdowne Club;

Lansdowne Row and Fitzmaurice Place were driven through to link Curzon Street with the square, and the Lansdowne House gardens were built over with flats and shops. (At the time of writing the whole southern side of the square is again under demolition.)

By 1935 the only trees left in the once charmingly wooded Berkeley Square were those in the central garden, thirty-three giant plane trees planted in 1789 by Edward Bouverie, a neighbour of Horace Walpole's. It was Michael Arlen in a short story published in 1923 who first invented the idea of a nightingale in Berkeley Square, later immortalized in the nostalgic wartime ballad by Eric Maschwitz.

On the eve of the Second World War Lord Rosebery's old town house on the north-west corner – the third house he had occupied in Berkeley Square during his lifetime – was pulled down and rebuilt as offices for the Berger paints group. Twenty-nine houses between Curzon and Clarges streets were demolished to build Curzon Street House, a faceless block of government offices. Residential Mayfair was fast disappearing. In the square itself the two most historic surviving houses remained in private hands: Number 44, Isabella Finch's beautiful William Kent house, continued until the late 1950s as the home of a family called Clark, and Number 45, where Clive of India had taken an overdose of laudanum in 1774, was lived in by his descendants, the Earls of Powis, until 1937. The Powis family was the last in London to maintain the old custom of having its name engraved on a brass plate fixed to the front door, instead of a street number.

In September 1929 the *Evening News* reported: 'Ancient families are leaving Mayfair and modern dressmakers or beauty or health specialists are arriving.' Town houses were indeed being sold for commercial use at an increasing rate. Only one important mansion destined to survive was built for private use in the inter-war period – 38 South Street, designed on an opulently Edwardian scale for Henry McLaren, later Lord Aberconway, who paid an estimated £40,000 for it in 1919–21. In 1974 *The Times* was still able to describe it as 'the last private house of great size to be built in London'. The McLarens moved into the spacious neo-Georgian house – only three rooms on the ground floor and three on the first floor, all designed to show off the owner's art collection – in 1922 and remained there until 1943. Five years later the house was bought by the J. Arthur Rank Organization, which still owns it.

As well as dressmakers and beauty specialists, the new businesses taking over Mayfair in the 1930s had a high proportion of interior decorators. As the Adam brothers had found two centuries before, it was a good plan to set up in the area where potential customers lived, and despite the exodus of families, there was no shortage of work for fashionable designers who had social connections with their clients. Lady Sibyl Colefax established her business about this time in Bruton Street, and Syrie Maugham, estranged wife of the novelist and playwright, had a shop behind 9 Grosvenor Square, from which she carried out a number of important commissions in neighbouring streets. In 1935 and 1936 she redecorated the Whighams' house at 48 Upper Grosvenor Street in her characteristic bleached style, with off-white furniture and sheepskin rugs; Marks and Spencer chairman Israel Sieff's flat in the new Brook House; and the Leveson Gower house at 47 Upper Brook Street. Her design for the Sieff flat, supervised architecturally by Lutyens, was typical of expensive 1930s taste. The drawing room was panelled in grey sycamore and hung with yellow taffeta curtains; the dining room had South American cedar panelling and green silk taffeta curtains; the master bedroom had white and cream satin draperies and bed furnishings, a white sheepskin carpet, chairs covered in lavender velvet and a white marble fireplace surmounted by a back-lit white statuette. Syrie Maugham's white decor became so identified with her that she renamed her firm White and Syrie Ltd when she moved it from Duke Street to Bruton Street in 1935.

Because her clients were leaders of society (George Hay Whigham's daughter Margaret, now the Duchess of Argyll, was a much-photographed debutante in 1930), Syrie's transformations were spread across the glossy pages of The Tatler, The Sketch, Harper's Bazaar and The Queen and had a great influence on their era. In the flats that were increasingly taking over from owner-occupied houses, Georgian pine panelling was ruthlessly treated to produce the bleached pale grey or honey-coloured look. Bathrooms were a particularly opulent speciality of 1930s designers. Mrs George Hay Whigham's was covered in mirrors; the banker's wife Mrs Leo d'Erlanger at 44 Upper Grosvenor Street commissioned the Paris firm of Jansen to design, among other rooms, a bathroom with coral and shell wall lights; while Samuel Courtauld of the textile family had his bathroom at 12 North Audley Street made in the form of a semi-circular temple. The d'Erlanger house was described by *Vogue* in 1935 as 'the new house all London is talking about . . . for it's unlike anything London has ever seen. The dining room is painted pink, and has a table of black glass. . . . Her bedroom is circular and done in a scheme of white, blue and green.' Of the bathroom, *Vogue* commented: 'Bathrooms nowadays look more expensive than any other rooms in the house.'

Murals were highly fashionable, and Rex Whistler the most fashionable of artists; among his commissions in Mayfair were the Courtauld master bedroom and Lady Mountbatten's boudoir in Brook House.

The Mountbattens lived in considerable style in their two-storey penthouse, which was served by a lift in which Queen Mary once got stuck. In October 1938, when he was already arranging for his best pictures and furniture to go to the country in the event of war, Mountbatten gave a lunch for the Hollywood studio boss, Jack Warner, with the object of getting films to show on Royal Navy ships. Andrew Cunningham, later Admiral Cunningham of Hyndhope, noted in his diary: 'Lashings of booze. . . . A most amusing lunch, and incidentally a very good one: half a dozen footmen in red and blue livery; and we ate off silver plate, etc., etc . . .'

One of the most spectacular private houses in Mayfair to change hands in the inter-war years was 69 Brook Street, now the Savile Club. When it was sold to the Savile in September 1927 it was described as 'one of the principal mansions in Mayfair'. Originally two Georgian town houses, Numbers 69 and 71, it had been thrown into one in the 1890s by the American banker Walter Hayes Burns, brother-in-law and partner of J. Pierpont Morgan. Burns had Number 71 completely rebuilt by the firm of G. H. Trollope, adding another storey to the combined house. He installed a lift and a magnificent sprung maple ballroom floor, still one of the Savile's glories. The interior of the double house was fitted out in the most lavish Louis XV style, dominated by a circular grand staircase with carved wooden balustrades opening straight into the first-floor ballroom, the whole effect being stagey and operatic. There were fine marble chimneypieces, delicately tinted 'fleur de pêche' marble pillars of a greyish mauve in the ground-floor rooms, carved dark oak panelling and masses of gilding. The house had more than thirty bedrooms, seven or eight reception rooms and nine or ten bathrooms.

Burns died in 1897, soon after the building work was completed, and the house eventually passed into the hands of his daughter, who had married the Liberal politician Lewis Harcourt, Colonial Secretary under Herbert Asquith from 1910 to 1915. Harcourt, nicknamed 'Loulou' since boyhood, had been elevated to the peerage as a Viscount in 1917, but in 1922, when he was fifty-nine, gossip had begun to circulate about him and an Eton schoolboy. As several recent biographies and memoirs have noted, Harcourt's sexual proclivities towards teenagers of both sexes had traumatic effects on the subjects of his advances – Dorothy Brett, one of the Bloomsbury fringe, was made deaf by the shock of her encounter – and though he remained a correct and dignified public figure, private pressures were undoubtedly building up. On the morning of 24 February 1922 Harcourt was found dead in bed by his valet at 69 Brook Street. The inquest on 28 February returned a verdict of death by misadventure, due to the effect of a sleeping draught called bromidia on what was described as a 'diseased heart'. The coroner referred several times to the unlikelihood of Harcourt having taken his own life, saying that he lived 'quite happily' with his wife, although the two had occupied separate rooms since Lady Harcourt suffered a breakdown some eighteen months before, and that he had been looking forward to an Easter break in Warwickshire, a guide to which was found on his bedside table.

Edward James, the Eton schoolboy concerned, who later became an international art dealer, said in his memoirs published in 1982 that the case did him a great deal of harm, because he was blamed by Harcourt's friends for his death.

But the scandal did not affect Lady Harcourt's position in society; she continued to live in the house for another five years, throwing dances and even entertaining Queen Mary there. When she did put the house on the market in 1927 the Savile Club, which had been looking for more spacious premises than it occupied at 107 Piccadilly (it had been founded as a literary club in Savile Row), acquired a singular bargain; the terms of the lease, which runs until the year 2017, fixed the annual rent at the 1927 level for the next ninety years.

The Savile has splendidly restored the original Louis XV interior, and the ballroom, which comes into its own at the Friday-night candlelit dinners when women guests are admitted, now shimmers in white-gold and sky-blue with a glorious painted ceiling; for years it was covered up in dull green and brown paint, the decision of some philistine prewar committee. The patio garden with its original *trompe l'oeil* trelliswork is another rarity in London's clubland. The Savile is one of London's best clubs for food and wine and maintains a determinedly convivial tradition by insisting that a member dining on his own take the first available seat at the long table and engage in conversation with his neighbour. But its greatest literary names are now in the past with the death in 1984 of its doyen, J. B. Priestley. There is still a fair sprinkling of distinguished writers, V. S. Pritchett and Vincent Brome among them, but most of the membership is now made up of editors, actors, BBC and other media men. The club tradition of authors contributing signed first editions of their works to the library has, however, built up a unique collection by past members like Kipling, Wells and Hardy. The Savile is unusual among London clubs in not using the black ball system; elections are openly discussed affairs. Long before the scandal that ruined him, Oscar Wilde was quietly 'warned off' applying for Savile membership; his name remains in the candidates' book.

H. G. Wells once left the Savile to join the Athenaeum but fled back to the Savile saying, 'Thank God I'm back. This is the Athenaeum of the living.' The story was told at a Savile dinner by Wells's son Professor George Wells, FRS, who was the only Savile member to have a bedroom permanently reserved for his use. (The club has only sixteen bedrooms in all.) Robert Louis Stevenson, a member between 1874 and 1894, once described the Savile as the centre of his London life. But society has changed, clubs now play a far more peripheral role and it is unlikely that the young generation of writers and composers (Andrew Lloyd Webber is a member) who are being increasingly sought to maintain the Savile's cultural character would subscribe to Stevenson's view. About a quarter of those admitted at one election in the early 1980s were under thirty. But it remains the only one of the elite male clubs of London to have its premises in the heart of Mayfair, though the Sesame Club at 49 Grosvenor Street, which admits both men and women, has often been a useful backstop for Savile members who find themselves locked out after their 11 p.m. curfew.

10

'ANGELS DINING AT THE RITZ'

*C*LUBS ruled Mayfair social life between the wars; not the men's clubs of London peopled by writers, bishops, explorers and administrators, but the night clubs that gave the West End its seductive glitter and filled it with dance music of such style and verve that, more than half a century later, a few bars of Ambrose, Harry Roy or Ray Noble have the power to summon up a whole era given over, for a fortunate few hundred, to the pursuit of pleasure and fun.

'Fun' is the word that recurs again and again in the conversation of those who were part of that gilded coterie, who spent their long nights of enjoyment in the 1920s and 1930s circulating between private dinner parties and clubs in the hinterland of Piccadilly. 'It was the most marvellous time; I wish I'd realized that it was all going,' sighed Lady Lindsay, thinking back to the time when she reigned over Mayfair society with her former husband Bendor, second Duke of Westminster. 'London has never been so much fun,' agreed Margaret, Duchess of Argyll, who pursued a headlong round of parties and night-clubbing between her coming-out in 1930 as Margaret Whigham and her marriage to the American golfer Charles Sweeny in 1933.

Night after night the taxis and chauffeur-driven cars disgorged their cargoes of white– or black-tied men and

evening-gowned women at the doors of the Kit-Cat in the
Haymarket, the Embassy in Old Bond Street, the Café de
Paris in Coventry Street, the Ambassador in Conduit Street,
the Silver Slipper in Regent Street, Ciro's and the
Monseigneur in St James's, the Five Hundred in Albemarle
Street, the Bruton in Bruton Mews, the Bag o' Nails off
Wardour Street and a whole flock of racier basement establishments in and around Soho. In these places, the owners
paid lip service only to the licensing laws, and the customary
night-club attractions of late drinking, sexual adventure and
hot jazz were liable to be sharpened by the risk of a police
raid.

Mrs Kate Meyrick, owner of the '43' at 43 Gerrard Street
(once the home of the poet John Dryden), was implicated
in the famous Goddard police corruption case of 1928 –
police bribery was rife on the night-club circuit. She was
imprisoned several times but never lost the loyalty of her
society clientele, who at different times included Augustus
John, Jacob Epstein, Joseph Conrad, June the musical
comedy star (Lady Inverclyde), Gordon Richards, Tallulah
Bankhead, the Crown Prince of Sweden, Jack Buchanan,
Michael Arlen, the flier Jim Mollison and the boxers Georges
Carpentier and Primo Carnera. Three of her daughters, who
went to Roedean, married into the peerage. The Kit-Cat,
opened in 1925, had a famous hot band in the late 1920s
assembled by Jack Hylton; it included Al Starita on clarinet
and alto sax, Ted Heath on trombone and Sid Bright, brother
of Geraldo, on piano. The club was raided one evening soon
after the Prince of Wales had paid it a visit: it later led a
quieter life as a restaurant with a conventional palais-de-
danse-style band.

Some clubs, like Uncle's in Albemarle Street, aped the
American speakeasies, with liquor served in tea cups; one
club owner circumvented the law by running his establishment on the principle of the bottle party – guests brought
their own. (Loelia Ponsonby, now Lady Lindsay, claims to
have invented the bottle party in 1926 when she was short
of money and wanted to throw a party in her parents'
apartments in St James's Palace. Michael Arlen, one of the
guests, contributed a case of pink champagne.)

Night clubs were a direct result of the licensing laws intro-

duced into Britain by the notorious Defence of the Realm
Act (DORA) in 1915. Before then, you could drink when you
liked, with or without food. There was a partial relaxation in
1921; you could drink until 12.30 provided you ordered a
sandwich with it, but properly licensed night clubs could
operate until 2 a.m., with extensions in some cases. The sort
of clubs that were raided tended, on the whole, to be what
Margaret Argyll calls the 'rougher' sort – the kind that a
debutante's escort might go on to, in anticipation of a pick-
up, after dropping his society girlfriend home. Uncle's and
The Bat came into this category. Membership was more
often than not a matter of instant registration at the door,
with the 'seconders' provided by the head waiter or a black
jazzband drummer. This sort of thing happened at the more
respectable clubs too, but was accepted only if the proposer
was someone well known in society.

Of all the respectable clubs none had a more glamorous
reputation, or is more affectionately remembered today,
than the Embassy at 6–8 Old Bond Street, where the Prince
of Wales, the Mountbattens and their friends and Bendor
Westminster all had permanently reserved corner tables and
the legendary Luigi presided over nightly gatherings that
had the air of private parties transported from a nearby
house. 'Everybody in the room knew everybody,' as the
Duchess of Argyll said. The charm of the Embassy lay not
in its surroundings – 'it had an extremely plain and rather
elegant decor, very simple, red velvet sofas, mirrored walls
and white and gold all over' – but in the quality of its food
and wine, the first-rate dance bands of Jack Harris and Bert
Ambrose, and the indefinable magic of a great maître d'hôtel
who could orchestrate his guests, knew everybody's social
connections with everybody else (including those the
involved parties might not want known) and above all, was
supremely discreet.

'The Embassy had all the people you wanted to see,'
recalled the Duchess of Argyll. She and her friends Lady
Bridget Poulett and Rose Bingham – who married the Earl
of Warwick after Margaret Whigham jilted him – were about
the only unmarried women to be given membership. 'It was
a place where married ladies in their thirties and forties went
with their boyfriends, and it never got in the press, it was

never discussed, so they felt safe. We *lived* there, we lunched and dined there. It had wonderful bands, and the most wonderful food and wine.'

'You saw all your friends,' agreed Lady Lindsay, who met her first husband, the Duke of Westminster, as the result of an evening at the Embassy. 'It was like a private party every single night, and all most decorously done, nobody misbehaved, it was just the most marvellous party.' Thursday was the most fashionable night to be seen there: 'No hostess would have been so stupid as to give a party on that night,' Barbara Cartland recalled in her memoirs. Habitués of the Embassy included Lady Diana Cooper; Thelma, Lady Furness, and Freda Dudley Ward, both intimates of the Prince of Wales; the young Prince Aly Khan; Cecil Beaton; Michael Arlen; Viscount Castlerosse, the gossip writer; Max Aitken, son of Lord Beaverbrook; and the Mountbatten circle, among whom were the Earl and Countess of Brecknock, and Lady Alexandra 'Baba' Metcalfe and her husband, Major Edward 'Fruity' Metcalfe, ADC to the Prince of Wales. Lady Alexandra was the younger daughter of the formidable Lord Curzon. Before she was married, someone told the former Viceroy of India and Foreign Secretary that his daughter had been seen at the Embassy. He misunderstood and inquired: 'Which embassy?' On hearing it was a night club he angrily forbade her to go to such places.

The sofas lining the walls were reserved by Luigi for royalty and the famous; the Prince of Wales always sat on the left as you went in. Around the tiny parquet dance floor, tables packed the rest of the room. A staircase led up to a balcony, but it was not considered smart to sit there. Ambrose's band, which later moved to the May Fair Hotel (he was offered the enormous salary of £10,000 to go there in 1927) was regarded as the best in London, in an era of superlative dance bands. Ambrose knew the favourite tunes of all the Embassy regulars. 'You just waved to him as you went in, and soon he was playing one of your favourites,' said Lady Alexandra Metcalfe.

Bert Ambrose, a Londoner born in 1897, had been lured back to the Embassy, after a spell at the Clover Gardens in New York, by a telegram from the Prince of Wales: 'Come

back, we need you. Edward P.' The Prince was an enthusiastic but not particularly skilful dancer, judged by the
exacting standards of the time when, as Margaret Argyll
says, '*Everybody* danced – and fast, there was no shuffling
around.' He did, however, leave a lingering impression on
his partners, and not only because of his rank and eligibility:
Margaret Whigham, as she then was, remained struck by
the intense blue of his eyes and the 'curiously wistful
expression' in them. While Edward was on the dance floor
it was understood that the band would continue to play for
as long as he stayed there: Jack Harris's band at the Embassy
once had to play without stopping for nearly two hours.
Ambrose recounted in his later years how he would start
off a waltz slowly when the Prince was dancing and 'watch
him like a hawk until he got into the swing of things, and
then I would increase the tempo until he went whirling
away'. No wonder Edward thought no band could play a
waltz like Ambrose's.

'The Embassy and the Café de Paris, those were the great
places; we went from one to the other,' said Margaret Argyll.
She often lunched and dined at the Embassy on the same
day; a friend once asked her why she didn't keep a camp
bed there. The Café de Paris, opened in 1924 by Martin
Poulsen, a former head waiter at the Embassy, shared many
of its eminent patrons for the very good reason that Poulsen
took a copy of his old employer's membership list when he
left. In the following year, 1925, he opened the Kit-Cat Club
underneath the Capitol Cinema on the corner of Jermyn
Street and the Haymarket.

The Café de Paris, underneath the Rialto Cinema, was a
place with a great sense of occasion. It had twin staircases
curving down to the dance floor from a tiered balcony, a
design said by some to have been copied, with ill omen,
from the Palm Court on the Cunard liner *Lusitania*.

The Café was given its glittering reputation by the Prince
of Wales, who kept a promise made at the Embassy, that if
Poulsen ever opened his own place he would visit it. He
came three nights a week for a month and put it on the
social map. Accompanied by Freda Dudley Ward or his other
companion of the 1920s, Lady Furness, he would sit with a
party of friends at the first banquette table on the right of

the dance floor; this was known as 'the Royal Box' and that side of the room as 'the Royal Enclosure'. A large circular table at the edge of the floor was reserved for members of Buck's Club, including its founder, Captain Herbert Buckmaster of the Household Cavalry. Another regular with his own table was Viscount Castlerosse, the enormous Irish peer who wrote the Londoner's Log in the *Sunday Express*. He was usually accompanied by Doris Delavigne, the society beauty whom he later married. (The two other gossip columnists who haunted Mayfair parties were the Marquess of Donegal, known as 'Don', who courted Sheilah Graham before she met F. Scott Fitzgerald in Hollywood, and Tom Driberg, later the Labour MP, who was the first to use the William Hickey byline.)

The cabaret acts were famous: Marion Harris, Layton and Johnstone, Marlene Dietrich, Maurice Chevalier, the Yacht Club Boys, Josephine Baker, Beatrice Lillie and Douglas Byng. Unlike the Embassy, the Café (supposed to have inspired the phrase 'Café Society') employed dance hostesses. One of these, a darkly attractive Anglo-Indian girl called Estelle O'Brien Thompson, was talent-spotted by a Fox film executive, given a walk-on part and later changed her name to Merle Oberon. Another, a vivacious girl named Nora Turner with swept-back fair hair, married the wealthy industrialist Sir Bernard Docker and became a byword for ostentatious glamour in the 1950s with her gold-plated Daimler.

One evening when the star attraction was Marion Harris, who sang 'My Canary Has Circles under his Eyes' and 'Miss Otis Regrets', there were four kings sitting at one table – Greece, Norway, Spain and Portugal – while at another sat Noël Coward, Gertrude Lawrence, Clifton Webb, Bea Lillie and Gloria Swanson. One could rub shoulders with all these celebrities and enjoy the best entertainment in London, along with a seven-course dinner, for one guinea (£1.05) a head.

Smaller, more intimate clubs had their devotees. A favourite of Loelia Ponsonby's before she married the Duke was the tiny Bruton, in Bruton Mews off Berkeley Square. It had a spectacular glass dance floor, lit up from below. So did the Silver Slipper, in Regent Street, where exuberant dancers sometimes cracked the glass rectangles of which the floor was composed. The resident attraction here for years was Teddy Brown, the enormously fat xylophone virtuoso who was also a hit at the Café de Paris and other night spots. The clubs were expensive to drink in; a bottle of champagne cost twenty-five or thirty shillings (£1.25 or £1.50), while at this time a working man's wage for a week was about £3.00.

The bands were as good, or better, in the hotel ballrooms, and Mayfair nights in the 1920s and 1930s were alive with sweet and hot syncopation: the Starita brothers, Ray and Al, with their jazzy Piccadilly Players and Piccadilly Revels at the Piccadilly Hotel; Ambrose and later Harry Roy at the May Fair; Roy Fox at the Monseigneur at 215 Piccadilly; the Blue Lyres (an Ambrose combination) at the Dorchester; Sydney Lipton and his sweet-voiced daughter Celia at the Grosvenor House. Of the band singers the most distinctive, and still immediately recognizable on 1930s dance-band recordings, was Al Bowlly, a dark, intense-looking young man from Lourenço Marques in Portuguese East Africa, who strummed a guitar and crooned wistfully with several of the big star bands, chiefly those of Lew Stone, Ray Noble and Roy Fox.

Some Mayfair socialites found the hotel scene sedate – 'for tourists' was Margaret Whigham's opinion. 'The Berkeley was the one place you were allowed to go before you came out, but I thought it dreadfully dull.' The Berkeley, on the corner of Piccadilly and Berkeley Street, had opened in 1898, renamed from the St James's Hotel, which had been built on the site of the old Gloucester Coffee House. It was very fashionable between the wars for lunch, particularly with couples in the early stages of courtship; lunch in a back room there was a recognized prelude to an evening at the Café de Paris as the relationship progressed.

The bandleaders were gods of the Mayfair night with their brilliantined hair and gleaming white tie and tails. Most were Londoners, like Harry Roy, born in 1900, who led a band called the Lyricals at the opening of the Café de Paris and became a household name ten years later in 1934 at the May Fair, when his dance music, along with that of other top West End bandleaders, filled the airwaves with nightly broadcasts from the big hotels and restaurants. The following year he married, in a much-publicized wedding, Elizabeth Brooke, known as 'Princess Pearl', the daughter of the 'White Rajah', Sarawak's British Governor Sir Charles Vyner Brooke.

Billy Cotton, born in 1899 in London and the leader of a sophisticated night-club band before he adopted his Cockney stage persona, played at Ciro's; fellow Londoner Sydney Lipton made his debut at Grosvenor House in 1932 and continued there in charge of musical entertainment until 1972, though by then dance bands in hotels were a thing of the past. Jack Jackson, a Barnsley man with a Yorkshire brass band training, led a smooth band at the Dorchester from 1933 until the spring of 1939. Maurice Winnick, a native of Manchester, modelled the sound of his band on that of the Canadian Guy Lombardo; he followed Harry Roy into the May Fair in 1935 and also featured at the Dorchester in the early years of the war. Ray Noble, born in Brighton in 1907, opened at the Monseigneur in the autumn of 1932, as did Lew Stone's band, which later played at the Café de Paris and moved to the Dorchester during Battle of Britain summer in 1940. Jack Harris of the Embassy was an American; so was Roy Fox, who opened at the Café de Paris in September 1930 as 'The Whispering Cornettist'.

In an era when 'everybody danced', Mayfair with its glittering hotel ballrooms and enticing rhythms was the magnet for young men with style, whether or not they were rich enough to live up to it. Stockbrokers' clerks and impoverished subalterns from Aldershot would save for weeks to take a girl out, sometimes finding it necessary, as my father once did after his date chose the most expensive items from the Berkeley menu, to telephone a trusty friend in the regiment to rush round in a taxi with extra funds. For those who lived in Mayfair, however, private entertaining formed the core of most evenings, rounded off perhaps by a visit to one of the night spots. Parties went on all the time in the tall Georgian houses in the hinterland of Berkeley and Grosvenor squares. 'There was something going on every single night,' recalled Margaret, Duchess of Argyll. 'Often there were two or three things – there was endless choice.' But convention was still prim: an unmarried girl was not supposed to dine alone with a man, but in a party with another couple.

As a debutante Margaret Whigham had been the sensation of 1930: 'The most photographed girl in the country', said the *Sunday Chronicle*. Cartoonists portrayed her rather unkindly, with large, baleful eyes and a jutting square jaw at the end of a long neck. Her coming-out ball at 6 Audley Square, which her parents, on returning from New York, had rented for the season, was a large and spectacular affair on 1 May 1930. Ambrose's band played and the party over-flowed into the street where, according to one society-page report, a peer's son who had not had time to change into white tie and tails 'and therefore could not enter the house', held court in his car and was brought relays of food and drink by friends.

Debutante balls were followed a few weeks later by the presentation at Court, a stiffly formal affair of long white gowns, head-dresses crowned by Prince of Wales feathers and deep curtseys to the King and Queen. At Margaret Whigham's presentation, when Queen Mary alone presided, the curtseying debutante caught the eye of her first serious admirer, Prince Aly Khan, who was standing behind the throne. He was just nineteen and living near the Whighams in Aldford Street. Her parents made her break off their unofficial engagement and Aly Khan, she recalled in her memoirs, would sit alone in the Embassy night after night drinking orangeade and asking the band to play 'I've Got a Crush on You'.

Debutante parties were supposed to lay the foundations for a successful social life and, of course, a suitable marriage. Most of Margaret Whigham's contemporaries, like herself, were married at or by the age of twenty-one. In her case, she had turned down Lord Beaverbrook's heir, Max Aitken, and jilted the Earl of Warwick (a month before their planned wedding in Westminster Abbey) before marrying Charles Sweeny in Brompton Oratory in 1933. Coming-out parties were succeeded in due course by those of the famous and often formidable Mayfair hostesses: Lady Londonderry, Mrs Ronald Greville, Lady Cunard, Lady Colefax and Mrs James Corrigan. They dominated the gossip columns and their reputation for political influence was considerable, if over-

rated by those Fascist diplomats in London who set out to
court their favours. Von Ribbentrop, Hitler's Ambassador to
Britain, was particularly adept on the London social circuit
with his wine-merchant's urbanity and mid-Atlantic accent.
He was so frequently a guest at Londonderry House on Park
Lane that the MP and diarist Chips Channon referred to
him as 'the Londonderry Herr'.

Some hostesses were openly pro-Nazi, Maggie Greville
among them. Harold Nicolson loathed the atmosphere at
her dinner parties at 16 Charles Street, where Ribbentrop
and the Italian Ambassador, Count Grandi, flattered and
were fawned upon by sycophantic socialites. He expressed
hope in his diary for 1939 that Berlin and Rome would realize
that British will-power was concentrated 'not in Mayfair or
Cliveden [the Astor estate by the Thames] but in the prov-
inces. The harm which these silly, selfish hostesses do is
really immense. They convey to foreign envoys the
impression that policy is decided in their own drawing-
rooms . . . these people have a subversive influence.'

Mrs Greville, whose husband had been a close friend of
Edward VII, owed her influence to the number of royal
acquaintances she cultivated, both at home and abroad. She
was small, round and fat and looked, in her god-daughter's
words, like 'a small Chinese idol'. She was possibly the
biggest snob in Mayfair and was noted for that memorable
piece of one-upmanship: 'One uses up *so* many red carpets
in a season.' Beverley Nichols, who recorded the remark,
said 'there were enchanted nights in the Twenties when the
people around Grosvenor Square were giving so many
grand parties that the pavements were as bright as a sunset'.
Indeed, a king or other crowned head was frequently in
attendance at Maggie Greville's dinners where, out of sixty
or so guests, fifty might be titled. The Duke and Duchess
of York spent their honeymoon in 1923 at her Surrey estate,
Polesden Lacey, and continued after they became King and
Queen to visit 16 Charles Street up until February 1939. (The
Queen, now the Queen Mother, was bequeathed all Mrs
Greville's magnificent jewellery.)

Other hostesses were less politically naive, and their
parties were also more fun. The two most fondly remembered today are Emerald Cunard and Florence de Peña.

Madame de Peña, the American widow of a rich Argentine, was neither so witty nor so famous as Lady Cunard, but the parties at her house in Charles Street were among the most sought-after invitations in Mayfair. They would begin with cocktails from 6 p.m. to 9 p.m., when a fresh group of perhaps fifty guests would arrive for dinner. Afterwards, a band would play for dancing until six in the morning. Favoured friends usually managed to stay on for the whole night's entertainment.

The secret of Emerald Cunard's success as a hostess (she had been born plain Maud Burke in California but acquired her nickname after she married the wealthy, middle-aged Sir Bache Cunard of the shipping family and became famous for her jewels) was not only her conversation, which was sparkling and faintly acid, like young champagne, but for her ability to orchestrate the conversation of others. 'She'd throw out some absolutely outrageous remark to stimulate people, and she had all the interesting people of the day: writers, painters, musicians,' recalled Lady Lindsay. 'She was also very interested in the young – I adored her.' Although she could put a young guest terrifyingly into the spotlight – 'Little Loelia will tell us what she thinks about Proust now' – she could make the most stumbling effort seem a sparkling contribution with a few witty comments of her own.

She lived at 7 Grosvenor Square on the corner of Brook Street, having left Sir Bache in 1911 to vegetate in his garden at gloomy Nevill Holt, the Cunard mansion in Leicestershire. Emerald was a chronic insomniac who spent her wakeful hours devouring the classics, from which she was liable to spring a Greek aphorism on her luncheon guests the next day. 'Emerald was a brilliantly clever woman, marvellously well read,' said Lady Lindsay. 'I remember going to one dinner party where Isaiah Berlin was one of the guests and she talked about a sonnet written by Pushkin and someone quoted the first verse in Russian. That was the sort of person she had at her parties.'

She was not a political hostess, though Chips Channon thought she was 'rather *éprise*' with Ribbentrop, and there was gossip that she influenced Edward VIII to pro-Nazi sympathies through Mrs Simpson. She did have some influence with the King because she openly backed Mrs Simpson when other London hostesses sided with the dislodged royal favourites Freda Dudley Ward and Thelma, Lady Furness. Channon recorded one white-tie dinner at his home in Belgrave Square when, arriving after the King was already seated at the table, Emerald slipped into the chair beside him and proceeded to 'put in a word' for one of her friends, Philip Sassoon, who wanted a civil service appointment.

After Emerald gave up her Grosvenor Square house at the outbreak of war, Channon wrote that it had been a place where

> statesmen consorted with society, and writers with the rich – and where, for over a year, the drama of Edward VIII was enacted. It had a rococo atmosphere – the conversation in the candlelight, the elegance, the bibelots and the books: more, it was a rallying point for most of London society: only those that were too stupid to amuse the hostess, and so were not invited, were disdainful. The Court always frowned on so brilliant a salon: indeed Emerald's only failures were the two Queens and Lady Astor and Lady Derby. Everyone else flocked, if they had the chance. To some it was the most consummate bliss even to cross her threshold. She is as kind as she is witty, and her curious mind, and the lilt of wonder in her voice when she says something calculatedly absurd, are quite unique.

She was small and birdlike, with glittering eyes heavily made up with mascara, and a 'pretty, wrinkled, Watteau face', as Channon described it. Her voice was birdlike too, trilling and swooping 'like the springtime song of a delighted canary', in Peter Quennell's words. She had tiny ankles and feet which she lifted up and down in an unmistakable, prancing gait 'like a temperamental racehorse being led to the paddock', recalled another friend. The many eminent men whom she enslaved were hyperbolic in their compliments. The novelist George Moore, who loved her for years, said her entrance into a room was like 'unpremeditated music'. Sir Harold Acton spoke of her quickening presence, like wind rustling through a room.

All sorts of nonsense sparkled off her like miniature fireworks [wrote James Lees-Milne]. Emerald gets gay on one sip of cherry brandy and pours forth stories helter-skelter, wholly unpremeditated in an abandoned, halting, enquiring manner that appears to be ingenuous, and is deliberate. Her charm can be devastating.

Flashes of her quicksilver, disconcerting conversational style are preserved by Brian Masters in his entertaining book *Great Hostesses*. She would introduce people with a flurry of *non sequiturs:* 'This is Mr Evan Morgan, who looks like the poet Shelley and whose mother makes birds' nests.' 'This is Lord Alington, dear. He drives in a taxi at dawn from Paris to Rome, wearing evening dress and a gardenia, *without any luggage.*' She once demolished a ponderously dull American businessman by asking him at dinner: 'Now Mr Taylor, what do you think about incest?' As the unfortunate man struggled with some solemn reply about genetic effects she broke in with 'But what about Siegmund and Sieglinde?' and proceeded to sing the finale to Act 1 of *The Valkyrie*, the scene where brother and sister go off into the night as lovers. When Somerset Maugham, whose homosexuality was discreetly veiled from public knowledge, left one of her parties early, explaining his early bedtimes by saying 'I have to keep my youth', she retorted: 'Then why don't you bring him with you?'

Other hostesses renowned for their parties included Mrs Richard Guinness of the brewing family, who had show-business stars like Noël Coward and Cecil Beaton. Coward and Emerald Cunard did not get on: she disapproved of his theatrical habit of calling her 'Darling' and thought him common. Mrs Laura Corrigan, whose parties had burst upon London in the early 1920s, was always regarded as some-thing of a joke, though few refused one of her lavish invi-tations. (An exception was George Bernard Shaw, who, on receiving an engraved card reading 'Mrs Corrigan At Home 6–8 p.m.', sent it back with the scribbled comment 'GBS

Ditto'.) The socially ambitious wife of a Cleveland steel
millionaire, she was the butt of many classic nouveau-riche
stories. When she was negotiating to rent Alice Keppel's
exquisitely furnished house at 16 Grosvenor Street for her
first London season in 1921, she was asked to look after the
Persian carpets with particular care. 'Why, they're not even
new,' she exclaimed. Nevertheless, she managed not only to
secure the services of Mrs Keppel's butler, cook and twenty
indoor servants, but also the use of Mrs Keppel's visitors'
book, which launched her into London society.

Laura Corrigan spent recklessly in pursuit of social
success: some of her 'surprise' parties, which might feature
night-club cabaret acts or mock raffles with 'prizes' of Cartier
jewellery for eminent guests, cost as much as £6000. She
paid nearly £500 a week for the Keppel house, a year's
salary in the early 1920s for many professional men. Her
malapropisms were retailed gleefully around Mayfair
drawing rooms. She said Mrs Keppel's Chippendale chairs
were spoiled by the 'petit pois' covering them, and that a
certain cathedral she had visited had magnificent 'flying
buttocks'. She told John Gielgud after his performance as
Hamlet that she knew the Danish royal family intimately,
and when someone asked whether she had seen the
Dardanelles while on a cruise of the eastern Mediterranean,
she replied that she had been given a letter of introduction
to them but hadn't sent it.

But few failed to be won over by her good-heartedness
and generosity, and her parties were exuberantly in tune
with the 1920s mood. Sometimes the guests provided their
own entertainment by singing, performing exhibition dances
– Mrs Corrigan excelled at the Charleston – or playing the
ukelele. The Mountbattens and their circle, Viscount
Weymouth (now the Marquess of Bath) and other young
socialites – Lygons, Barings and Plunkets – took part with
relish, and occasionally there would be a minor member of
the royal family such as Prince George of Kent.

Fancy-dress parties were the Mayfair vogue in the 1920s:
the grandest, according to the then Loelia Ponsonby, being
those given by the Duchess of Sutherland at Hampden
House in Green Street, which had a garden and a tennis
court at the back. At her 1926 ball a party of girls dressed

up as the Eton rowing eight and 'rowed' themselves into the ballroom in a real boat, coxed by Duff Cooper. Lord Birkenhead, the famous advocate F. E. Smith, went as Captain Hook and his twelve-year-old daughter Pamela (later Lady Pamela Berry) as Peter Pan. In 1928 the young dress designer Norman Hartnell threw a 'Circus Party' at Strathmore House, the Duke and Duchess of York's town house at 17 Bruton Street where Princess Elizabeth had been born. He turned the ballroom into a circus ring; Ferraro, the head waiter of the Berkeley, provided a buffet decorated by circus animals carved in green ice; there were real performing wolves and acrobats, and Lady Eleanor Smith, Lord Birkenhead's elder daughter, who had worked for a time in a circus, rode a white pony up the stairs.

A frequent *pièce de résistance* at Laura Corrigan's parties was the sight of the hostess standing on her head; peculiarly fascinating in view of the fact that all London knew she wore a wig, or a series of wigs, depending on the occasion. There was a windswept one for visits to the country, a freshly coiffeured one for town, a dishevelled one for sleeping in. Only once was it known to have been dislodged, when she dived into a friend's swimming pool at Henley: stoically, as Brian Masters related in *Great Hostesses*, she stayed under water until 'she had retrieved the soggy object and replaced it firmly on her head'.

Mrs Corrigan was fortunate in acquiring, along with Alice Keppel's butler, Rolfe, the services of his wife, an exceptional cook. In the 1920s and 1930s the eating-out habit was not yet developed. Opportunities were limited to hotel dining rooms, old-fashioned chop-houses and a few solid, traditional restaurants like Rule's, Simpson's, Frascati's and Oddenino's. For women lunching together the Ritz was a favourite with its pretty, painted dining room overlooking Green Park. But people with houses in Mayfair and the staff to run them usually lunched and dined at home and entertained each other. 'The food was very good in the private houses,' said Loelia Lindsay. Twenty for luncheon was nothing unusual, and the guests might include a good sprinkling of businessmen, MPs and government ministers. 'People had more leisure then, they lunched all over the place.' There was usually a white wine such as hock at luncheon parties, but comparatively abstemious drinking; at balls, however, it was different. 'People got drunk at balls, but drugging was *totally* out,' said Lady Lindsay.

Mayfair women in the 1930s dressed, as their Edwardian predecessors had done, for separate parts of the day. 'We changed four times a day if we were going out to lunch as well as dinner,' said Margaret Argyll. 'We dressed to the nines for lunch, with hats that would be too grand for Ascot now. One never went to dinner in a short dress, or to cocktails in a long one.' Maids were still cheap and plentiful to care for all these formal clothes: the pleated silks and crêpes-de-chines, the linens and lamés and slipper satin, the georgettes and starched piqués. 'Even those who lived in flats had a cook and a maid, and there were wonderful maids to wash and iron – one didn't have any wrinkle-proof clothes then,' said Lady Lindsay. 'I can remember the white kid gloves we all wore, and how they smelled to high heaven when they came back from the cleaners, so hard, like steel, that you could hardly jam your fingers in.'

Men were also on sartorial parade throughout the prewar Mayfair day. In the early 1930s they wore hats and gloves with lounge suits, carried canes and sported a rosebud or carnation in the lapel, bought from one of the many flower-sellers in the West End. At night they wore white tie, stiff wing collar, boiled shirt with ornamental studs (until soft piqué shirts came in for the adventurous), white waistcoat and tails, all this for dinner parties as well as formal balls, the theatre or a West End night club. The heir to the throne was responsible for loosening up much of this starchy formality, though his taste for American fashions was not wholly approved by Mayfair society. 'All those loud checks,' said Lady Lindsay. 'He wasn't admired for his dressing, but he was very much talked about.' According to her it was not the Prince of Wales who was the first to start wearing a dinner jacket to white-tie occasions, as others have said, but the Duke of Marlborough's younger brother, Lord Ivor Churchill. He wore a white waistcoat with it, as did Michael Arlen, the dandyish Armenian-born novelist of whom it was unkindly said he was more 'brilliantine' than brilliant.

The second Duke of Westminster, the richest man in Europe, whose income was reputed to be twice that of King

George V, rarely dined out in restaurants when he was married to his third wife, Loelia Ponsonby. In the two or three days a month which were all they would spend in London, they usually lunched and dined with guests in the panelled splendour of Bourdon House in Davies Street, which was kept fully staffed (including six housemaids) whether or not the Westminsters were in residence. On the rare occasions when they dined out together it was invariably at the Savoy, where Bendor always ordered the same dish, boiled chicken and rice with onion sauce. Bendor became quickly bored by London, preferring Paris, his villa in the south of France, his Scottish retreat at Lochmore or, best of all, being on the move around the playgrounds of Europe in one of his yachts, *Flying Cloud* or *Cutty Sark*. During their marriage, the longest he and Loelia were ever in one place together was three weeks.

They had met early in 1929 in appropriately glamorous circumstances. Loelia was in a party at the Embassy Club when a message arrived to say the Duke of Westminster and Lord Beaverbrook would shortly be joining them. 'The Duke of Westminster!' wrote Loelia in her memoirs.

> But how can I explain what he represented? He stood for dash, glamour and fast living. . . . I had a vague idea that he was immensely rich, owned great slabs of Mayfair and Belgravia and shot, hunted, played polo, cruised about the world in a yacht, had been married twice and was a legend, almost a myth. . . .

(Noël Coward's comedy *Private Lives*, produced in 1930, had the warring ex-spouses, Elyot and Amanda, refer to a yacht in the bay beneath their hotel balcony: 'Whose yacht is that?' 'The Duke of Westminster's, I expect, it always is.') The meeting in fact took place not at the Embassy but later that evening at Bourdon House, which still retained something of the style of the country house it had been in early Georgian times among the fields and farms north of Grosvenor Square. (It is now occupied by Mallett's, the fine art dealers.) Loelia was struck by its beautiful old panelling, with 'a patina like an old bronze statue', and by the works of art with which the house was crammed, including ranks of Grosvenor family portraits by Gainsborough. The Duke, then nudging fifty, was an imposing figure with fair to reddish hair, blue eyes and a debonair manner. With him were Beaverbrook and Loelia's cousin Valentine Castlerosse, the gossip columnist. They all went on to the Café de Paris and when that closed its doors at 2 a.m., the Duke swept them back to Bourdon House where he had summoned up an elaborate cold buffet, a dance band and the black crooner Hutch (Leslie A. Hutchinson), the most popular entertainer in Mayfair. The Duke drove Loelia home in his Rolls-Royce and invited her to a shooting party the next day at Eaton, his Cheshire estate.

From then on she was showered with invitations and flowers, yet the courtship was curiously restrained for a man of Bendor's reputation. Loelia records in her memoirs that it was not until the following Christmas that he kissed her goodnight for the first time – after casually proposing marriage as they drove past Caxton Hall. They were engaged that week, married in February 1930 at the register office in Buckingham Palace Road, and Bendor gave all his tenants a free week's rent and cancelled all arrears.

It was a disastrous marriage. Loelia herself, living in old age in an unpretentiously comfortable Georgian rectory in the depths of Surrey, remained discreetly reticent about its worst excesses, but she and Bendor had blazing rows. There were black explosions of jealousy on his part, and on one occasion a Cartier clock she prized was splintered against the bedroom wall. At fifty Bendor could not accept that he was middle-aged: his daughter Ursula was older than his bride. The marriage essentially ended in 1935 although it was another sixteen years before it was formally dissolved. At the height of the Blitz Loelia was forced to sell her magnificent jewellery for £8000; its value today, she estimated, would be around £500,000.

As landlord of Mayfair and Belgravia, Bendor took little interest in the business side, though he cared for the architecture and its preservation. He left the finances to factors and estate managers and, not surprisingly, was spectacularly bilked by one of them. 'He was like a king, without the responsibilities of a king,' said Loelia. Chips Channon described him as 'a mixture of Henry VIII and Lorenzo Il

Magnifico . . . restless, spoilt, irritable and rather splendid in a very English way. He was fair, handsome, lavish; yet his life was an empty failure.' He scoffed woundingly at his wife when she tried to do good works on the estates. 'He would tell me they were sniggering behind my back for trying to play Lady Bountiful.' His one abiding interest outside his own pleasures was the Empire, and he sent an astute agent around the Dominions buying property, which resulted in the Grosvenor estates overseas becoming greatly enlarged under his stewardship; they own half of Sydney to this day. When he died in 1953 the £1 million of property he had inherited from 'Daddy Westminster' in 1899 stood at a value of £10 million overseas and £6 million at home – some compensation for the loss of 'The Blue Boy' to America.

Mayfair society continued its nightly revels as the Czechoslovakia crisis of 1938 deepened, trenches were dug in the parks and sandbags distributed in unreal preparation for war. Three months before Chamberlain's flight to Munich, Chips Channon (who wrote admiringly of the Prime Minister, 'I don't know what the country has done to deserve him') recorded a vignette of the Establishment at play on the night of 22 June 1938:

> We dined with the indefatigable Laura Corrigan, a
> festival of 137 people, all the youth and fashion of
> London with the Kents enjoying themselves wildly and
> leading the revels. . . . There is a new dance called The
> Palais Glide which smacks of the servants' hall, and,
> lubricated with champagne, the company pranced
> about doing this absurd 'pas' till 4 a.m. Leslie (Hore)
> Belisha was in the gayest of moods and 'cracked the
> dawn', as did half the Cabinet. In spite of the general
> frivolity of the evening, I gleaned some news – i.e., that
> the King is sound, and is very against Anthony Eden,
> who, in two years, has caused us more trouble than
> any Foreign Secretary since Palmerston.

11

'GIVE US BACK OUR BAD, OLD WORLD'

WAR came to London in a burst of brilliant sunshine, following a mighty thunderstorm on the night of Saturday, 2 September, a real as well as symbolic clearing of the atmosphere after weeks of humid cloud and uncertainty. But the air of unreality persisted. 'It was an awful anti-climax,' said Margaret, Duchess of Argyll, then Mrs Charles Sweeny and a leader of Mayfair society. 'We were all geared up and nothing happened. One siren went off.' After that first false air-raid warning, as Neville Chamberlain's weary tones faded from the nation's wireless sets, no one quite knew what to do next. Some sat with their gas-masks on, expecting London to be deluged with the invisible weapon that had been dreaded since its first use on the Ypres salient in 1915. Others, like Margaret Sweeny's father, George Hay Whigham, methodically set about moving their families to safety in the country.

Whigham himself took a suite in the Dorchester, whose pre-stressed concrete construction was reputed to make it the safest hotel in London. His daughter, who also stayed at the Dorchester on weekdays, recalls the efficiency with which he taped up the windows of their narrow house (just eighteen feet across its frontage) at 48 Upper Grosvenor Street against bomb blast, disconnected all the telephones and electrical appliances, turned off the water, locked up and left. At the end of the war Margaret Sweeny walked back in and found everything undamaged and in working order. 'Nobody could get a telephone just after the war and I had at least eight. People could have killed me!'

Some Mayfair residents had no option but to give up their homes. Lady Freda Valentine, daughter of the Earl of Lanesborough and married to a London doctor, had been warned by a German fellow guest at a country-house party in August to move herself and her children out of their Green Street home. Heinrich Brüning, the German Chancellor who had been forced out of office in 1932, told her that the Nazis would not declare war but would arrive without warning and bomb London to destruction. The Valentines began house-hunting immediately and found a suitable retreat in Northamptonshire. Their house at 26 Green Street, however, was already one of several in that area earmarked for government requisition as billets for foreign diplomatic and military personnel. Lady Freda found lodgings elsewhere, moving in the winter of 1941 into the lofty set of chambers in Albany which she still inhabited in her ninetieth year in 1985. Albany had been hit by a stick of incendiaries shortly before she arrived and several sets destroyed at the Vigo Street end; Lady Freda's kitchen roof in A11 was partly burned out and all the windows were broken and patched with brown paper. From her sitting room she saw, across the rooftops to the north, the raids on King's Cross and Euston railway stations lighting up the horizon like a titanic fireworks display. During raids she was a familiar if eccentric sight to other residents, bustling about in her tin hat and Schiaparelli silk dressing-gown. (Edith Evans, appearing in *Heartbreak House* in 1943, also had her Albany chambers blitzed.)

Those first days of brilliant weather brought a procession of slow-moving vehicles on the arterial roads out of London; coaches full of children bound for indefinite exile in the country, cars and London taxis heavily laden with luggage. The diarist Henry 'Chips' Channon noted how the great houses of Mayfair were being closed down one by one: Hampden House in Green Street, where the Duke and Duchess of Sutherland, Lady Freda Valentine's cousins, had presided over brilliant prewar parties; Londonderry House in Park Lane. There were 'house-coolings', farewell parties marking not only the end of the feverish summer season of 1939 but that of a world about to be swept away. 'It is said that the houses of the great will never again open their hospitable doors,' lamented Channon. 'Emerald [Cunard], too, is trying to sell her house. It would indeed be the end of a chapter, were that to go.'

Yet West End social life continued, transferred to hotels, restaurants and night clubs. The Ritz, Claridge's and the Berkeley were heavily booked, their stately commissionaires quickly adapting to the sight of fashionable young women, now engaged in government jobs, riding up for luncheon dates on bicycles. In the evening dinner dresses and black ties mingled with uniforms on the dance floors of the Embassy, Hatchett's, Ciro's, Quaglino's and the Café de Paris. Noël Coward and Ralph Richardson joined the navy, but Charles Cochran announced in a letter to *The Times* that his young ladies were standing by for the autumn revue he still intended to produce. The West End theatres did close for a few weeks, but most reopened in October. Business thrived in the West End shops, though displays of jewellery and pigskin in Bond Street were heavily framed by protective boarding. Mollie Panter-Downes, the Englishwoman who reported the home front for the *New Yorker* magazine in her weekly 'Letter from London', said women were buying 'sensible things like tweed suits tough enough to last the three years for which everyone has been told to prepare, and smart slacks or house coats in which to brighten up their air raid shelters'.

A month after the outbreak of war, she reported:

In London one never hears an airplane. . . . the
fashionable periodicals, such as *Tatler* and *Sketch*, are
carrying on gamely, though in somewhat leaner form,
since the death of the social season did them out of
most of their glossy prey. Unable to photograph peers
on shooting sticks, they get along as best they can with
peeresses driving ambulances, debutantes trundling fire
hose, and young Guardees trundling debutantes
around the Café de Paris. . . .

Elizabeth Arden advertised her Bond Street salon as a place where members of the women's services could meet their friends, take a shower and telephone. (She also recommended 'Burnt Sugar' as the lipstick colour to go with khaki.) Mayfair hat and dress designers including Digby Morton and Aage Thaarup joined Miss Arden in taking touring fashion shows to the women's forces. Scott's, the Bond Street hatters, continued their prewar custom of making deliveries in a smartly turned out horse-drawn carriage, the only difference being that the coachman and footman on the box wore tin hats instead of cockaded toppers.

Battle of Britain summer in 1940 brought noticeable changes. The fear of an imminent invasion caused a rush to travel agents by parents wanting to evacuate their children to a safe neutral country; Thomas Cook's office in Berkeley Street was inundated. Italy's entry into the war on the side of the Axis powers brought the internment on the Isle of Man of many popular Italian restaurateurs like the Bertorelli brothers, Charles Forte (who has never quite got over the experience), Ferraro of the Berkeley and the Quaglinos. It also brought about curious changes of employment. When Alfredo Campoli, the concert violinist, was released from internment on condition that he worked anonymously, he took a job with Victor Silvester's dance band.

The great hostesses of Mayfair continued to hold court, but from suites in the 'safe' Dorchester rather than Georgian houses in Grosvenor Square or Charles Street. Emerald Cunard returned from the United States to find that bombs had destroyed 7 Grosvenor Square. She moved what furniture she could salvage into suite 707 on a seventh-floor corner of the Dorchester overlooking Hyde Park. Here, with paintings stacked underneath her bed and the three rooms filled to bursting with buhl and ormolu furniture, she gave dinner parties almost nightly at which Cabinet ministers and war leaders mixed with writers, painters and attractive women. Even on the night in February 1943 when she learned that her great love of thirty years' duration, Sir Thomas Beecham, had married in New York, she kept up a sparkling facade, doing what Lady Diana Cooper called 'a

Marie Antoinette' and directing a stream of brilliant conversation that ranged from Henry James to cock-fighting.

In another Dorchester suite Emerald's great rival Sibyl Colefax, who set out single-handedly to cement Anglo-American understanding while wartime links still largely depended on sentiment and Lend-Lease, held monthly suppers she called 'Ordinaries', for which guests were each sent a bill for 10s. 6d. Harold Nicolson called them 'ghastly functions', but they were always packed and appeared to fulfil their purpose. 'She manages us firmly as if we had all come to the Dorchester to give a blood-transfusion,' grumbled Nicolson.

The third legendary hostess to hold court at the Dorchester was the last of the Edwardians, Maggie Greville, who had cultivated the Nazi diplomats before the war but now rose to the shattering turn of events with indomitable spirit. Very old, lame and nearly blind, confined to a wheelchair but still bravely decked out in the dazzling Greville jewels, she continued to attract the great to her salon until her death in September 1941: the King of Greece, whom Chips Channon said was embarrassed by the rich food because it made him think of his starving compatriots; the Mountbattens, the Kents, Churchill's right-hand man Brendan Bracken. The author Beverley Nichols wrote of her courage in choosing to live high up in the hotel and of her delight in inviting nervous friends or those of whose war record she disapproved to come and keep her company during raids. They seldom refused: 'It was easier to brave the Luftwaffe than to incur Maggie's displeasure.'

Lady Cunard viewed the war as a vulgar inconvenience and tried to make the best of it, enjoying those occasions when air-raid warnings prevented dinner guests from leaving; ringing friends like Cecil Beaton at 4 a.m. for ninety-minute chats; retreating, when the bombs came uncomfortably close, under a table to read Shakespeare or Proust in preference to making for the Dorchester's air-raid shelter. This was situated in what had been the hotel's Turkish baths in the basement. Conditions there were sardonically contrasted by the American journalist Ralph Ingersoll with the sweaty, overcrowded shelters in the East End and the tube-station platforms lined with sleeping bodies:

A neat row of cots, spaced about two feet apart, each
one covered with a lovely fluffy eiderdown. Its silks
billowed and shone in the dim lights in pale pinks and
blues. By each cot the mules and the slippers.
Alongside, the little table with the alligator-skin dressing-
case. The pillows on which the heads lay were large
and full and white. . . . They did not sleep as well as
the heads slept in the Liverpool Street tube. Even
though it was 3 a.m. and we tiptoed, most of them raised
off the pillows and eyed us defensively. There was a
little sign pinned to one of the Turkish-bath curtains. It
said, 'Reserved for Lord Halifax'.

Halifax was not the only government minister to take up
residence in the Dorchester, which advertised itself as being
safe from anything short of a direct hit and was also
convenient for Whitehall and Westminster. (When the
bombing began in earnest, the grill room and restaurant,
covered only with roof gardens and outside the central structure of the hotel, were transferred to the ballroom lounge
and another large ground-floor room, protected by the thick
concrete raft which carried the eight bedroom floors above.)
Duff Cooper with his glamorous wife Lady Diana, Oliver
Stanley, Oliver Lyttelton (later Lord Chandos) and Lord
Portal, Chief of the Air Staff, were others who found it a
convenient haven. Portal had a third-floor semi-suite
protected enough from the noise of the raids to allow him
four hours' sleep a night. It consisted of bedsitting room,
bathroom and lobby, with access to another room which he,
his wife Joan and their daughter Rosemary, when on leave
from the WAAF, could use when it was not otherwise
required by the hotel. For this accommodation, obtained for
them through the King's air equerry, Group Captain Sir
Louis Greig, who was a director of the Dorchester, they paid
£5 a week, flowers included.

Many others, of less value to the war effort, had flocked
to this bastion of luxury and security in the first days of
war. In September 1940 the young Canadian diplomat
Charles Ritchie wrote in his diary:

In the Dorchester the sweepings of the Riviera have been

washed up . . . pot-bellied, sallow, sleek-haired
nervous gentlemen with loose mouths and wobbly chins,
wearing suede shoes and checked suits, and thin
painted women with fox capes and long silk legs and
small artificial curls clustering around their bony,
sheep-like heads.

In October, dining there, he observed that the hotel
resembled

a luxury liner on which the remnants of London society
have embarked in the midst of this storm. Through the
thick walls and above the music of the band one could
hear the noise of the barrage and at intervals the
building shook like a vibrating ship with the shock of an
exploding bomb falling nearby.

A month later he wrote:

It certainly feels safe in this enormous hotel. I simply
cannot believe that bombs would dare to penetrate this
privileged enclosure or that they could touch all these
rich people. Cabinet Ministers and Jewish lords are not
killed in air-raids – that is the inevitable illusion that this
place creates. It is a fortress propped up with money
bags.

Cecil Beaton was another who took a jaundiced view of
his fellow guests at the Dorchester.

The noise outside is drowned with wine, music and
company – and what a mixed brew we are! Cabinet
ministers and their self-consciously respectable wives;
hatchet-jawed, iron-grey brigadiers; calf-like airmen off
duty; tarts on duty, actresses . . . *declassé* society people,
cheap musicians and motor-car agents. It could not be
more ugly and vile, and yet I have not the strength of
character to remain, like Harold Acton, with a book.

Chips Channon saw the hotel as 'a modern wartime
Babylon'. One evening in November 1940 he wrote: 'London

lives well: I've never seen more lavishness, more money spent, or more food consumed than tonight. The dance floor was packed. There must have been a thousand people.'

Girls went out for the evening knowing that the safest place to be caught in a raid was one of the big hotels or night clubs. The American journalist Basil Woon wrote at the height of the Blitz in September 1940:

> You can dance, dine and sleep at Hatchett's, the Hungaria, the Lansdowne, the Mayfair and Grosvenor House. When a girl goes out for the evening these days she brings her pyjamas and make-up with her. This has led to some interesting situations, and it certainly gives the girls an excuse for not getting home till morning.

The Grosvenor House provided a scene of less febrile glamour than the Dorchester, but it saw more momentous comings and goings among the exiled leaders of occupied Europe. Like the Dorchester, it was buttressed with sandbags – ten thousand of them – and darkened at night with over five miles of blackout material. The Great Room, once a fashionable playground for young Mayfair society, was turned into a vast dormitory for ARP wardens and then, in the summer of 1940, became a special annexe to the US immigration department where hundreds of anxious mothers and children waited for visas to the States. After the fall of France and the Low Countries, resistance groups gathered there for rallying addresses: the Dutch Cabinet made the hotel its wartime headquarters; General de Gaulle gave a rousing speech to 700 Free French on Bastille Day, 1941; General Sikorski rallied the exiled Poles, King Haakon the Norwegians and Queen Wilhelmina of the Netherlands, on a visit to London from her exile in Canada, received members of the Dutch colony.

In 1943 the Great Room underwent vast structural alterations to become the main US officers' mess in London. It was known, from its vast size, as Willow Run – a place outside Detroit famed for producing B24 Liberators – and before it reverted to civilian use at the end of 1945 more than five and a half million cafeteria meals were served there. The Turkish baths became a gas decontamination

centre and thirty-eight of the hotel's depleted staff formed
a Home Guard platoon, often drilling on the roof, where a
miniature rifle range had been installed for firing practice.

In September 1940 London's phoney war came violently
to an end with the massive air-raids on the docks and the
East End. On the 13th Buckingham Palace was dive-bombed
and three days later Mayfair was hit for the first time when
an explosion in Park Lane blasted Londonderry House.
General Raymond E. Lee, the US Military Attaché in
London, observed tartly in his journal: 'I could only wonder
what that chump Londonderry thinks now of his friends
Hitler, Ribbentrop and Goering, with whom he was so
chummy a short time ago.' Raids on that and ensuing nights
also destroyed the John Lewis department store and two
others on Oxford Street; reduced a beautiful block of Georgian houses on the north-west corner of Berkeley Square to
rubble, and gutted the historic Bond Street premises of
Gieves, the naval and military tailors. The northern end of
the Burlington Arcade was shattered, and Georgian houses
on Dover and Albemarle streets were 'opened up like doll's
houses', as Mollie Panter-Downes recorded.

General Lee, who was occupying a fourth-floor corner
suite in Claridge's for one and a half guineas a day (other
American officers paid £1 a day for room and bath), noted
with curiosity how the bombing revealed eighteenth-century
jerry-building behind the elegant facades. 'The materials
from which these Georgian buildings were constructed were
shockingly second-rate. . . . This goes even for houses in
fashionable squares. The lumber is cheap, splintery and full
of knotholes.'

He was more impressed by the durability of one of
Mayfair's oldest institutions, the prostitutes. 'I particularly
admire the little tarts who wander about the streets of
Mayfair every afternoon and evening in their finery. When
everyone else is hurrying for the air-raid shelters, they are
quite indifferent and continue to stroll unperturbed.'

October brought more widespread destruction. The
former Rothschild mansion at 145 Piccadilly, home of the
Duke and Duchess of York before they became King George
VI and Queen Elizabeth, was destroyed; General Gort's
house in Hill Street was hit twice, 'as though the Germans

knew its exact location', remarked Lee. On the night a bomb went through the roof of St Paul's and wrecked the high altar (precursor to the more serious raid of 29 December), two huge bombs fell at the junction of Davies and Grosvenor streets. Savile Row was 'fairly battered to pieces', wrote Lee, adding, 'All the glass is out in Bond Street and Regent Street. Not a shop in Conduit Street has any glass in it.' Brook Street received four hits and Bond Street was again badly damaged on 15 October, the night St James's, the Wren church in Piccadilly, was hit along with the Carlton Club and 10 Downing Street. The 'In and Out' Club at 94 Piccadilly was virtually sliced in half. On the 25th a bomb hit 6 Grosvenor Square, the former home and embassy occupied by US Ambassador Walter Page during the First World War; it had been used as a barracks for the balloon company which tended the great silver barrage balloon tethered in Grosvenor Square's central garden.

Saddest of all, perhaps, was the destruction of Mayfair's village heart which began that October. The night the In and Out was wrecked saw the end of Shepherd Street in Shepherd Market, which still had its butcher's shop, fishmonger, greengrocer, oil and candle store and two pubs. After the raid, as the writer Robert Henrey, who lived in the neighbourhood, reported, boxes of sardines mingled in the road with smashed bottles of perfume from the ladies' hairdresser. Mayfair's oldest house was gone. Once a shepherd's cottage when fields surrounded it, the little building had 'The Cottage, 1618 AD' written over its oak postern gate, from which hung a brass lantern. That night it was smashed to matchwood, its James I rafters scattered amid rubble in the tiny garden. The bomb had struck a pub opposite, killing the barmaid as she sheltered under a billiard table in the cellar. A saddler's shop nearby was also destroyed.

A few months later, walking through the rubble that had been Jermyn Street's smart shops, and watching Christie's burning fiercely, its great staircase outlined redly in the heart of the fire, Robert Henrey commented sadly: 'The West End was writhing. . . . Its ancient landmarks were passing away. The next generation would not know it as we had.'

General Raymond E. Lee, the detached American

observer, saw things a bit differently. From his eyrie in
Claridge's, where one night he saw fifteen buildings blazing
round about, with the hotel at the eye of the storm, he
perceived that the ruin of the West End brought at least one
consolation – it equalized the suffering of London's people.
'Had they [the Germans] continued to batter the East End
and kill and destroy among the slums, there would certainly
have been great discontent.' Something of the same feeling
perhaps prompted the Queen to make her famous remark
when the Palace was bombed: 'Now I can look the East End
in the face.'

Brook House on Park Lane received a direct hit in
November 1940, badly damaging the Mountbattens' thirty-
room penthouse. The couple had, however, prudently
moved out in the autumn of 1938, a year before war was
declared, and their pictures and furniture including the
famous Rex Whistler murals were in storage in the country.
Park Lane fared particularly badly in the raids; the famous
mirrored ballroom and the art gallery in Dudley House were
lost for ever, and seven Regency houses adjoining Dunraven
Street so badly damaged that they were demolished after
the war and replaced by the 1950s office block Avenfield
House. But the full fury of the Blitz was yet to come.

In January 1941 Lee recorded bombs dropping 'all over
Mayfair'. The evening of the 11th was particularly bad, with
Berkeley Square hit again, havoc in Piccadilly and Stratton
Street, and a massive explosion a block away from Claridge's
which caused the nine-storey, steel-framed Victorian
building to sway 'like a tree in the wind'. The tube station
in Down Street was destroyed and never rebuilt – a ghostly
reminder of it can still be seen in the series of arches built
into the brickwork.

The coming of spring brought Mayfair's worst ordeal. In
April Grosvenor Square was heavily bombed. John G.
Winant, the wartime American Ambassador who committed
suicide in 1947 after returning to the States, was working in
his embassy office at 1 Grosvenor Square when the raid
began. His flat was next door at Number 3. 'Afterwards I
went out and walked through the streets. I was struck by
the number of houses ablaze which had to burn themselves
out because of the lack of fire-fighting equipment.' A

member of Winant's staff put out a fire in the vacant Italian Embassy at 4 Grosvenor Square and was amused next day to receive a note of thanks from the Brazilian Embassy, which was acting as 'protecting power' for Italy's property during hostilities.

Grosvenor Square was the hub of Anglo-American co-operation before America's entry into the war in December 1941 – later General Eisenhower had his headquarters there and US troops nicknamed the square Eisenhowerplatz. The British, Winant recorded, were already planning to erect a statue there after the war to President Roosevelt. The area was heavy with Anglo-American history: John Quincy Adams had lived at Number 9 from 1786 to 1788 as the first US Ambassador to the mother country, and Walter Page at Number 6 as Adams's successor during the Great War.

Of his flat, 'my workshop and my living quarters', Winant recorded:

There are few men in British public life, whether in the government or in the armed forces, who have not stopped in at some time, and none in our High Command, nor on special missions from the United States, who has not made his way here, and many in the services have found here a night's lodging.

Eleanor Roosevelt stayed there in 1943 when she came to pay tribute to the women of Britain in the war.

The lack of fire-fighting equipment noted by Ambassador Winant caused the death of the heart of old Mayfair in May 1941. A rain of incendiary bombs fell on the northern part of Shepherd Market, where the old village connected with Curzon Street by a narrow covered passage. It had been a picturesque part of London, reminiscent of Montmartre with its open-air flower market, tall red chimneys and red-tiled roofs, a variety of village shops, Paillard's the hairdresser's with its cased display of magnificent tortoiseshell combs, and the Bon Viveur Club on the corner of Market Mews with its striped awning and interior painted to resemble a Riviera beach scene.

Close by, facing Crewe House across Curzon Street, was Sunderland House, which in prewar days had been a

favourite place for charity balls and debutante parties, hired
out by the evening. Before that it had been the town house
of the Duke of Marlborough, having been built for the
Duke's bride, the New York heiress Consuelo Vanderbilt,
by her father as a wedding present. On the night of 11 May,
when the House of Commons was destroyed, it was set
alight by incendiaries and burned unchecked. At the height
of the fire Robert Henrey recalled a man shouting: 'This
building is doomed. It was built on consecrated ground –
on the site of May Fair Chapel.'

The Market, too, was left to burn itself out. Henrey wrote
in 1942:

> For two days after the great fire in our village our
> courtyard was filled with soot, charred fragments of
> bills and cheques and documents of every kind. . . .
> Soon the demolition squads came along, and of the old
> houses there remained nothing but holes in the ground,
> the cellars open to the sky. How small these squares
> looked! It seemed impossible to believe that so many
> people had lived here, so many flourishing shops done
> business in so small a space.

Paillard the hairdresser, a small, neat, elderly man with
carefully trimmed moustaches, arrived on the afternoon
after the bombing, a Sunday, to inspect what was left of his
famous shop. Fragments of its light blue and gold facade
clung pathetically to its neighbouring buildings. 'I was
intending to hold a slight celebration,' he told Henrey with
a bitter smile. 'I started here forty years ago this very day.
I'm afraid the Nazis have celebrated for me with fireworks.'

In many ways the most devastating loss for Mayfair was
not within its own boundaries but in Leicester Square on
the night of Saturday, 8 March, when the Café de Paris,
crowded with revellers on leave, received a direct hit. It had
been advertised as London's safest restaurant, twenty feet
underground in a basement beneath the Rialto Cinema. It
was entered by a long flight of stairs leading from an anony-
mous-looking doorway between the Rialto and Lyons'
Corner House in Coventry Street. The stairs descended to a
foyer and bar, from which one stepped out on the balcony

of the restaurant, which legend (perhaps subsequently) had it was modelled on either the Palm Court of the *Lusitania* or the ballroom of the *Titanic*. Charles Graves's book on the Café de Paris, *Champagne and Chandeliers*, says the former; Constantine Fitzgibbon's account, *The Blitz*, favours the latter. In fact the Café's interior with its oval dance floor and curving staircases down from the balcony does not match any photographs of public rooms on either of the ill-fated liners, but it is possible that in 1911 when the Elysée, the first restaurant on the site, was opened, the opulent design of the *Titanic*, then being built for the White Star Line, had some influence.

Along with the Embassy Club in Bond Street, the Café had been the focus of West End night life in the 1920s and 1930s. Closed in the summer of 1940, it had reopened three months later at the height of the Blitz, and was still the smartest place for young officers on leave to take their girls for an evening of dining and dancing. The resident band, a Caribbean swing ensemble led by Ken 'Snakehips' Johnson, a native of British Guiana, was regarded as London's best. Down here, amid the infectious rhythm, the popping of champagne corks and the happy buzz of conversation, you could not hear the noise of the raids.

Margaret Sweeny, now the Duchess of Argyll, had been planning to go with a party of friends that Saturday night, but 'We changed our minds and didn't – that's fate for you.' One of her friends, Pat Bray, later Lady Cullen, did go and lost a leg in the bombing. Among those who survived was Lady Betty Baldwin, daughter of the former Prime Minister; she was off duty that evening from her ambulance unit in Berkeley Square and remembered that the men, nearly all in uniform, were remarkably handsome, the young women in their evening frocks very beautiful, the atmosphere full of gaiety and youth. The Café was so crowded that she could not get her usual banquette table; as it happened, all the people who did sit there were killed. Others who survived included Fulke Walwyn, the racehorse trainer, bandleader Nat Allen and Noel Streatfeild, the children's novelist, who later included the episode in a book. Douglas Byng should have been the cabaret star but that evening had agreed to appear at a charity ball in Grosvenor House.

It is often thought that Mayfair's favourite night-club singer, Al Bowlly, was killed that night. Bowlly often sang with Johnson's West Indian Orchestra but on that evening he was in his Jermyn Street flat, where he died in another raid five weeks later, when much of Jermyn Street and St James's was laid waste.

Earlier that Saturday evening Snakehips Johnson had been playing at the Embassy Club; at the height of the raid he ran from Bond Street to Leicester Square after joking with a friend at the Embassy who tried to persuade him not to go that no one would notice his dark skin in the blackout. He arrived, breathless, around 9.30 p.m., wearing his usual jaunty red carnation, and said to his trumpeter Leslie Hutchinson (no relation to the singer Hutch), 'Man, it's terrible outside, just terrible.' About twenty minutes later the band was playing a popular quickstep, 'Oh, Johnny'. There was a curious pinging sound – one dancer thought it was the signal for a novelty number – and a blue flash, and then everything blew up. Two fifty-kilo bombs had fallen down an air shaft through the Rialto and directly on to the dance floor of the Café de Paris.

One bomb exploded in front of the bandstand, killing Snakehips, his tenor-sax player Dave Williams and more than thirty diners and dancers. Sixty more were seriously wounded. Martin Poulsen, the restaurant's owner, and his Swiss head waiter Charles were killed outright as they stood side by side on the balcony – where, otherwise, people were only slightly hurt. The other bomb did not explode – it burst as it hit the dance floor, spilling its reeking yellow explosive over the dead and dying.

Survivors spoke of darkness, dust, bodies all around, groaning and whimpering, and a macabre light shining from somewhere above, 'like one's imagination of hell'. One man remembered seeing glasses full of champagne still on his table, the foam on the wine grey with dust. The waiter who had been pouring it a moment before lay dead across his feet. A girl celebrating her twenty-first birthday had all her clothes stripped off her by the blast. Covered in a tablecloth, she died in a stranger's arms. A Dutch officer washed a woman's broken leg in champagne, the only liquid available since the kitchens were wrecked. Her face was full of splinters of glass from the shattered, bloodstained mirrors. Sir Vyvyan Cory, a Welsh baronet who was off duty that evening from the Special Police (flat feet had kept him out of the armed services) and had been sitting at a table by the band, was so badly injured that he was taken with the dead to the mortuary. Protesting that he was still alive, he was moved to Charing Cross Hospital but died a week later from his injuries.

A radio actor called Anthony Jacobs, then serving as a private in the infantry, saw the crowd of sightseers jamming the entrance to the Café and people in evening dress staggering out. Bodies were being laid out on the pavement 'like bright, dead dolls with dust on them'. Lady Betty Baldwin was badly cut about the face and head and was subsequently treated by the plastic surgeon Sir Archibald McIndoe. The cab driver she hailed to take her to her doctor in Culross Street, Mayfair, told her brusquely not to bleed over his seat. In the darkened chaos of the dance floor two men in flat caps and working clothes were glimpsed rifling the handbags of the dead and injured women. Martin Poulsen's cuff links were ripped from his dress shirt. For some, it was not London's finest hour.

The horror of the Café de Paris brought the war home in a very personal way to the café society to which it had given its name. Nearly everyone, it seemed, knew someone who was there, had been there shortly before or had narrowly avoided going on the fatal night. With wartime censorship in force, however, nothing was published in the newspapers except the brief mention of a hit on a West End restaurant; the death of its most celebrated victim noted simply in the deaths columns of *The Times* as 'Kenneth Johnson – by enemy action'. There was an official inquiry into why the ambulance service took so long to rescue the seriously wounded on the dance floor while spending forty-five minutes among those less badly hurt on the balcony, but the file dealing with it was later lost.

The Café was so badly damaged that it was left derelict for two years, reopening in 1943 as a patched-up shadow of its prewar self: a dance hall for the troops, run by the Nuffield Centre. Entrance was sixpence for anyone in uniform and it was nicknamed the Café de Khaki. After the war it was refurbished to something approaching the old glamour, once more attracting top-line entertainers like Marlene Dietrich, Bea Lillie and Tallulah Bankhead and patrons like the Mountbattens, as well as nurturing new talents – Shirley Bassey and Tommy Steele among them – but it consistently lost money and closed in 1957. A restaurant of the same name was subsequently opened and still exists today.

London's night life was never seriously interrupted during the war, despite the shock of the Café de Paris. Much of it went on in tiny dark clubs around Shepherd Market and Jermyn Street – 'a world of hotels and bars and little pubs that have become clubs, run by gangsters who make a nice profit out of prostitutes and the dope racket', wrote Charles Ritchie in October 1941. Hotels, clubs and theatres remained open through the Blitz; the *Melody Maker* gave details of nightly dancing to resident bands in the Dorchester, Berkeley, Savoy and May Fair, where Ambrose and Jack Jackson played. Some musicians were accused in the popular press of avoiding military service; the pianist Charlie Kunz was even rumoured, on no evidence whatever, to have been arrested for sending musically coded messages to the enemy. In fact Ambrose and other bandleaders lost key personnel early in 1940 to the RAF, where they became members of the Squadronaires dance band, the morale-boosting brainchild of Squadron-Leader O'Donnell, leader of the RAF Central Band at Uxbridge.

Wartime Mayfair was undoubtedly a playground for some. 'London's never been so much fun' is the verdict of Margaret, Duchess of Argyll. 'We had the Milroy, now Les Ambassadeurs, with Harry Roy playing. We had the Orchid Room just up on Brook Street, a wonderful place to dine and dance quietly. There were no private parties but the restaurants were packed and there were Americans everywhere, of all classes. The heads of the American army and navy came over and stayed at the Dorchester.' (General Eisenhower in fact stayed first at Claridge's but complained that his gold and black room there looked like 'a goddamned fancy funeral parlour' with a bedroom decorated in 'whorehouse pink' that made him feel as if he was 'living in sin'. He felt more at home in the Dorchester, where he had suite 104/5 over the front entrance. At Winston Churchill's request a wall was built to screen his balcony from the adjoining room: it is still there today and a plaque on the suite commemorates Ike's wartime occupancy.

In certain occupations there was more money to spend than ever before, and prices of essential goods were held down by government decree. There was a five-shilling limit on restaurant meals, but it was astounding what some establishments could provide: in February 1943 the Dorchester's dinner menu ('not more than three courses may be served at a meal') included native oysters, cold lobster, smoked salmon, braised ham in madeira sauce, roast grouse and pheasant. Luxury food was still obtainable in the shops at a price. A year after being badly damaged in the spring Blitz of 1941, Fortnum and Mason was selling lobster and salmon, along with grapes at 35s. a pound and caviar at £5. The writer who noted this, Vere Hodgson, was taken to the flat of a titled woman living above Fortnum's in August 1943. The rooms were decorated in off-white with furniture upholstered in rich red material costing £3 a yard; the floor was of parquet, the chairs by Hepplewhite and the door knobs of solid crystal. 'So there is still some money left in England. . . .'

In March 1943 Chips Channon celebrated his forty-seventh birthday with a party for thirty guests at which the gin flowed, and the food included oysters, salmon, dressed crab and minced chicken. 'I counted nineteen cars parked outside my house,' he wrote in his journal. 'No raid disturbed our revels, and we all wished that Hitler could have seen so luxurious a festival in London at the height of the war.'

As time went by, however, it became harder for West End hotels to keep up appearances. Vere Hodgson fulfilled an ambition in October 1944 of having tea in the Dorchester. The surroundings were luxurious enough but the tea

very inferior. . . . Sandwiches, thin and beautifully cut, but the insides had no flavour of any kind at all. I think it was just soya bean. The waiter then appeared with a tray full of cakes and pastry – we were allowed two. They were awful. The cups were plain white – I expect

all their own were broken. . . . At a quarter to five we
asked for our bill, and felt lucky to get out at 4/6d each,
for a tea the like of which I should have been ashamed
to serve in my flat.

Ernest Bevin had called up employees in the retail trades,
and the luxury shops of Bond Street and Regent Street lost
all their counter staff under forty-five. (Hairdressers were
exempt, for morale-boosting reasons.) In one Regent Street
men's shop Mollie Panter-Downes saw customers 'timidly
selecting ties with the help of a commanding, white-haired
dowager in a velvet train'. Where it wasn't bombed and
boarded up, London had grown noticeably shabbier. The
gardens in Berkeley Square and Grosvenor Square, shorn
of their iron railings, lost their air of shut-in mystery and
exclusivity; at least one grand town house in Grosvenor
Square had a hen-house on its roof in response to the
government's exhortation to foster domestic egg production
– an ironic echo of the early Victorian householder there
who got in trouble with the Grosvenor estates for keeping
a cow, which his lawyer had claimed was quite customary
for any gentleman.

The flying bombs, Hitler's last throw, brought a final burst
of destruction to Mayfair. One Sunday morning in March
1945 Park Lane was hit without warning, the blast killing
eight people out walking their dogs in Hyde Park. 'The lie-
abeds were all safe,' wrote Chips Channon, 'and all the
Dorchester inmates unscathed. I rang Emerald to ask her if
she had been all right and she answered insouciantly,
"Quite. I was under the table with the telephone and
Shakespeare." '

In April 1945 the lights were symbolically switched on
again, though street lighting remained sporadic. The Budget
that month revealed other changes wrought by the war. In
1939 there had been 7000 people with an annual income of
£6000 or more; in 1943 there were just eighty. But fully three
million more people than in 1939 earned between £250 and
£500.

VE Day came in with 'intense, Wagnerian rain' which
reminded Chips Channon of the night before war was
declared, when it had seemed to him 'as if the very gods

were weeping'. The Ritz was decorated with flags but there were no buses, on account of a strike, and taxis refused to venture out. Peace was restored, but not to the same world: the six-year abyss had changed everything, more than the four years of the Great War which had left London largely unscathed. In December 1941 the diplomat Charles Ritchie had lamented the passing of the once-privileged, elegant Mayfair and yearned for its return:

> Oh God, leave us our luxuries even if we must do without our necessities. Let Cartiers and the Ritz be restored to their former glories. Let houseparties burgeon once more in the stately homes in England. Restore the vintage port to the clubs and the old brown sherry to the colleges. Let us have pomp and luxury, painted jezebels and scarlet guardsmen – rags and riches rubbing shoulders. Give us back our bad, old world.

SQUARE MILE OF MONEY

12

BONANZA IN BRICKS AND MORTAR

MAYFAIR was never to be the same after 1945. Charles Ritchie's beloved 'bad, old world' of luxury, style and privilege survived in patches or returned, a trifle threadbare, after the bombing: the expensive shops and hotels, a few exclusive clubs, the tarts of Shepherd Market and the pockets of private wealth in serviced apartments, hotel suites and the smaller houses between Bond Street and Hyde Park. But the essential change could be seen in the empty houses whose owners had not returned after the war; houses that had become too big and expensive to run without a full domestic staff. They represented a way of life that had vanished with the Anthony Eden hat, spats, wing collars, liveried delivery boys and the flower-girls of Piccadilly. Many of the big Georgian houses had been badly damaged in air-raids, others had become rundown and neglected through six years of abandonment or requisition.

Grosvenor Square was one of the worst-hit parts of Mayfair. 'We took a terrible hammering in the war, especially on the Park side and where the Britannia Hotel is now,' says the Duke of Westminster, one of whose family was bombed out there. The whole of the damaged west side was swept away in the late 1950s to make way for the grandiose new US Embassy designed by the Finnish archi-

tect Eero Saarinen. Its formal composition of Portland stone
and serried ranks of tall windows, was intended, under the
terms of the US Government's competition for the building,
to conform as far as possible with the scale and materials of
the rest of the square, while representing the essence of
contemporary America. The site was acquired by the American Government in 1957 on a 999–year lease – the only non-
freehold site in the world, it is said (including Moscow)
to be occupied by a US embassy. The deal was forced on
Washington by a canny offer from the Grosvenor estate
trustees: the freehold could be had in return for Grosvenor
family lands in Florida confiscated during the American War
of Independence – lands which now include Cape Cana-
veral. The former American Embassy at 1–3 Grosvenor
Square, on the east side, became offices for the Canadian
High Commission.

Those houses whose owners had deserted them reverted
to the ground landlords and were soon transformed in the
great influx of commerce from the bombed-out City. All
sorts of companies and professional businesses migrated to
the West End after the war; an estimated two million square
feet of floor space on the Grosvenor estate alone went to
business use on so-called 'temporary' office permits. Some
of these permits have lasted more than forty years and will
not run out until 1990; even then it is unlikely that Mayfair's
offices will revert more than marginally to residential use.
Without single-family occupancy – 'a very slim market
indeed', as the Duke of Westminster remarks – many great
interiors would be destroyed were the buildings to be
converted to residential use as flats. The 1971 Town and
Country Planning Act brought in the graded listing of
historic buildings, but it has been corporate money in the
main that has preserved many classical houses with their
finely proportioned public rooms and graceful central
staircases.

It is only a half-life, of course; great stretches of Mayfair
at night are like beautifully preserved sarcophagi from which
the living presence has fled, their brilliantly lit windows
and fanlights giving on to empty, chandeliered rooms with
echoing floors and blank, unlit fireplaces. But this, as the
Duke points out, is also true of stately homes open to the

public where velvet ropes and curators replace the bustle and warmth of family life, the boots in the hall and the dogs on the rug. 'If we want to conserve we have to pay a price somewhere,' he observes. In his view, office use has done more to preserve some of the great interiors of Mayfair than almost any other single factor: 'Imagine what the row would have been if we had gone in for lateral conversions and started tearing the interiors about!'

But Brigadier Gordon Viner, founder and former chairman of the Mayfair Residents' Association, takes a different view. 'A very clever deal, in my opinion, was made with the Westminster City Council, which allowed the Grosvenor Estate to extend a great many of these temporary office permissions, in some cases to 1990, in others for the life of the building. It should never have happened; by the Seventies, offices were being built all over the place.'

Brigadier Viner says he has lots of examples from the late 1970s and the early 1980s where the Grosvenor Estate 'fought to keep the office permission because they knew that reversion to residential use would mean a lowering of the income they were getting'. In answer to the argument that corporate money preserves the buildings and their interiors, Viner asks: 'What are they being preserved for?' Many interiors, he says, have been altered anyway, with plasterboard partitions and lowered ceilings.

Custom and practice as 'established office use' has thrown up some oddities. For example, Lansdowne House (the block of 1930s flats recently demolished on the south side of Berkeley Square) was requisitioned for war use in 1939 and became established thereafter as offices. Hence the block that will replace it needs no permission to be used as offices; the residential right has long been waived because of some emergency arrangement nearly fifty years ago.

Some Mayfair streets lost all vestiges of residential use after the war. Brook Street is occupied today by property, oil and construction companies, PR and advertising agencies, lawyers and professional consultants. Number 74, Sir William Gull's home in the 1880s (and in Stephen Knight's theory the West End lair of Jack the Ripper) is occupied by a clutch of whisky and cognac companies. At 69–71 the Savile Club preserves the illusion of a millionaire banker's

town mansion at the turn of the century, but otherwise
the street is populated by antique dealers, decorators (Sibyl
Colefax's firm, Colefax and Fowler, survives at Number 39),
solicitors, travel agents, international bankers, fashion firms,
chartered surveyors, ladies' hairdressers and estate agents.
In Upper Brook Street the eccentric collector William Beckford's old home at Number 12, rebuilt in 1948–9 as the
official residence of the Canadian High Commissioner, went
on the market at £2.75 million in 1985.

Grosvenor Street also went over to commerce after the
war: the 1983 *Kelly's Post Office Directory* listed not a single
private residence. Instead there were airline offices, shoe
companies, designers, executive search consultants, oil and
shipping companies, cosmetics firms, merchant banks,
chemical companies and dozens of businesses in advertising
and PR, two industries which scarcely existed before the
Second World War. Number 75, where Clementine Hozier,
later the wife of Winston Churchill, was born prematurely
in the drawing room on 1 April 1885, is now occupied by
Chesterton's, the estate agents. Alice Keppel's old home at
Number 16, the scene of Laura Corrigan's brash social coups
in the roaring twenties, has become the offices of the English
Property Company.

Dunraven Street, off Park Lane, was badly bombed and
changed from private houses to blocks of flats and offices.
In South Street, now a totally featureless canyon except for
Skittles's charming little house on the corner of Rex Place
(still, apparently, in private occupation), the dead hand of
redevelopment had begun in 1929 when Florence Nightingale's house at Number 10 was demolished. A hideous red-
brick building with crude painted ironwork now abuts the
site, commanding Miss Nightingale's once-verdant back
view over the gardens of Dorchester House, vestiges of
which survive behind the hotel. Green Street, where that
amiable lover of Mayfair, Sydney Smith, once lived, was
thoroughly rebuilt in Victorian red brick before the
depredations of the mid twentieth century: the neighbouring
address to Smith's, Number 54, is a trichological clinic and
most of the street, appears to be occupied by companies in
the food and confectionery business. *Kelly's* lists the UK
Association of Frozen Food Manufacturers, the Ice Cream

Federation, the Cocoa, Chocolate and Confectionery Alliance, the Cake and Biscuit Alliance and the Confectioners' Benevolent Fund, along with Hambro Life Assurance and the Brazilian Embassy, which occupies the sixth Earl of Harewood's old home at 32 Green Street. Hampden House at 61 Green Street, the scene of grand prewar balls given by the Duke and Duchess of Sutherland, has become the conference centre of the British Standards Institution.

In 1948, as London's social life picked itself up, St Mark's Church in North Audley Street witnessed packed memorial services for two great Mayfair hostesses, Emerald Cunard and Laura Corrigan. Lady Cunard never recovered her spirits or health after the shock of her beloved Tommy Beecham's marriage to another woman in 1943 – he had denied all rumours of it to her two days before it happened. In the summer of 1948 she lay dying in her suite in the Dorchester. With her were her maid Gordon, her doctor and a nurse. Gordon recorded later how her employer seemed to be muttering the word 'pain' over and over. The doctor asked where the pain was. She shook her head and scrawled on the fly-leaf of a book the word 'champagne'. A bottle was brought and a teaspoon of the wine held to her lips. Emerald again shook her head and pointed first to the bottle, then to each of them in turn. At last understanding, they fetched glasses and drank a toast to her. 'Our beloved, dazzling, bright, fantastic Emerald dying. I cannot believe it,' lamented Chips Channon. He had been with her at a fashionable wedding in January 1946 and provoked a typical Emerald riposte by commenting how quickly London society had resumed its glitter after the war. 'After all,' he remarked, gesturing around the crowded reception, 'this is what we have been fighting for.' 'What?' retorted Emerald. 'Are they all Poles?' Emerald's ashes were scattered in the garden of Berkeley Square.

Laura Corrigan, the much-mocked American with her malapropisms and travelling wardrobe of wigs, had a brave war. Trapped in Paris when the Germans marched in, she worked for Allied prisoners of war held by Vichy, paying out of her own pocket for medical supplies and food. Petain awarded her the Légion d'Honneur (later rescinded, with other Vichy honours, by de Gaulle) and she used to wear the red rosette when she lunched at Claridge's, along with the King's Medal she was given for founding the Wings Club for RAF officers. She died in 1948 on a visit to New York; her memorial service at St Mark's was crowded out, perhaps a gesture of remorse by those who had taken her generous hospitality while exchanging the latest cruel Corrigan jokes behind her back.

A new, less flamboyant generation of hostesses tried, here and there, to restore Mayfair's reputation for the smartest parties in town. The Honourable Mrs Dorothy Burns, daughter of the art dealer Joseph (later Lord) Duveen, lived in Mayfair for all but four of her eighty-two years and well into the 1980s was giving three dinner parties a week at her house in Chesterfield Hill. They were formal, black-tie occasions mingling writers, dukes, politicians, journalists, ambassadors and businessmen, marked by a lively intellectual atmosphere and serious discussion. 'Frilly conversation is not expected, and she will not listen to gossip,' wrote Brian Masters, biographer of great hostesses, in a description of her style of entertaining in her eightieth year. When 'Dolly' Burns died in 1985 it was announced that part of her considerable bequests would be used to launch a charity to maintain the intimate panelled Chesterfield Hill house for regular dinners and discussions of the kind at which she presided for nearly sixty years. But the project had to be abandoned and the house was put on the market in 1986.

In 1945 Margaret Sweeny, who married the eleventh Duke of Argyll after divorce from the American golfer Charles Sweeny, returned to her parents' old home, the tall, narrow brick house at 48 Upper Grosvenor Street, and continued to live there for more than thirty years, entertaining lavishly throughout the 1950s and 1960s. Her cook remained with her for nearly fifty years, though her domestic staff of five was half that of her father's in the 1930s. The Duchess of Argyll was one of the last prewar Mayfair socialites to maintain a private house in Mayfair up to the late 1970s. Luncheon and dinner parties there often numbered anything from eighteen to forty guests. The house was deceptive in its eighteen-foot-wide frontage; it went back as far as Reeves Mews and there were large rooms at the back overlooking a pretty garden with two cottages and a garage.

'The fun didn't go out after the war, it was just different,' she recalled. 'You don't have less fun because men are in black ties instead of white. What changed were the Courts; afternoon Courts were deadly dull.' (Evening presentations of debutantes at Court were never revived after the war.) 'But a lot of entertaining went on in the fifties. Many people were still quite well off and living in big houses. We wore beautiful evening dresses, big, stiff crinolines. Men put on black ties for the theatre and for a first night there were still some who wore white tie and tails. What stopped it all were the sixties – the Beatles, pop music, the punks. Everything changed, *everything*.'

In her last years at 48 Upper Grosvenor Street, where she believed she was the last private householder, the Duchess, who had been through a notorious divorce case with the Duke in the scandal-ridden summer of 1963, threw the house open to paying visitors. She had redecorated it, bringing back colour to the bleached Syrie Maugham interior her mother had commissioned. 'Marg of Arg' was much criticized for her commercial attitude, though many owners of historic houses in the country were doing or would soon be doing the same thing; nevertheless, the opportunity to see one of the last authentic private houses in Mayfair and sip good champagne with a star of the gossip columns came to be quite a tourist attraction while it lasted. In 1978, when she was nearly seventy, the Duchess sold the house (it is now two large flats) and moved into a balconied, eighth-floor permanent suite in Grosvenor House, one of the top-priced apartments originally built as service flats for the wealthy American trade in the year before the Wall Street Crash. Her neighbours past and present – there are about a dozen permanent residents among the serried ranks of company flats – have included an elderly heiress to the Chivers jam fortune, Henry Ford II (who also owns a house elsewhere in Mayfair), Dame Margot Fonteyn, Sir Geoffrey Kitchen, former chairman of Pearl Assurance, Viscount Leverhulme (whose grandfather planned to buy old Grosvenor House from the second Duke of Westminster in 1925),

Owen Aisher, the Marley Tiles tycoon, and the Marquess of Exeter.

The Park Lane hotels survived the war unscathed and a semblance of prewar glamour returned within months in a flurry of charity balls and parties graced by members of the royal family. Princess Elizabeth attended her first public dance at the Dorchester on the first anniversary of VE Day in 1946: the Royal and Merchant Navy Ball, held in aid of King George's Fund for Sailors. Ambrose's band played and Arthur Askey was the cabaret star. Tickets were five guineas a double and many parents used the occasion as a coming-out dance for their daughters. In the grey postwar years the Dorchester had an average of one charity ball a week, most of them attended by a member of the royal family. A year after that naval ball Princess Elizabeth was dining with thirty friends in the Dorchester's Park Suite, prior to going on to a debutante dance at the Duke of Wellington's home, Apsley House. At half-past midnight news of her engagement to Prince Philip of Greece broke and the hotel was besieged by photographers and onlookers. In 1957 the McAlpine family, which had owned the Dorchester for twenty years, antici- pated heavy death duties by acquiring an 'off-the-shelf' company and registering the Dorchester shares in it. As a public company the Dorchester attracted several takeover bids but it was not until 1976 that McAlpine's, who still held the controlling interest, sold the hotel to an Arab consortium for £9 million. It was the most spectacular acquisition of the Arab invasion of the 1970s and caused some consternation among old patrons of the Dorchester, not least Marks and Spencer with its Jewish family connections. Since then the Dorchester has changed hands twice in the space of a year, first to the American Regent Hotels group for £40 million and then to the Sultan of Brunei for a rumoured £56 million. Lord Forte, whose Trusthouse Forte company owns Grosv- enor House, missed the chance to buy the Dorchester in the late 1970s for about £16 million; perhaps his one big lost opportunity in a long career of shrewd takeover strategy. (The Sultan, who already maintained a regular suite at the Dorchester, had a sentimental reason for his purchase; his parents had spent their honeymoon there.)

Jimmy Welch, front hall manager of the Grosvenor House,

recalled arriving as a junior in 1947, 'straight off a farm in Rutland, not qualified for anything'. There was still an air of wartime austerity about, but to the farm boy all was luxury and splendour. American and South American guests would telephone ahead of arrival and ask if they could bring steaks or butter. The coronation of 1953 marked the final shedding of austerity for both the Dorchester and the Grosvenor House; the hotels were crammed with dignitaries, everyone in full evening dress or uniform. The Moores, the publicity-shy Littlewoods Pools millionaires from Liverpool (Sir John Moore was reputedly worth £400 million), rented a suite in Grosvenor House overlooking the procession route in Hyde Park but left it, all laid out with a sumptuous buffet, for the hotel staff to enjoy while they went off to seats in a stand along the way.

But the rising property boom and predatory developers of the late 1950s and early 1960s were about to change the character of Park Lane for the second time in thirty years, bringing brash new rivals to the two great hotels which had dominated the scene almost by *droit de seigneur*. In 1956 Tim Abel-Smith, heir to a banking fortune who had recently inherited a chunk of Mayfair bounded by Park Lane, Hertford Street and Shepherd Street, found himself harassed by death duties and heavy mortgages on the Mayfair properties. He sold the Park Lane end to the millionaire shoe retailer and property developer Charles Clore for £550,000. Clore demolished the stretch of bomb-damaged Regency terrace houses facing the Park and on the site built the twenty-eight storey London Hilton for £5 million. Sidney Kaye's Y-shaped design was the tallest building seen in London when it went up (builders on its upper storeys in the last great London smog in 1962 were working in bright sunshine above the black lid of pollution) and there were fierce protests, which have never entirely died away, at the destruction of the bosky skyline of Hyde Park seen from the Serpentine, and the fact that hotel guests on the upper floors could peer into the gardens of Buckingham Palace.

Soon after the Hilton went up the Marquess of Londonderry sold his great, gloomy Park Lane mansion to a developer named Isaac Klug for £500,000. It had been requisitioned for government use during the war and had never returned to private occupation, though it was occasionally hired out for charity events. It was pulled down in 1962 and rebuilt two years later as the Londonderry House Hotel, a mundane building of no architectural distinction which in fact was not opened as a hotel for another four years; in the interim it was used as a government hospitality centre.

Southern Park Lane's transformation into a colony of luxury hotels continued in 1970 when the Canadian-owned Inn on the Park replaced a row of houses on Hamilton Place, part of the Crown Estates. The process was completed in 1975 when the Duke of Wellington opened the Intercontinental, designed by Sir Frederick Gibberd, on a Crown Estates site flanked by Piccadilly, Park Lane and Hamilton Place. Numbers 1, 2 and 3 Hamilton Place were demolished but Number 4, one of the most elegant private houses in prewar Mayfair, and since 1939 the headquarters of the Royal Aeronautical Society, survived along with Number 5, a former Rothschild mansion. Now splendidly restored with its magnificent marble staircase, it houses Les Ambassadeurs club and adjoins the Intercontinental at the rear. A stretch of walled garden amid the river of traffic provides a flicker of memory of the gracious town houses that once lined this end of Park Lane.

The Intercontinental replaced the rest of 'Rothschild Row', the terrace of imposing houses along Piccadilly occupied by bankers and financiers in the 1900s. They had been bomb-damaged and had degenerated into a squatters' paradise for the hippies of the 1960s. Some were used as temporary offices but most were deserted, their stone cladding disintegrating and rats infesting their interiors. Neither the Georgian nor the Victorian Societies showed any interest in their fate until the Intercontinental group applied for planning permission. The most famous of the Piccadilly houses had already gone, partly wrecked in the Blitz and swept away in the 1959 redevelopment of Hyde Park Corner and the new Park Lane carriageway. This was 145 Piccadilly, where the Duke of York had lived with his family before the abdication of Edward VIII thrust him on to the throne as George VI.

Mayfair's biggest landlords, the Grosvenor family, had undergone a series of upheavals to the succession in the

1950s and 1960s. Bendor, the flamboyant second Duke whom Chips Channon described as a mixture of Henry VIII and Lorenzo the Magnificent, was a man who lived for pleasure and to avoid being bored, but his dislike of change had the effect of preserving the Grosvenor Estate in Mayfair from the kind of brutal redevelopment Lord Bearsted's historic properties on Berkeley Square suffered in the 1930s. Bendor died in 1953 without a son to inherit; his heir was a cousin, William Grosvenor, a reclusive bachelor in poor health approaching sixty. When he in turn died in 1963 the dukedom again passed sideways to a cousin, Colonel Gerald Grosvenor, a professional soldier who had been badly wounded in the D-Day landings. He lived only four years after inheriting. The fifth Duke was his brother, Lieutenant-Colonel Robert Grosvenor, who had served with the Royal Artillery in the war and then gone into politics as Unionist MP for Fermanagh and South Tyrone in Northern Ireland, and parliamentary private secretary to the Conservative Foreign Secretary, Selwyn Lloyd. Inheriting in his late fifties, he was active as Duke for only six years or so before suffering a stroke which brought his young son Gerald, now the sixth Duke, prematurely into the running of the estate.

For some twenty years, therefore, during which large tracts of historic London were being pulled down and redeveloped in all directions, the key figure in Mayfair changed four times, three of them being elderly, ailing men whose responsibilities in running the estate must have been something of a burden. The second Duke had resisted several applications to redevelop the south side of Grosvenor Square including the Waterloo House, Number 44, but in 1959 the Grosvenor Estate proposed demolishing it with others as far westward as Number 38. Both internally and externally Number 44, which was owned for a hundred years until 1903 by the Earls of Harrowby, had changed substantially from the building where the Waterloo victory dispatch had been received and where the Cato Street conspirators planned to assassinate Lord Liverpool's entire Cabinet at dinner. The Grosvenor Estate trustees took the view that to retain these houses would prevent the grand design of the square's rebuilding begun in the late 1920s and early 1930s, and that the houses were no longer original enough to warrant preservation. They were blocked, however, by the Minister of Housing and Local Government in Harold Macmillan's Government, who slapped a preservation order on Number 44.

In 1961 the trustees appealed, and were supported by both Westminster Council and the London County Council, as it then was. The minister gave in, and the Waterloo House and its neighbours were duly demolished in 1967–8 to make way for the neo-Georgian Britannia Hotel. The final occupants of the Waterloo House, the last private house in the square, were Margaret, Lady Illingworth, widow of a Yorkshire businessman and politician, and Princess Lalla Aisha, the Moroccan Ambassador. Lady Illingworth occasionally opened the house to the public and in 1960 discovered a mural painting by William Kent concealed behind the drawing-room wall. It was presented on demolition of the house to the Victoria and Albert Museum. Today this and a bit of the original paved courtyard garden, preserved at the back of the Britannia Hotel, is all that remains of a Mayfair landmark connected with two key events in British history.

The present Duke of Westminster, who inherited in 1979, concedes that some major architectural losses occurred in the 1960s, a period he views as driven by the desire to 'put the ball and chain in and start again' and which was a disastrous time for architecture generally, its sad monument the shoddily fabricated tower block. In Mayfair, which suffered some ugly 1960s infilling in its Georgian streets, the Grosvenor Estate failed to exercise the degree of control it does today over design and sympathy with the environment. This may well have been due to the fact that the fourth Duke, the present Duke's uncle, who inherited late in life and was in perpetual pain from the war wounds which eventually killed him, found it difficult to get to grips with the complex estate business.

But social and cultural change was also at work in the 1960s and 1970s. As well as a desire to chuck out the past, one of the greatest changes in Mayfair's golden acres was to be a foreign influx bigger in its impact than anything yet contributed by the diplomatic colonies of a dozen countries.

13

ARABIA WEST ONE

*T*HE first Arabs were seen around the streets of Mayfair in the middle of 1974, a few months after the oil-producing countries of the Middle East had quadrupled the price of oil and thrown the economies of the industrialized world into a tailspin of recession. Almost overnight, un-dreamed-of riches were flooding into near-primitive com-munities; Dubai in the 1960s had been little more than a trading entrepot on the Gulf with camels in its sandy streets and a water supply dependent on a handful of standpipes. The new wealth drew many sheikhs and their families into a cosmopolitan world of consumer spending, investment in European and American real estate and the forbidden delights of gambling and alcohol. These were the successors to the Indian maharajahs (fifteen of whom were said to have lived in Mayfair after the Second World War), but far less sophisticated or able to manage their wealth in a foreign culture. With the sheikhs, as they moved into suites in the Dorchester and Hilton, bought houses off Park Lane, made spectacular forays into Harrods and jammed the back streets of Mayfair with huge limousines bearing diplomatic plates, came retinues of wives, children, servants and servants' dependants, the latter often setting up sub-colonies in less affluent districts like Paddington or Notting Hill Gate.

The first Arab residents bought houses and apartments as holiday homes, to escape the punishing desert summer heat.

In 1976 it was estimated that Arabs owned 10,000 flats in London. In Mayfair they settled predominantly in Chesterfield Hill, where the veteran musical comedy star Cicely Courtneidge lived but subsequently moved out, in Curzon Street and Hertford Street, the centre of Mayfair's gambling and prostitution. By 1976, in one of the hottest summers of the century in Britain, old Mayfair residents were complaining bitterly about the peasant habits of some Arab millionaires and their entourages; of cooking fires lit on the expensive parquet flooring of service apartments and Park Lane hotel suites; of Arabs squatting on pavements and doorsteps; of washing lines strung with djellebahs; of rowdy all-night parties and dangerously inexpert driving; of Arab graffiti sprayed on walls and the unthinking arrogance of the new rich. A passing British clergyman, the *Daily Telegraph* reported, was outraged to be asked by a small Arab child for change of a twenty-pound note. 'I don't carry that sort of money,' he snorted. Hoteliers in Mayfair still recall with a shudder the worst excesses when rooms had to be redecorated completely after Arab occupancy. Like some Aladdin's lamp fable, the oil billions had pitchforked the Middle Ages into the late twentieth century, and neither could cope with the other.

The Arab presence in fashionable quarters of London – Belgravia and St John's Wood as well as Mayfair – diminished dramatically at the end of the 1970s, an exodus partly attributed to the angry diplomatic reaction to a BBC television film, *Death of a Princess*, which portrayed rough justice in Saudi Arabia including medieval scenes of a judicial beheading. When the Arabs began to return in the mid 1980s they tended to be more urbane and discreet, serious investors looking for a long-term safe base for funds which now would have to earn their keep, not just be spent as if the oil would last for ever. But the earlier influx had left a permanent legacy of inflated property prices. These surged anywhere in London where Arab custom was to be had: estate agents' advertisements from the early, pre-Arab 1970s now seem from another era altogether – four-figure sums which have turned into six. Although the first 'million-pound flat', a penthouse overlooking Green Park by the Ritz, was in St James's, it was Mayfair that felt the first accelerating thrust of Arab buying power and which became the pace setter for the 'telephone-number' prices that have now spread far beyond the purviews of W1 and SW1.

The most spectacular Mayfair property to go to the second wave of Arab buyers, apart from the Dorchester, was Crewe House in Curzon Street, now owned by the Saudi Government and designated as its next embassy in London. Much altered and enlarged from Edward Shepherd's 'long, low, white house' and set back behind velvet green lawns, it is the last of Mayfair's great private palaces to survive as it looked in the days of its last aristocratic owner, the Marquess of Crewe. His family had it as their town house from 1899 to 1937, when it became the headquarters of the Thomas Tilling group of companies; when Tilling was taken over in 1985 by the multinational BTR it was the prime asset to be sold off. Dudley House, the other surviving grand mansion at 100 Park Lane, lost its picture gallery and incomparable mirrored ballroom in the Blitz but the rest of it has been handsomely restored as the head offices of the Hammerson property group.

Arab sheikhs have poured millions onto the gaming tables of Mayfair, which has a long tradition of fortunes won and lost on the turn of a card or the throw of a dice. The surge of affluence and quick property-development fortunes in the 1960s encouraged the growth of casinos and gambling clubs around Berkeley Square and Shepherd Market. (About eleven clubs licensed by Westminster Council now exist in Mayfair.) In 1964 Jack Cotton applied to pull down the mansion at 45 Park Lane built by the ill-fated Barney Barnato and subsequently acquired by the Sassoon banking family, and build offices on the site. The *Architectural Journal* noted that the building would be the first in London to be designed by Walter Gropius of the Bauhaus movement. In 1966 the new building was leased by Hugh Hefner's Playboy Club, and the bunny-emblazoned flag, symbol of sanitized sexual fantasy for a generation of businessmen, flew above Park Lane for fifteen years until the club lost its gaming licence and closed, the building lease then being sold to Land Securities for £14.6 million.

The most famous and elegant of the Mayfair gambling clubs, one in which it is easy to imagine Brummell and

Byron at the tables and Watier presiding over the kitchens, is the Clermont Club at 44 Berkeley Square, Lady Isabella Finch's magnificent 1742 mansion with its painted ceiling and staircase admired by Horace Walpole as a 'beautiful piece of scenery'. It is undoubtedly the best-maintained town house of the eighteenth century left in London and until 1959 was owned and lived in for three generations by a family called Clark. Wyndham Damer Clark, a former High Sheriff of Glamorgan, was the last private resident to own a house in Berkeley Square; when he died in 1959 the house was acquired by John Aspinall and turned into the Clermont, named after a nobleman who had owned it in Regency times. Annabel's, the night club in the basement, was started by Mark Birley as a meeting-place for his friends and named after his wife, who later married Sir James Goldsmith. Founder members of Annabel's included Sir James (now Lord) Hanson, Prince George Galitzine, Lord Hambledon, (a director of the newsagents W. H. Smith and descendant of its founder), Norman Parkinson, the society photographer, and Sir Anthony Berry, the Conservative MP who lost his life in the IRA bombing of the Grand Hotel at Brighton during the 1984 Conservative Party Conference.

The Clermont members provided as dashing and exotic figures as any in Regency London, among them Jimmy (later Sir James) Goldsmith, the Earl of Suffolk, Dominic Elwes the painter, William Shand Kydd and Daniel Meinertzhagen. All were intimates, mainly from schooldays at Eton, of the man who became the Clermont's most notorious member – Richard John Bingham, seventh Earl of Lucan.

'Lucky' Lucan, whose great-great-grandfather sent the Light Brigade on its doomed charge at Balaclava, was a committed gambler. His impassive exterior and heavy features which rarely betrayed emotion were well suited to his particular passion, poker. His life moved in a regular daily cycle between the Clermont, the St James's Club, Annabel's, the Portland Club, the Mirabelle Restaurant in Curzon Street and his home in Lower Belgrave Street. After leaving Eton, Lucan had served in the Coldstream Guards and achieved some sporting eminence in bobsleigh and powerboat racing. He worked for a spell in a merchant bank but after winning £20,000 at chemin de fer in 1960 took up gambling as a serious way of life.

In the early 1970s his day would begin around noon with a vodka martini at the St James's or the Clermont, where he invariably lunched, choosing always the same meal – smoked salmon, followed by lamb cutlets. (In summer the cutlets were served in aspic.) There might be a game of backgammon after lunch. Lucan spent most evenings at the Clermont, except for Mondays and Thursdays when he played bridge at the Portland Club. In the early days of the Clermont, before John Aspinall sold it to Hefner's Playboy Club in 1972, Aspinall, who had known Lucan since the early 1950s and regarded him as someone, like himself, 'born out of his own time', often staked him when his funds ran low at the tables. Lucan was a popular figure in the club, though his wife Veronica found the place oppressive and would sit in silence most evenings when dining at a large table dominated by Lucan's male gambling cronies. The couple's marriage was in deep trouble by 1973, when Lucan attempted unsuccessfully to gain custody of their three children.

On Thursday, 7 November 1974, Lucan had booked a table for dinner at 11 p.m. at the Clermont for a party of friends who had earlier spent the evening at the Mermaid Theatre. Lucan said he would join them later, but when his four guests turned up at 10.45 p.m. they discovered the table had been booked for only four. Their host never arrived. About 9 p.m. that evening Lady Lucan, with blood pouring from her head, had burst distraught into the Plumber's Arms, a pub in the street where they lived. She screamed, 'He's in the house, the children are in the house. He's murdered the nanny.' Then she collapsed. Police went to the Lucans' house and in the basement found the badly beaten body of the family's nanny, Sandra Rivett, stuffed into an American canvas mailbag. The murder weapon was there, a length of lead piping wrapped in bandages.

At 11.30 p.m. Lucan, driving a friend's car, arrived at the Sussex home of Susan Maxwell-Scott, another friend, where he wrote three letters, two of them to his brother-in-law, William Shand-Kydd, and one to the friend whose Ford Corsair he had borrowed. He explained that he had surprised an intruder in his house attacking his wife, but that the man had escaped. 'I have had a traumatic night of unbelievable coincidence,' he wrote, adding that things looked bad for him and that he intended to 'lie doggo for a while'. He left the Maxwell-Scott home at 1.30 a.m., Mrs Maxwell-Scott told detectives later, planning to return to London and contact the police. But the car was found near the harbour at Newhaven, departure point for the ferry to Dieppe. Lucan has never been seen again, though countless false sightings have been reported around the world.

Three days after his disappearance a warrant was issued for his arrest for the murder of Sandra Rivett and attempted murder of the Countess of Lucan. The murder file is still open although both detectives in charge of the case have long since retired. Lucan's son and heir George, Lord Bingham, became technically eligible to succeed to the earldom seven years after his father's disappearance, but the seventh Earl is still listed in *Debrett's* and *Who's Who*. Veronica, Countess of Lucan, has had a history of hospital and psychiatric treatment since the tragedy. Dominic Elwes was pilloried by the Lucan circle for talking to newspapers, and committed suicide. Most people who knew Lucan or who were connected with investigating the case appear to believe he is dead, probably having jumped from the Newhaven ferry en route to France. Yet one may ask whether such a seasoned poker player would have given up while some odds of escape remained in his favour. . . . And there is a sharp divergence of opinion between the two senior policemen in charge of the case. Former Detective Inspector David Gerring, who now runs a pub in his retirement, still believes Lucan is alive; his ex-colleague Detective Chief Superintendent Roy Ranson thinks he killed himself in the Channel and that his body was subsequently devoured by crabs.

By one of those bizarre coincidences that often haunt the chronicles of murder, another Lucan family nanny of the time, who might well have been on duty instead of Sandra Rivett, died at the hands of her husband in 1985 in particularly grisly circumstances, her body being dismembered and distributed round a number of dumping-grounds in London. Christabel Boyce's diary for 1974 revealed conversations with Lady Lucan after the murder in which she said the Earl had suggested a suicide pact with sleeping pills following the struggle in which he injured her head. Lady Lucan agreed to fetch the pills, then, according to the entry in Mrs Boyce's diary, 'got up and ran like hell downstairs and out of the house to the Plumber's Arms to raise the alarm'.

If the Lucan case cast a glaring light on the lifestyle of a small group of Mayfair gamblers, plenty of less notable but equally serious crime was rife in the area around Shepherd Market in the 1970s, when a Maltese vice gang was running prostitution rackets that put its parallel operation in Soho into the shade. During four years in the late 1970s there were five murders, three cases of arson, one suicide of a ponce and thirty-five violent incidents, all in the limited area between Shepherd Market and Park Lane. In June 1978 three five-gallon petrol bombs were hurled from the roof of the Hilton into the bedroom of a mews flat belonging to the owner of the 21 Club in Chesterfield Gardens. Official crime figures for 1977 showed that 2200 prostitutes were arrested or cautioned by police in Park Lane and Shepherd Market, four times the number in Soho. On Saturday nights anything up to 250 women 'on the game' could be counted in Park Lane, patrolling outside the big hotels.

Prostitution and vice are still a problem, though far less obtrusive than ten years ago. One exception was the fatal shooting of a call girl in Park Lane in late 1985. Park Street, Park Lane and Curzon Street are the main areas affected; Shepherd Market itself now tends to be quieter since the girls operate from houses rather than openly touting on the streets. On a hot summer night the tiny squares of the Market are like a stage set with women seated in the lighted, upper-floor windows, sometimes exchanging gossip across the street. The occasional ponce sits warily in a car with the engine running, but a relaxed, even homely atmosphere prevails, more reminiscent of Amsterdam's cosy red-light district than the sinister, gang-ridden scene of twenty years ago. A male hairdresser who worked in the Market some years ago tells of drinking in one of the old pubs there with a regular practitioner of 'the game' who insisted on buying her round of drinks. Finding herself short of ready cash on one occasion, she excused herself for about ten minutes, returning to her friends at the bar with a wad of notes from which she peeled off payment for the round. The louche spirit of the old May Fair is never far away. These days, however, the trade is more often conducted discreetly through hotel doormen, 'escort services' advertised to visiting businessmen, and telephone numbers slipped slyly into the hand.

There are still brothels in the area, as well as signs advertising 'French lessons' and suggestive red neon lights winking from basement doorways, but not so many to concern the Mayfair Residents' Association as in the late 1970s when an estimated fifty brothels were operating on a 'bedshift' basis, using relays of girls to occupy a limited number of beds. (At that time, also, one flat in Shepherd Market and another in Curzon Street still had as their listed ratepayers two known former members of the infamous Messina Gang, which was driven out of Britain in the 1950s.)

Mayfair residents today have other worries: protest marches spilling over from the Park and shattering the Sunday quiet, the spread of rubbish from takeaway food shops and restaurants, the noise and late-night traffic caused by casinos and the lack of residential parking space. 'There are four permits issued for every space,' complained one resident. The vast explosion of traffic, especially of tourist coaches since the de-regulation of buses, has gone higher up the list of priorities for action in the Grosvenor Estate's strategy for Mayfair, first published in 1971 and reviewed in 1983. The estate's hope, says Stanley Coggan, the surveyor, is for heavy traffic eventually to be diverted out of the main residential areas. Yet Mayfair, unlike its sister district in the Grosvenor Estate, Belgravia, has commerce inextricably linked with its residential addresses. One of the most difficult tasks for local council officials is trying to determine breaches of residential use; a Mayfair address is a valuable asset for the kind of small service industry, often consultants of one kind or another, which thrives in the area. One man in the 1970s was said to have a £250,000 turnover making diamond-studded golf balls for Texans; council inspectors face a daunting task trying to track down people like him posing as bona fide residents. In 1986 it was likely anyway that new legislation would soon permit many householders to use their homes for business purposes, blurring the lines still further in the same way that increasing numbers of residential flats were being hired out as short-let service apartments – in effect, becoming little more than hotels.

14

LEASEHOLD ON HISTORY

*M*ARGARET, Duchess of Argyll, remembers the time – only just prewar – when Mayfair had no real contenders as the best address in London, when Knights-bridge and Belgravia were 'very nice and respectable places' to live, but when it was damning to say of a debutante that 'she came out in Pont Street.' In 1931 it was better to say you lived in Mayfair than Belgravia, as a character remarked in the Jessie Matthews film of that year, *Evergreen*. Today, however, the ultimate owner of Mayfair and Belgravia, the Duke of Westminster, has his London residence in Eaton Square (more fashionable now than Grosvenor Square), and it is no longer a town house but a flat three floors above that occupied by his mother, Viola, Duchess of Westminster. The Dukes of Westminster have not maintained a Mayfair house since the 1960s, when the fourth Duke, the present Duke's uncle, lived at 68 Brook Street, adjoining the Grosv-enor estate offices at 53 Davies Street.

Belgravia has far more homes in private ownership than Mayfair – 50 per cent of its total floor space compared to one-third in Mayfair – and its relative quietness, freedom from wartime damage (which resulted in the great switch to commercial use in Mayfair) has given it the residential edge since 1945. Its more spacious nineteenth-century layout has ensured less traffic congestion, particularly by the tourist coaches which clog the narrow Georgian streets of Mayfair and the entrances to its squares. 'Mayfair,' says Margaret Argyll, meaning the sort of society once associated with the district, 'has moved down to Chelsea and Belgravia now.'

So who lives in Mayfair these days? The answer is, probably more people than you think. The ratio of floor-space within the Grosvenor estate part of Mayfair of one-third residential use, one-third offices and one-third non-office commercial use (shops, hotels, restaurants and clubs), has remained little changed since the war; if anything, the residential element is very gradually increasing. It is not, of course, the same kind of residential use as in the 1930s; a house like 15 Grosvenor Square, once occupied by the in-laws of the present Duke of Westminster, is now divided into several flats and accommodates more people than when a single family lived there. Still, 'you would be surprised how many private houses there still are,' says Malcolm Lothian, chairman of the Mayfair Residents' Association, which was founded in 1977. Mr Lothian's full-time occupation is headmaster of St George's Primary School in South Street, which is attended by 190 pupils of different nationalities, many of them from embassy families. (There are twelve embassies in Mayfair including those of Italy, Egypt, Yemen, Japan and Burma. The Italians struck a remarkable bargain in 1931 when they acquired a 200-year lease on 4 Grosvenor Square for £35,000 and an annual rent of £350.)

Stanley Coggan, the Surveyor to the Grosvenor Estate, believes that, apart from temporary office permits, the estate is probably the one area in Westminster where residential use has constantly, if gradually, increased over the years. About 3000 people live on the Mayfair estate compared with 4354 in 1961 and 8775 in 1931, and between 2500 and 3000 people are employed in offices there. In 1976 the proportions of floor space were made up of 45 per cent offices and 36 per cent residential, compared with 48 per cent offices and 11 per cent residential in St James's. Precise statistics about residence are hard to establish, partly because wealthy people with houses or flats in Mayfair often have property elsewhere and may be registered there on the voters' rolls; partly because many owners are domiciled abroad. But a good number of the smaller houses on the estate, particularly in Hill Street, are still owned and occupied by single families. The leasehold system established under Sir Richard Grosvenor in the early eighteenth century means that very few houses in Mayfair are freehold, in itself a deterrent to buyers looking for long-term investments. A typical price in early 1986 for a sixty-year lease on a four-storey Georgian house in Hill, Charles or South Audley streets was somewhere between £500,000 and £1 million, with £250,000 a common figure for a stylish converted two- or three-bedroom flat. Service and rental charges on flats might easily exceed £6000 on top of the purchase price, with the steep Mayfair rates on top of that.

Grosvenor Square, now entirely given over to apartments where it is not hotels or diplomatic territory, is popular with wealthy Greeks and Indians, many flats selling at above £1.5 million. A flat briefly owned by Christina Onassis, the shipping heiress, at 15 Grosvenor Square changed hands in the early 1980s for £875,000 for a fifty-year lease. A one-bedroom apartment reputed to be the most expensive of its kind in London was on sale in 1983 at 17 Grosvenor Square for £295,000 plus outgoings of £8000 a year. In Chesterfield House, the 1937 block of flats built on the site of the fourth Earl of Chesterfield's handsome mansion, £100,000 was the minimum in 1986 for a small, unmodernized two-bedroom flat. The house in Dunraven Street once occupied by the Edwardian beauty Lillie Langtry and now converted into four flats went on the market in the mid 1980s for £1.6 million. Several Georgian houses in Charles Street changed hands at the same time for prices ranging from £875,000 to £1.25 million; they were snapped up by corporate buyers rather than individuals, a growing trend. Flats for rent in 1985 could command anything from £250 a week upwards, and a large house cost £1500 a week.

Some residents in Mayfair have done very well on long leases acquired years ago. So have some shops. Asprey's of Bond Street have a lease with a nominal ground rent stretching well into the next century, One private leaseholder with a two-level maisonette in Hays Mews, off Berkeley Square, bought a twenty-five year lease in 1969 for £9,500 at a ground rent of £270 a year. (His rates, however, are

£1,500 a year now.) His next-door neighbours include a couple of Anglophile Canadians and a journalist on the *Daily Telegraph*.

A glance at the electoral register for Mayfair – officially, Westminster South, West End ward – gives an impression of mainly obscure, plain Anglo-Saxon names, few of them titled, with a sprinkling of Arab, Greek, Indian and other foreign nationalities, though many titled or foreign residents with second, third or fourth homes would not necessarily appear there. The register in force until February 1986 showed eighty-two residents in Grosvenor Square, all in flats, including Earl Spencer, father of the Princess of Wales. Brook House in Park Lane, with its once-vast apartments occupying a floor apiece, is all offices now, although Westminster City Council has stated that it should return to residential use when the 'temporary' office permit expires in 1990. The former Mountbatten penthouse on the seventh and eighth floors is an executive suite for the building's current owners, the property company MEPC, which occupies most of the other floors as well. The Mountbattens' splendid curved staircase with its art deco ironwork is still the dominating feature of the seventh floor, where the five main reception rooms (which could once be linked into one vast room for entertaining, with matching carved chimney pieces at either end) now serve as MEPC's boardroom, executive dining-room and senior offices. The eighth floor, badly damaged by a wartime bomb, has been sub-divided into anonymous offices.

The only duke still to have a Mayfair address is the Duke of Marlborough, who lives in Shepherd's Place. Mrs Betty Kenward, 'Jennifer' of the *Harper's and Queen's* social diary column, lives in Hill Street and Prince and Princess Galitzine, who run a public-relations business, are among the fifty-four inhabitants of Curzon Street. Fifty-four is also the number listed for Charles Street, while a mere thirteen residents are given for the lofty, red brick mansion flats of Down Street, among them Princess Pauline Melikoff.

Albany has a huge waiting list of applicants for its sixty-nine sets of apartments. Copies are lodged with the bursar of Peterhouse College, the leading freeholder, and with Knight, Frank and Rutley, the London estate agents, as well as with the three trustees of Albany, but the list is not precisely what it seems. Names are not necessarily taken from it when 'sets' change hands; it is, as a trustee explained, 'guidance' for people wishing to dispose of their sets, but they would not be bound to sell to someone on the list. To get rooms in Albany, as with so many other desirable things in life, personal contacts and recommendations are invariably the key.

Albany was once one of the cheapest places to live within a stone's throw of Piccadilly; Cyril Ray bought his present set, K1, in 1950 for £5500 freehold. Today, freeholds are around a quarter of a million pounds and rents on leaseholds £5000 to £6000 a year plus rates. Albany freeholds tend to be passed down families and a few residents own several sets which they let out; the attic rooms which go with each set are profitable lets on their own, though the climb of seventy-two steps deters the unfit. Middle and top sets have an extra attic room, originally intended as a kitchen; ground floor sets have a basement instead, which Cyril Ray has converted into a comfortable dining room and compact fitted kitchen.

Ray's first set, C6, had a colourful history. Lord Clanricarde, the miserly collector, left it so filthy that his priceless paintings had to be chipped off the walls, an old Albany retainer told Ray. During the Second World War part of the D-Day operations was planned there by Lord Louis Mountbatten, Sir Harold Wernher and the brilliant, eccentric scientist Geoffrey Pyke. Later, it was the home of Graham Greene, the novelist, and is now occupied by Michael Colston of the dishwasher family.

Albany is still a quirky sort of place to live; not everyone's idea of a luxurious Piccadilly address. The stone staircases are cold and dank in winter, the collegiate atmosphere forbidding to some. It is very dark in the ground-floor sets; even on sunny days there is only a short time in each day when you do not need the lights on. There is no central heating, Westminster rates have risen to around £1500 a year and maintenance outgoings, once very low, have caught up with the costs of modern labour and the chronic ailments of an old building. The cost of repairs is levied by the staircase, not as a proportion of the total, so a resident might have to find £5000 for dry-rot damage as one-sixth of the bill instead of one-sixty-ninth.

But the advantages are inestimable – convenience and history. Who could resist living in Byron's rooms, as the publicist John Addey used to, or in one of Macaulay's sets, F3 and E1 – no longer, however, giving inspiration to men of letters – or in the converted ballroom of the original Melbourne House, as the American author and journalist Fleur Cowles does? Edward Heath rashly decided to give up his rented Albany set, now occupied by a Rothschild, when he moved into 10 Downing Street in 1970; when his premiership ended unexpectedly early at the hands of the striking coal-miners in 1974 he found himself homeless. To Cyril Ray the advantages far outweigh the disadvantages, though his wife, cookery writer Elizabeth Ray, is not so sure. 'I love it dearly,' he says – the quiet, the high-ceilinged rooms, the short walking distance to his clubs, the Athenaeum and Brooks's, and to art galleries and theatres; the round-the-clock watchfulness of the six green-liveried porters (once all ex-Guardsmen), the back-door short cut to Vigo Street and the food shops of Soho a few hundred yards away.

About one hundred and twenty-five people live in Albany today, some for only part of the year. They include six peers, a former private secretary to the Prince of Wales, (who occupies the set Oscar Wilde gave to Ernest Worthing in *The Importance of Being Earnest*), three MPs, the philosopher Sir Isaiah Berlin, publishers Sir Robert Lusty and George Rainbird, author Peter Coats, actor Terence Stamp, designer David Hicks, industrialists, merchant bankers and the inventor of lateral thinking, Edward de Bono, who lives in the young Gladstone's rooms, now filled with the clatter of word processors and the production of books and lectures.

The Piccadilly frontage of Mayfair is a jigsaw of ownership, as is most of the district outside the boundaries of the Grosvenor estate. One major freeholder with properties that stretch intermittently from Sackville Street to Old Park Lane is the Sir Richard Sutton estate, a formidably private, publicity-shy business dating back to 1808 when it was joined to the historic Pulteney estate, part of Mayfair's earliest development in 1664. Under the will of an eighteenth-century

Pulteney heiress, Lady Frances Johnstone-Pulteney, the London properties were left to her cousin and trustee, Sir Richard Sutton, while the better-known Bath estate (commemorated today in such names as Pulteney Bridge and Great Pulteney Street) went to the Vane family. The last Sir Richard Sutton, who succeeded as sixth Baronet on his birth in 1891, served in the Life Guards and the Machine Gun Regiment in the First World War and won the Military Cross for gallantry; he was killed, aged twenty-seven, just before the Armistice in November 1918.

The Sir Richard Sutton Estate has been selling off some of its freeholds along Piccadilly, notably to a property company called Stockley PLC, which has acquired the freeholds of both the RAF Club at 128 Piccadilly and the Cavalry and Guards at 127. The RAF Club already had a lease to the year 2025, but has bought its freehold from Stockley nonetheless for £1.6 million. The Cavalry and Guards, however, is nearing the end of its lease and in a weak position. Stockley wants to turn the property into an eighty or ninety-bedroom hotel.

Of the other big Mayfair landlords, one of the largest is the BP Pension Trust, which has extensive holdings in Charles, Farm and Hill streets, a chunk of Bruton Street and the Berkeley Square garden. The trust's thirty acres are estimated to be worth over £100 million.

Mayfair's chief landowner, the Duke of Westminster, is reputedly the richest man in Britain, though at least one Arab grandee would dispute the title. The Grosvenor family's wealth has been legendary for generations; in 1865 it was described as 'the wealthiest family in Europe – perhaps . . . the wealthiest uncrowned house on earth'. The sixth Duke, however, has no pretensions of grandeur whatsoever. Born in 1951, he is an engagingly boyish, good-looking man, tall and lean with an eager, friendly manner and an infectious laugh. He is also patently dedicated to the business to which he came by an accident of birth, several preceding dukes having lacked direct heirs, but which he would most probably not have chosen by temperament. Like all his immediate forebears, Gerald Cavendish Grosvenor is a countryman by nature whose favourite leisure hours are spent fishing and shooting and who, if the succession had not come his way, would doubtless now be contentedly farming in the Northern Irish county of Fermanagh, which his father once represented in Parliament. Like his great-uncle Bendor, he finds two days in London about as much as he can take though there is scant resemblance otherwise between the two. 'He was a restless soul; I'm not nearly so restless, but I'm uninterested in the extreme in the social life of London and I come down here from Eaton at the latest possible hour I can and get out again at the first opportunity.' London, he says, is a place 'to which I come to do a job', but he does that job with extreme conscientiousness. It occupies about a third of his year in chunks of between two and four days a week, and he is very much in control of the new complicated conglomerate structure of the Grosvenor Estate.

He still thinks of it as a family business, but it has changed immensely from the way it was run in the 1970s and before on a 'family care-and-maintenance basis.' Leaning back in his shirtsleeves with his office window open to a freezing January day, smoking intensively, he explains the change. 'It's much more business-oriented today than it has ever been, and more so, I would guess, than other comparable family estates. But one does business to survive. The days have gone when one could just sit back on the flat green acres and hope for the best. My long-term objective is to keep the base assets of the London estates, the historical assets, alive and kicking. And to do that, we have to diversify into other areas.'

These areas involve hotels, office developments and shopping centres around the world, and property investment portfolios stretching from central London through western Canada to Australia. The six trustees of the Grosvenor Estate, headed by the Duke, form a board of directors over a fully fledged corporate structure whose asset base is reckoned (though never by the estate itself) to be worth around £2000 million, Mayfair and Belgravia being, as the Duke says, 'the jewel in the crown'. (Mayfair is itself virtually run as an investment company with Stanley Coggan as chairman.) The trustees include two merchant bankers, a solicitor and an estate agent, as well as Jimmy James, the chief executive. They meet once a month and exert far more control over developments in the face of Mayfair and Belgravia than their predecessors did in the brutalist 1960s. Like the Victorian first Duke, who rejected a pub design as 'too gin-palacey' for Mount Street, they will send an architect back to his drawing board. A number of architectural details were changed, for example, in the Bond Street underground station redevelopment. Certain applications for redevelopment or change of use come directly to the Duke for decision: a hotel, for instance, a restaurant or a club would certainly do so, 'anything big or different', as the Duke says, or outside the normal run of estate management.

Gerald Grosvenor was about fifteen and a schoolboy at Harrow when he first learned, on the death of the third Duke, of the responsibilities that would one day fall upon him. 'My father had in part protected me from knowing, but it came as a bit of a shock at the time.' The fifth Duke was taken ill by a stroke when Gerald was in his early twenties, forcing him to become involved in the business earlier than he might have wanted to. As a child on school holidays he remembers Bourdon House, 'pitch dark with long passages, heavyweight tapestries and the lights permanently on. It was tremendously grand, full of the pictures we now have at Eaton, but for a small child it was gloomy and very depressing.' Later, the family moved into 68 Brook Street as their London residence; this was abandoned for an Eaton Square flat in the 1960s and the estate offices at 53 Davies Street now spill over into the adjoining Brook Street house, where the Duke has his office. A small sitting room that once connected to the family dining room through double doors, it has twin alcoves of beautifully bound books, a portrait of the second Earl Grosvenor ('it helps to fill a wall'), family photographs, a broad antique desk and comfortable easy chairs around a coffee table.

Does he feel at all proprietorial as he walks or drives through his London domains in his Aston Martin or slate-blue 'stretched' Range-Rover, registration plate GRO 1? Loelia, Duchess of Westminster in the 1930s, used to joke with friends about being their landlady. Gerald Grosvenor has plainly never entertained the thought. 'No, I don't. To run an estate of such complexity causes many problems; it's much more impersonal from a landlord's point of view than the agricultural estates, where you know all the people so much better. This is a great shifting, cosmopolitan society.'

His position is light-years removed from that of his great-grandfather, the first Duke, whose vision and imagination in developing the estate he much admires. Things were never the same for the landed estates of England after the First World War and the double yoke of estate duties and increased income tax that followed it. Trusts were the vehicle devised to enable landed families to pass on their inheritance; these have now evolved in the Grosvenors' case to a complex web of holding companies and directorships. A watershed occurred in 1953 when the second Duke, Bendor, died leaving his heirs with more than £19 million in death duties. 'We had to find a down payment of marginally over £4 million and make stage payments over the next five or six years. We managed without selling too much because we decided to try to trade our way out of it, to generate cash, which we could do with the London estate supporting us. If we had been an entirely agricultural estate we would have had to sell.'

Gerald Grosvenor's naturally buoyant temperament betrays an undertow of serious concern for the future. 'It is difficult to plan for the estate because we are living in a society that is becoming increasingly polarized politically.' It has been reported that he would consider moving to an offshore base if things got really rough for the family business. 'I've always maintained that I want to go on living in this country and I have consistently refused to move overseas for tax reasons. I just don't want to do it. That was one of the first major decisions I had to take. But I've also said that if the historical, base assets of the estate were at risk, then perhaps I might be persuaded to move overseas, if it was right and if it would be beneficial in order to retain those assets for future generations. But I don't want to – I like living here too much.'

He admires his great-grandfather as 'a man of astonishing vision and tremendous social conscience'. The working-class housing the first Duke caused to be built on the Grosvenor estate, both in Mayfair and Belgravia, will endure well into the twenty-first century as low-rent flats. The Peabody Trust, founded by the Baltimore philanthropist George

Peabody (who lived at 15 Cork Street for a while and died in Eaton Square), manages most of the blocks for the Grosvenor Estate under an arrangement dating from the late 1960s. Given their prime position between Oxford Street and Grosvenor Square they must represent a vast, locked-up profit potential for the Grosvenor Estate, but the intention, says Stanley Coggan, is always to keep them as low-income rented property. There is a long waiting list, now closed, for these flats, which rent for no more than £25 a week. The list, says Mr Coggan, consists of 'people we think are good, deserving cases'. They do not necessarily have to live or work on the estate, but most of them are of pensionable age.

The sixth Duke would like to be remembered, like his great-grandfather, as a man of vision, and as a man who cared, like him, about 'quality and standards. Those are the hallmarks of his which I would endeavour to keep up on the London estate and elsewhere.' This doesn't, in the young Duke's eyes, mean necessarily preserving everything that past generations have done. He grows quite impassioned about the need to foster good contemporary architecture· – his own stately home, Eaton in Cheshire, was once a monumental piece of Victorian Gothic by Alfred Waterhouse but is now a low-slung, austere concrete building and the object of much criticism from estate workers. 'One must go forward in architecture,' he argues. 'There is bad architecture from Victorian, Edwardian, Queen Anne times. It wasn't all great by any stretch of the imagination. We must beware of just looking back and fossilizing, we must create something for the future as well. We do it in the artistic world, with pictures and opera, but in architecture we seem to have an awful lot of trouble. Yet our children and our grandchildren will not thank us for leaving them a legacy of nothing. We must leave something. It is frankly our duty to do so.'

Architecture apart, the Duke also wants to leave a different sort of legacy, to ensure that the supply of rented accommodation in central London, already near vanishing point, survives. For all the rush towards a property-owning democracy, an idea beloved now of all political parties, he is convinced that many people prefer not to have the responsibility for their own bricks and mortar, burst water pipes or windows that need replacing. The leasehold system, with its management of services and maintenance, has the same attraction for some over freehold, and in the Duke's view is seriously threatened by legislation introduced in 1967 enabling leaseholders to have a legal right to buy the freehold. To this end he recently pleaded his case personally in the European Court of Human Rights and was sharply criticized by those who saw his motives as purely selfish on the part of the wealthiest landlord in London after the Queen. The Court rejected his case, holding that the British Parliament was right in 1967 in its view that long leaseholds were unfair to tenants, and that, as the majority of MPs voted at the time, 'in equity the bricks and mortar belong to the qualified leaseholder'. The Duke, however, has already lost some 200 leaseholds, mainly in Belgravia, only to see many of them resold for huge capital gains, and his concern, apart from the loss of a profitable asset, is for the erosion of a cohesively managed system which has largely been responsible for preserving the character of estates like Belgravia. (Of his two estates in London he admits to preferring the Regency terraces and squares of Belgravia, their grandeur contrasting with the intimate jumble of mews and courtyards behind.) If it hadn't been for the war, he says, Mayfair would be far better architecturally than it is today.

Bombs and commerce have changed Mayfair's character since 1939, though many of the elegant old shops remain, providing old-fashioned style and personal service: Asprey, Truefitt and Hill, George Trumper, Sulka, Purdey and Thomas Goode among them. Some historic names have gone, squeezed out in the 1970s by steeply rising leases, notably Savory and Moore and Scott's, the hatters. But other things remain constant: the suits that Savile Row tailors have been cutting and stitching since the trade was established there in the 1850s; the poultry and game and old-fashioned gas jet on the wooden counter at John Baily, opposite the Connaught; the sleek barbering and elegant hair preparations of Trumper and Truefitt; the exquisitely embroidered children's clothes at the White House in Bond Street; the whimsical, Fabergé-like extravagances dreamed up in

Asprey's workshops, and Heywood Hill, the Curzon Street bookshop which Nancy Mitford ran from 1942 to 1945 while Mr Hill was away at the war, and which remains a favourite haunt for writers..

On a humbler level, too, there is heartening continuity: the tiny, cluttered ironmonger's shop in Weighhouse Street, more Fulham or Hammersmith than Mayfair, handy for the Peabody flats nearby; the coffee shop next door to the Grosvenor Estate's grand offices, where workmen come in for egg, chips and beans; the priests of Farm Street presbytery going about their parish duties as well as running Jesuit affairs in England. (It is said their advantageous rent is due to a friendship struck up on the battlefield of Gallipoli between the second Duke of Westminster and the chaplain who subsequently became Superior at Farm Street.)

Mayfair is still, to a surprising extent, a village in spirit; the Arab and Indian and Greek billionaires come and go, and the Georgian portals of Curzon Street resound with the costly click of gambling chips, but trading, gossip, good living and an eye for business were always part of the Mayfair mix. (Today there is something else; Britain's spy masters of MI5 occupy the bland 1930s bulk of Leconfield House in Curzon Street and the MI6 master computer system is reputedly housed in Mount Row.) But there are, of course, missing parts of the old mosaic. The older Mayfair residents, living now on fixed incomes, find the steeply rising cost of rents, leases and rates a progressive anxiety: the Grosvenor Estate's new business approach means paying attention to market forces, and corporate buyers are powerful factors in the market-place. Then there is the disappearance of the lively literary and theatrical presence that has fled to Hampstead, Islington, Chelsea and other fashionable enclaves in the great web of London villages. In the 1930s writers like P. G. Wodehouse, musical comedy stars like Jack Hulbert and Cicely Courtneidge and Vesta Tilley, could afford to live in Mayfair and it matched their public image to do so; today's creative talent wears jeans rather than silk dressing-gowns, prefers gardening and home decorating in Wimbledon or Fulham to night-clubbing off Piccadilly. And the pop industry's millionaires who could afford a Mayfair house have nearly all chosen to move out of

London to stockbroker-belt manors near Weybridge and Farnham.

Much of Mayfair's cheek-by-jowl diversity that allowed a mix of social classes and enabled even a writer with a few hundred a year to rent a couple of rooms in Half Moon Street vanished with the pressure on property values caused by the postwar business invasion. It will always be, as Stanley Coggan says, a very expensive place to live. As the leases come up for renewal, a few blocks each year, the two-thirds dominance by commerce is not likely to change now. A few more houses may be turned back to residential use and converted to flats, but to survive architecturally, the old Mayfair mansions with their gracious interiors are now inevitably fated to an existence as prestige company offices. At least corporate money will preserve them from threats of redevelopment like that hanging over Avery Row, a charming jumble of eighteenth-century cottages and work-shops behind Bond Street whose developers, the Co-op Insurance Society, planned to build a two-storey shopping centre with offices on top. That particular plan was rejected by Westminster City Council, but it may only be a stay of execution, as many residents and shopkeepers believe.

Mayfair today may have too much business in its heart to be again the vibrant, varied community it once was. Yet as one wanders at night round its deserted rows of empty mansions, voices from the past still whisper – just loud enough to convince us of Sydney Smith's 'parallelogram' of intelligence and ability, wealth and beauty. Pockets of enchantment remain. History is just around the corner, and the place still has the power to cast a spell.

INDEX